The
OXFORD
Children's Encyclopedia of
History

OXFORD
UNIVERSITY PRESS

OXFORD
UNIVERSITY PRESS

Great Clarendon Street, Oxford OX2 6DP

Oxford University Press is a department of the University of Oxford.
It furthers the University's objective of excellence in research, scholarship,
and education by publishing worldwide in

Oxford New York

Athens Auckland Bangkok Bogotá Buenos Aires Calcutta
Cape Town Chennai Dar es Salaam Delhi Florence Hong Kong Istanbul
Karachi Kuala Lumpur Madrid Melbourne Mexico City Mumbai
Nairobi Paris São Paulo Singapore Taipei Tokyo Toronto Warsaw

with associated companies in Berlin Ibadan

British Library Cataloguing in Publication Data

Data available

ISBN 0-19-910669-X

1 3 5 7 9 10 8 6 4 2

Typeset by Oxford Designers and Illustrators
Typeset in Photina and Rotis
Printed in Britain by Butler and Tanner

Contents

Contributors

Editor
Ben Dupré

Coordinating editors
Ian Crofton
Joanna Harris

Proofreaders
Helen Maxey
Susan Mushin

Indexer
Ann Barrett

Design
Jo Cameron
Oxford Designers and Illustrators

Art editor
Hilary Wright

Assistant art editor
Jo Samways

Cover design
Jo Cameron

Photographic research
Charlotte Lippmann

Consultants
John R. Brown
Professor Warwick Bray
Professor Adrian Brockett
Gal Gerson
Naranjami Gupta
Professor David Harris
Rosemary Kelly
Myrtle Langley
Colin Mills
Professor Kenneth Morgan
Padraig O'Loingsigh
Stewart Ross
Elspeth Scott
Dr Harry Shukman
Peter Teed
Bob Unwin
Elizabeth Williamson

Authors
Dr Michael Benton
Arthur Swift Butterfield
Mike Corbishley
Ian Crofton
Tony Drake
Neil Grant
Dr Alastair McIntosh Gray
Gerald Haigh
Rosemary Kelly
Margaret Killigray
Haydn Middleton
Peggy Morgan
John Robottom
Dr Alisdair Rogers
Stewart Ross
Theodore Rowland-Entwistle
D. Sehbai
Peter Teed
Elizabeth Williamson

Acknowledgments

Key t top; b bottom; c centre; r right; l left
AAA = Ancient Art and Architecture; BAL = Bridgeman Art Library; NGIC = National Geographic Image Collection, RH = Robert Harding

Photos are reproduced by kind permission of:
Front cover AAA. 6t Michael Holford. 6b RH, Sassoon. 7b Magnum, Ian Berry. 8t Getty Images. 8b BAL, Museo e Gallerie Nazionali Di Capodimonte Naples. 9t Peter Newark's Pictures, Mathew Brady. 9b BAL, Yale University. 11t, b, 12t Michael Holford. 12b St Edmundsbury Borough Council/West Stow Anglo-Saxon Village Trust. 13t NGIC, Kenneth Garrett. 14t NGIC, Sam Abell. 14b E. T. Archive. 15t Katz Pictures/Mansell. 15b Michael Holford. 16b E. T. Archive. 17t Topham. 17b Getty Images. 18t Q. A. Photos Ltd. 18b RH, Advertasia. 19t RH, Robert Frerck. 19b BAL. 20 Peter Newark's Western Americana. 21t Getty Images. 21b AKG photo. 23t Michael Holford. 24t The National Museum, Copenhagen. 24b Mary Evans. 25t RH. 25b NGIC, James L. Stanfield. 26t AKG photo. 26b David King Collection. 27t RH, Adam Woolfitt. 27b E. T. Archive. 28t Getty Images. 28b RH, Gavin Hellier. 29t Science Photo Library, Los Alamos National Laboratory. 29b Science Photo Library, Los Alamos National Laboratory. 30t Rex Features, Mckiernan. 30b Mary Evans/Explorer, Plisson. 31t Getty Images. 31b Popperfoto. 32tr Mary Evans. 32b Mary Evans. 33t BAL, Towneley Hall Art Gallery and Museum. 33b BAL, Bibliotheque Nationale, Paris. 34b BAL, British Library. 35tr Michael Holford. 35bl AAA. 36br Michael Holford. 37t BAL, Woburn Abbey, Bedfordshire. 37b AAA, Ronald Sheridan. 39t BAL, The British Library, London. 40t BAL, Bibliotheque Nationale, Paris. 41t National Maritime Museum Picture Library. 41b Getty Images. 42t Michael Holford. 42b E. T. Archive. 43t Getty Images. 43b Rex Features. 44t Topham Picture Point. 44b BAL, Crown Estate/Institute of Directors. 45t Mary Evans. 45b Mary Evans. 46t BAL, Schloss Augustusburg. 46b Getty Images. 47t Getty Images. 47b Rex Features. 48b, 49t Michael Holford. 50t RH, Tony Gervis. 51t Topham. 51b BAL, Walker Art Gallery, Liverpool. 52t Images Colour Library. 52b David King Collection. 53t Corbis/Getty Images. 53b, 54c Getty Images. 54b NGIC, Stephen L. Alvarez. 55t Michael Holford. 55cr Images of India. 55b Link Picture Library. 56t Images of India. 56b E. T. Archive. 57t BAL, Walker Art Gallery, Liverpool. 57b Michael Holford. 58t Corel. 58b Getty Images. 59t Image Bank, Marc Romanelli. 59b Palazzo Publico Siena/E. T. Archive. 60t Michael Holford. 60b BAL, Private Collection. 61t RH, E. Simanor. 61b BAL, Jean Auguste Dominique Ingres. 62t Topham. 62b Topham, Ray Hutchinson. 63l Mary Evans. 64t David King Collection. 64b Getty Images. 65t BAL, Giraudon. 65b Topham. 66t David King Collection. 66b BAL, Castle Museum and Art Gallery Nottingham. 67tr RH, Christopher Rennie. 67b BAL, The British Library, London. 68t BAL, Lambeth Palace Library, London. 68b BAL, Private Collection. 69b RH, Peter Scholey. 70t Mary Evans. 70b BAL, The British Library, London. 71b Getty Images, Nabeel Turner. 72t Getty Images. 72b Popperfoto. 73t Mary Evans. 73b Image Bank, Wendy Chan. 74t BAL, Private Collection. 74cl Peter Sanders. 75t BAL, Christie's Images. 75b South American Pictures, Charlotte Lipson. 76t BAL, National Maritime Museum, London. 76b BAL. 77tr RH, Adam Woolfitt. 78t Michael Holford. 79t, 79b Mary Evans. 80t BAL, The British Library. 80b RH, Paolo Koch. 81t Rex Features. 81b National Maritime Museum. 82tr AAA, Ronald Sheridan. 84cl RH, Adam Woolfitt. 84b Hanny/Gamma/FSP. 85tr BAL, City of Bristol Museum and Art Gallery. 86tr BAL, Biblioteca Ambrosiana, Milan. 86br BAL, Bibliotheque Nationale, Paris. 86bl Charlotte Lippmann. 87b Michael Holford. 88t BAL, Museo Archeologico Nazionali, Naples. 89t Michael Holford. 89b Getty Images. 90t Mary Evans. 90b Novosti. 91t Image Bank, Harald Sund. 91b Rex Features. 92t RH, C. Bowman. 92b Corbis/Bennet Dean/Eye Ubiquitous. 93t Mary Evans. 93b BAL, The British Library, London. 94t Getty Images. 94b Popperfoto, Juda Ngwenya, Reuters. 95t South American Pictures. 95b Corel. 96t Mary Evans. 96b Rex Features. 97t BAL. 97b Tony Stone, Robert Freck. 98t Popperfoto. 98b David King Collection. 99t BAL, Private Collection. 99b, 100t Getty Images. 100b BAL, Museum of Fine Arts, Budapest. 101t E. T. Archive. 101b Getty Images. 102t BAL, National Maritime Museum, London. 102b Getty Images. 103t Museum of London. 103b BAL, Victoria & Albert Musem, London. 104t Getty Images. 104b Getty Images/Tony Stone, Peter Seaward. 105t Science Photo Library/NASA. 105b Topham. 106t United Nations. 106b Topham. 107, 108t Peter Newark's Western Americana. 108b RH, Simon Harris. 109t BAL, Stapleton Collection. 109b BAL, Royal Holloway and Bedford New College, Surrey. 110t Getty Images. 110b Weidenfeld Archives. 111t Topham, Associated Press. 111b York Archaeological Trust. 113t Corel. 113b, 115t Mary Evans. 115b Getty Images. 116t Popperfoto. 117t David King Collection. 117b Topham Picture Source. 118t Getty Images. 118b Matsumoto/Sygma. 124tr, 124l Rex Features. 124c Press Association, John Stillwell.

Illustrations are by:
Ambrus, Victor: 50b
Berridge, Richard/Sneddon, James: 82l
Connolly, Peter: 49b, 88b, 112
Cottam, Martin: 38
Hook, Richard: 83b, 114
Oxford Illustrators: 125
Parsley, Helen: 36cl
Polley, Robbie: 22, 36t, 78b, 120, 121, 122, 123
Raw, Stephen: 119b
Sneddon, James: 48t, 85b
Wheatcroft, Andrew: 13b
Woods, Michael: 23b
All maps by Olive Pearson and Phoenix Mapping.

Finding your way around

The *Oxford Children's Encyclopedia of History* has many useful features that will help you find the information you need quickly and easily.

The articles in the encyclopedia are arranged in alphabetical order from Africa to Writing. When you want to find out about a particular topic, the first step is to see whether there is an **article** on it in the A–Z sequence. If there is no article, there are two things you can do.

First of all you can look at the **footers** at the bottom of the page.

These may include the topic you want, and give you the name of the article where you can find out about it. If there is no footer, the next thing to do is to look the topic up in the alphabetical **index** at the back of the book. This will tell you which page or pages you can look at to find out what you want to know.

The **header** tells you what articles are on the page, for quick reference.

Articles are arranged alphabetically, so that they are easy to find.

The **opening paragraph** gives a friendly introduction to the topic.

The **main text** gives an account of the topic in a continuous and readable way. Key terms are picked out in *italic text*.

Ottoman empire

A Turkish leader, Uthman, founded the Ottoman kingdom in north-east Turkey in the 14th century. The Ottoman empire was at the height of its power in the 16th and 17th centuries. Altogether the Ottoman family ruled for more than 600 years.

The Ottoman Turks and their empire took their name from Uthman (1258–1326). The capital of their empire, Constantinople, was captured from the Byzantine emperor in 1453. To win the city, Mehmed II, the Turkish sultan, had his ships dragged overland to the harbour to bypass Constantinople's sea defences.

The sultan was the religious head over all Muslims within the empire. All his ministers and servants were originally military slaves, and so were his personal troops, the Janissaries. They were taken as boys from the Balkan lands, spent all their lives in barracks and were not allowed to marry.

In 1683 the Ottoman army threatened to capture Vienna but Austrian and Polish troops turned them back. From about 1800 the empire began to break up. The Greeks fought and won their independence in 1829.

In World War I, the Turks fought on the side of Germany

▶ The greatest of the sultans was Suleiman the Magnificent, who ruled from 1520 to 1566. He filled his court with painters, poets and craftsmen, and employed architects to build aqueducts, bridges, public baths and mosques.

and Austria and were defeated in 1918. The lands of the old empire became independent countries and the new Republic of Turkey was created in Asia Minor.

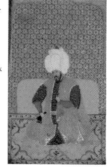

• Constantinople actually became Istanbul after the Turks took over in the 15th century, but the name was not officially changed until the Turkish Post Office changed it in 1926.

find out more
Balkans
Byzantine empire
Holy Roman Empire
Middle East
Muslims

Margin notes provide nuggets of extra information and amazing facts.

The **find out more panel** points you to other articles related to the topic.

Pakistan

The Indus valley was the site of the great civilization of Harappa and Mohenjodaro (about 2500–1600 BC). The invasion of Alexander the Great in the 4th century BC was the first of a series of invasions into the rich lands of the Indus valley and the Punjab (the land of the five rivers). Muslim rulers controlled the region from the 13th century until the 1750s, when the British East India Company began to take control.

From 1858, for almost a hundred years, Pakistan was part of British India. From the 1920s Indian nationalists campaigned for independence from Britain. But the Muslim minority in India demanded the

creation of a separate country for Muslims. When in 1947 India gained independence, it was divided into two nations: India, which was mainly Hindu, and Muslim Pakistan. Pakistan was in two parts, West and East, separated by Indian territory. India and Pakistan both claimed the territory of Kashmir, and went to war over it in 1948 and 1965.

There were also difficulties between West and East Pakistan. The people in the East campaigned for independence, but in 1971 West Pakistani forces invaded. Millions of refugees fled to India. This led to another war

▶ Part of the remains of Mohenjodaro. Four thousand years ago Mohenjodaro was an important trading city on the River Indus.

between India and Pakistan, in which the West Pakistani forces were defeated. In 1972 East Pakistan became independent as Bangladesh.

Since the creation of Pakistan, democratic government has alternated with times when the army has had control. Pakistan's constitution is based on Islamic (Muslim) law.

find out more
Ancient world
India
Muslims

• The name Pakistan comes from two words in the Urdu language. *Pak* means 'pure', and *stan* means 'land'.

Colour illustrations, photographs and **maps** bring the topic to life.

Captions not only describe the photographs and illustrations but give additional information on the topic.

The **footer** provides a short cut to topics that do not have their own articles.

Africa

Archaeologists have found more hand axes and other stone tools in East Africa than anywhere else on Earth. Fragments of fossils of early humans have also been discovered. So scientists believe that human beings evolved in Africa and spread out from there to other parts of the world. It was in Africa that prehistoric people developed skills of shaping tools, hunting, learning to use fire and living in groups.

◀ The royal court of Benin in West Africa produced quantities of fine bronze casts from the 16th to the 19th centuries. This head was made in about 1550.

Most Africans, over the centuries, lived in small settlements and villages, and very little is known in detail of prehistoric times. From about the year 4000 BC powerful empires grew up beside the River Nile, because the soil along its banks was very rich and fertile. The most famous was Egypt of the Pharaohs. Further south, Meroe grew rich, trading up and down the river. Its people smelted iron, built cities and buried their kings under pyramids. The Meroitic language was engraved on walls and stones, but today no one can understand what is written. Meroe's rule ended when other trading kingdoms invaded, from Ethiopia in the east. These kingdoms became Christian, and one, in the highlands of Ethiopia, lasted into the 20th century.

Cities and kingdoms

Trade was important in West Africa, too, and increased when traders began to use camels to cross the Sahara Desert with gold, salt and slaves. In the grasslands south of the Sahara, city states grew rich and powerful. Many of their kings adopted the Muslim religion, which traders and scholars brought with them from North Africa. Mansa Musa, the king of Mali, made a pilgrimage to the holy city of Mecca in Arabia in the 14th century, paying everyone with gold on the way.

Other states grew up in the forest areas nearer to the coast. These had also grown rich, from trading in gold, slaves, leather goods and cloth. In Benin richly clothed kings ruled from a magnificent palace, and craftspeople and artists produced fine ivory carvings and bronze sculptures.

City states on the east coast, such as Kilwa and Sofala, sent ivory, gold, copper and gum by sea to Arabia, India and China. The gold came from the powerful inland state of Zimbabwe. Its great drystone granite buildings, over a thousand years old, still remain. Kilwa had grand houses and a large Muslim mosque built of coral stone. During the 16th century Portuguese guns and ships destroyed the wealth of these coastal states.

Slavery and wars

Slavery had long existed in African societies. Slaves were also exported, north across the Sahara to the Mediterranean and east to Arabia and India. But the slave trade grew greatly during the 16th, 17th and 18th centuries, when European ships took large numbers of Africans across the Atlantic to the cotton and sugar plantations of the Americas and the Caribbean. In this period the Dutch, English and French, as well as the Portuguese, sent their ships to buy and sell slaves on the West African coast, building forts to control the trade.

In the 19th century there were serious wars and disturbances in various parts of Africa. Passionate Muslims fought to control states in the interior of western Africa, wanting Islam to be the only faith of the people. In southern Africa the Zulu people attacked and conquered

▼ Ethiopia has been Christian since the 4th century AD. In the late 12th to 13th centuries, 11 churches were carved out of solid rock in the town of Lalibela. The expertly crafted buildings still attract thousands of pilgrims today.

neighbouring African groups, and also fought the Dutch (Boers) and British who were settling on their lands.

European rulers

In the late 19th century most parts of Africa were conquered and divided up by France, Britain, Portugal, Germany and Belgium. For over 60 years Africa was under European rule. The white colonists imposed new systems of law, government, language and education on the African people and often tried to stamp out their religion and culture. The boundaries Europeans drew on the map ignored the shapes of former kingdoms and empires. Artificial frontiers separated people who spoke the same language. Some colonies, including Uganda and Nigeria, were made of groups of people (tribes) who had nothing in common and were hostile to one another. A few African kings survived, in Buganda and Swaziland for instance, but they had lost their power.

Resistance and independence

Many Africans continued to resist colonial rule, but they were not strong enough at first to free their lands. Nationalist groups were formed to campaign for independence, and from 1956 onwards one by one the states of Africa achieved their freedom. Some had to fight the colonial powers, who did not want to lose their African colonies. There were long wars in Algeria against the French, and in Mozambique and Angola against Portugal.

Most African countries became politically independent of European rule, but serious problems remained. The newly independent countries kept the territorial boundaries which the European colonists had drawn, and these did not correspond with the territories of ethnic groups (tribes). Until 1994 the white minority in South Africa kept political power for itself.

In the years after independence cities grew, railways and roads were improved and new industries began. The countries of Africa sent their representatives to the United Nations and took part in world politics. But although politically independent, they were dependent on the prices that other countries gave them for the products they were able to export. Difficult climates, fast growing populations, lack of resources and local wars and rebellions have caused widespread famine and unrest in many parts of Africa.

▶ At a conference In Berlin in 1884 European countries agreed on frontiers for their colonies. By 1913 most of Africa was ruled by Europeans.

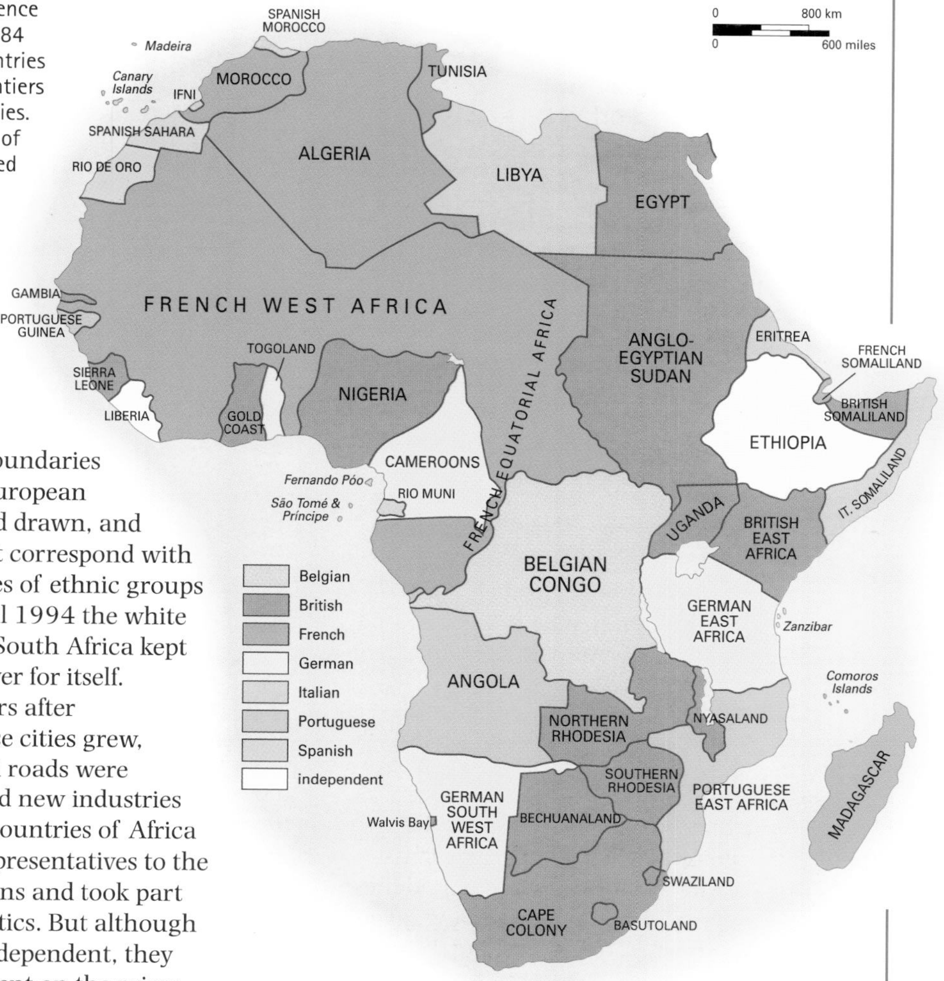

0 800 km
0 600 miles
SPANISH MOROCCO
Madeira
Canary Islands
IFNI
MOROCCO
TUNISIA
SPANISH SAHARA
RIO DE ORO
ALGERIA
LIBYA
EGYPT
GAMBIA
PORTUGUESE GUINEA
FRENCH WEST AFRICA
FRENCH EQUATORIAL AFRICA
TOGOLAND
SIERRA LEONE
LIBERIA
GOLD COAST
NIGERIA
ANGLO-EGYPTIAN SUDAN
ERITREA
FRENCH SOMALILAND
BRITISH SOMALILAND
ETHIOPIA
CAMEROONS
Fernando Póo
São Tomé & Príncipe
RIO MUNI
IT. SOMALILAND
UGANDA
BRITISH EAST AFRICA
BELGIAN CONGO
GERMAN EAST AFRICA
Zanzibar
Comoros Islands
Belgian
British
French
German
Italian
Portuguese
Spanish
independent
ANGOLA
NORTHERN RHODESIA
NYASALAND
SOUTHERN RHODESIA
PORTUGUESE EAST AFRICA
MADAGASCAR
GERMAN SOUTH WEST AFRICA
Walvis Bay
BECHUANALAND
SWAZILAND
CAPE COLONY
BASUTOLAND

◀ The Belgian Congo (now the Democratic Republic of Congo) became independent in 1960. Immediately a vicious civil war broke out between various ethnic groups (tribes). Many other African countries have suffered civil war since gaining their independence.

find out more

Egyptians, ancient
Explorers
Mandela, Nelson
Prehistoric people
Slaves
South Africa

Agricultural Revolution

Huge changes took place in farming methods and machinery in the 18th century – known together as the Agricultural Revolution. This revolution started in Britain and spread to other countries in Europe and America.

◀ This threshing machine was driven by a steam engine. Engines like this were used on farms in Britain and North America in the second half of the 19th century.

At this time the population of Britain was rising very quickly. To meet the new demand, farmers developed ways of increasing the amount of food they could grow. They drained their fields and enclosed them with hedges. They found that by growing turnips, clover, barley and wheat in successive years, they could use their land all the time, instead of letting it lie fallow for a year. At the same time, stock breeders developed larger and fatter animals.

But some people suffered from these changes. In Scotland, sheep farming led to the Highland clearances, in which many small farmers were forced off the land. In England the enclosures of fields deprived cottagers of the right to graze their animals on common land.

Farm machinery developed during the late 18th and early 19th centuries, much of it in the rapidly growing United States of America. Reapers, threshers and combine harvesters followed in quick succession. Steam engines were used to power the traction engines used for ploughing and threshing. In the early 20th century petrol-driven tractors appeared. All these machines meant that more food could be grown by fewer people. There were fewer jobs in the countryside, and more people moved to the towns to find work in factories.

• In 1701 Jethro Tull, an Oxfordshire barrister and farmer, invented a seed drill. A blade made a small furrow, and the seed was fed into the furrow at an even rate down a tube. Modern seed drills work in much the same way.

find out more
Georgian Britain
Industrial Revolution
United States of
   America
Victorian Britain

Alexander the Great

Born 356 BC in Pella, now in Greece
Died 323 BC aged 33

find out more
Ancient world
Egyptians, ancient
Greeks, ancient

Alexander the Great was perhaps the most famous and greatest soldier of the ancient world. By the time he died, when he was only 33, his vast empire stretched from Greece in the west to India in the east.

Alexander became King Alexander III of Macedonia at the age of 20 after the death of his father, Philip II. He soon set about expanding his empire, and in 332 BC he conquered Egypt. Within the next two years he defeated the Persian army and became king of Persia (modern Iran). He even ordered the magnificent Persian city of Persepolis to be burned and destroyed as a sign of his power. (The ruins of the city are still visible today.) He also invaded northern India, but his exhausted soldiers refused to carry on and he agreed to turn back. He died of a fever shortly after returning to Persia.

Alexander rode into most of his battles on his horse Bucephalus. When the old horse died, Alexander built a city and named it Bucephala after him. He also built many new cities which he named Alexandria, after himself. The most famous is the one in Egypt, which is still an important city today.

When he was a young boy, Alexander had been taught by the philosopher Aristotle to be proud of being Greek. Although he was proud, he also wanted all the people in his new empire to live in peace as friends, not as enemies as before. To help achieve this, he gave important jobs to Persians as well as to Greeks, and even took a Persian princess to be his second wife.

After Alexander's death, no one was able to keep his empire together. After years of war amongst his generals, it was split up into smaller kingdoms, including Macedonia, Egypt and Babylonia.

◀ This Roman mosaic from about 100 BC shows Alexander the Great riding into battle against the Persian ruler Darius III.

American Civil War

The American Civil War lasted for four years, from 1861 to 1865. It was fought between the southern states and the northern states. In the South the big landowners owned many black slaves. The southerners relied on slaves to work their land. In the North most people believed that slavery was evil.

In 1860 Abraham Lincoln became president of the United States of America (the Union). Southerners thought he was a threat to their way of life, and the southern states withdrew from the Union. Instead they formed their own nation, the Confederate States of America (the Confederacy). The North went to war against the Confederacy to maintain the Union and to free the slaves.

In the early years of the war both sides won several battles. In 1863 the Confederates, under General Robert E. Lee, invaded the North, but the Union armies defeated them in a three-day battle at Gettysburg. This was the turning point of the war. The richer North had more men and more factories, while the South became weaker and weaker. The northern armies were led by two generals, Ulysses S. Grant and William T. Sherman. Grant attacked the Confederacy from the north, and Sherman marched in from the west, destroying everything in his path. Eventually, on 9 April 1865, Lee surrendered to Grant. A few days later Lincoln was assassinated.

▲ A wounded soldier is given water. This and other photographs by Matthew Brady showed the reality of suffering in the war.

The slaves were freed, and in time all the southern states rejoined the Union. But the white people in the South remained bitter for many years.

• There were heavy losses on both sides in the Civil War. Altogether 529,332 soldiers died.

find out more
Lincoln, Abraham
Slaves
United States of America

American Revolution

• British historians used to call the Revolution the American War of Independence.

find out more
Georgian Britain
United States of America
Washington, George

In the American Revolution Britain's American colonies rebelled against their British rulers, and fought for their independence. The colonists defeated the British and set up a new country: the United States of America (USA).

Each of the 13 British colonies had its own local government, but Britain made all the important decisions. In particular, the British taxed the colonists to pay for their defence against the French, who also had colonies in North America. The colonists wanted to make their own decisions. They objected to being taxed when they were not represented in the British Parliament. In the end they rebelled.

The fighting began in April 1775 at Lexington in Massachusetts. The colonists organized their militias (part-time soldiers) into an army, led by General George Washington. The British won the first major battle, at Bunker Hill, near Boston. The following year, on 4 July 1776, the colonists declared their independence, and in 1777 they defeated the British at Saratoga.

At this point the French declared war against the British, and later Spain and the Netherlands also joined in on the American side. From then on there were no more big campaigns in the north, but many battles at sea and fighting in the south. Eventually, in 1781, the British army surrendered to the Americans at Yorktown, Virginia. Peace talks began, and in 1783 Britain agreed to the independence of the new United States of America.

◄ On 16 December 1773 a group of Boston citizens disguised as Mohawk Indians boarded British tea ships and threw tea into Boston Harbour. They were protesting against the tax on tea. This incident, which became known as the 'Boston tea party', brought the Americans and British closer to war.

Ancient world

By about 5000 BC human beings in Africa, Asia, Europe and America had learned to farm crops and keep animals. This was the first step towards civilization, because it allowed people to live together in communities. Full civilization appeared when villages grew into towns and cities, with government, laws and record-keeping.

The best-known early civilizations are those of the 'ancient world' of Mesopotamia (now Iraq), Egypt, Greece and Rome. But other remarkable cultures flourished elsewhere.

The first civilizations

The first towns were built between about 8000 and 6000 BC. Two of the earliest were Jericho on the River Jordan and Çatal Hüyük in Turkey.

The world's first civilization emerged along the rivers Tigris and Euphrates in an area of Mesopotamia called Sumer. The Sumerians built large cities and pyramid-shaped towers or 'ziggurats'. They dug canals, and traded by sea and land. They also developed the first form of writing.

The second and longest-lived ancient civilization grew up in Egypt beside the River Nile. By 2000 BC other civilizations were spreading across the Middle East and the eastern Mediterranean. The Babylonians took over Mesopotamia. Their king, Hammurabi, was one of the first rulers to write down his laws. Further north, the Hittites, who were fierce warriors, built up an empire in what is now Turkey.

A string of wealthy trading cities emerged in the region called Phoenicia, now Syria and Lebanon, including the great ports of Tyre and Sidon. The Phoenicians were a trading people. They were also great explorers, and settled colonies right across the Mediterranean.

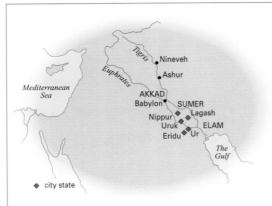

▲ The Sumerian civilization in Mesopotamia.

about **2600**	Egyptian pyramids being built
about **2500**	Indus civilization begins
about **2000**	Early Minoan civilization on Crete
about **1790**	Beginning of the reign of King Hammurabi of Babylon
about **1600**	Mycenaean civilization flourishing
about **1595**	Hittites attack Babylon
about **1500**	Shang civilization begins Phoenicians trading in the eastern Mediterranean

area of Olmec influence

▲ The Olmec civilization in Mexico.

Time-line of the ancient world

BC

about **10,000**	Farming begins in Asia
about **8000**	City of Jericho built
about **3500**	City of Ur founded Sumerian writing appears
about **3200**	Egyptian hieroglyphic writing begins

area of Shang civilization

▲ The Shang civilization in China.

about **1200**	Olmec (Mexico) and Chavin (Peru) civilizations beginning
about **1120**	Mycenae destroyed
about **900–650**	Assyrian power at its height
814	Phoenicians establish the city of Carthage
about **800**	Etruscan civilization beginning in Italy

776	First Olympic Games in Greece
about **753**	Rome founded
605	Nebuchadnezzar becomes king of Babylon
557	Cyrus the Great becomes king of Persia
490	Greeks defeat Persians at Marathon
336–323	Reign of Alexander the Great
146	Romans destroy Carthage
27	Augustus becomes first Roman emperor
AD	
400	Roman empire in decline

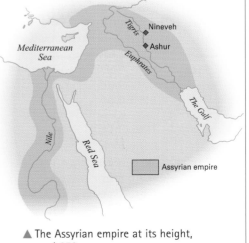

Assyrian empire

▲ The Assyrian empire at its height, around 650 BC.

◀ The Standard of Ur is a richly decorated box which was found in one of the 16 magnificent tombs discovered at Ur, one of the greatest of the early cities. Dating from 2500 BC, the two long sides of the box show the Sumerians at war and in victory.

China, India and America

The Chinese were growing rice in about 5000 BC. Their first true civilization, the Shang civilization, flourished some 3000 years later, around the Huang He (Yellow River) and the city of Anyang. The Shang made objects from bronze and invented a very complicated writing system based on pictures. Around 1045 BC the Shang kings were conquered by the Zhou from the west.

Meanwhile, further west, another great river civilization had grown up around the Indus, which lasted for almost 1000 years. At its heart lay the great cities of Harappa, Mohenjo-daro and Lothal. Perhaps 40,000 people lived in Mohenjo-daro. The straight streets were laid out in a grid pattern and larger houses had bathrooms and toilets. The people's wealth came from trade. The Indus culture began to crumble about 1700 BC. After the invasion of Aryans from the north, a new and even richer civilization appeared that gave the world the Hindu and Buddhist religions.

American civilization developed separately. By about 1200 BC two cultures had emerged, the Olmecs of Mexico and the Chavins of Peru. Neither had writing, the wheel or metal tools, but they put up huge buildings and carved stone sculptures of their mysterious, half-human gods.

The glory of the ancient world

The Greek and Roman civilizations (about 900 BC to 400 AD) are the best known of the ancient world. But many other important cultures flourished around the same time.

The warlike Assyrians once controlled an empire that swallowed up Babylonia and reached from Egypt to the Persian Gulf. They too traded widely and built impressive stone palaces. When the Assyrian empire broke up in 612 BC, the Babylonians returned under King Nebuchadnezzar II. He rebuilt the city of Babylon, including a massive, nine-storey ziggurat known as the Tower of Babel.

The Babylonians finally fell to the equally remarkable Persians. Darius I (521–486 BC) ruled the largest empire the world had ever seen, stretching from Egypt and Turkey to the borders of India. It was governed from Persepolis in modern Iran, a city linked to the rest of the empire by a system of royal highways.

The Minoan civilization, on the island of Crete, began in about 3000 BC and survived for over 1500 years. The remains of its stately palaces at Knossos, Mallia and Phaistos survive to this day. Like the Phoenicians, the Minoans grew rich through trade. Their craftspeople were much admired for their pottery and gold working. In about 1450 BC Crete was settled by Mycenaeans from northern Greece, who took over the island's trade and set up markets across the Mediterranean.

The City of Carthage began as a trading post, founded by the Phoenicians in about 814 BC. Until it was destroyed by the Romans in 146 BC, it possessed strong armies and a large fleet of merchant ships. The Etruscans of central Italy were another important civilization overthrown by the Romans. They produced beautiful art and impressive architecture. The Romans copied a great deal from the Etruscans – their capital, Rome, was originally an Etruscan city.

find out more
Africa
Alexander the Great
China
Egyptians, ancient
Greeks, ancient
India
Prehistoric people
Romans
South America
Writing

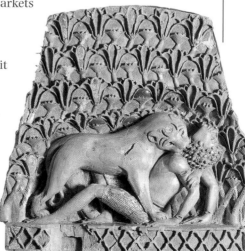

▼ A Phoenician ivory furniture panel showing a lion attacking a slave. The Phoenicians were most famous for trading in luxuries like glassware, carved ivory, dyes and jewellery made of precious metals.

Anglo-Saxons

find out more
Archaeology
Dark Ages
Normans
Roman Britain
Vikings

The name Anglo-Saxon describes a number of different peoples from Germany and Scandinavia called Angles, Saxons and Jutes who settled in much of Britain from the 5th century AD. The English spoken today comes from the language Anglo-Saxons spoke 1500 years ago.

In the late 4th and early 5th centuries, Anglo-Saxon soldiers, with their families, were brought over by the Romans as paid fighters to help defend the south and east coasts against pirates and other Saxons. By about 410 the last Roman troops had left Britain. Although some people continued to live in a Roman way, many places began to change and become Anglo-Saxon, as more and more new settlers came from across the English Channel and the North Sea.

▲ This warrior's helmet was found in the remains of an Anglo-Saxon ship at Sutton Hoo, an archaeological site in Suffolk, England. Sutton Hoo is thought to have been the grave of Raedwald, who was not only king of East Anglia but was also High King of Britain. He died in 624 or 625.

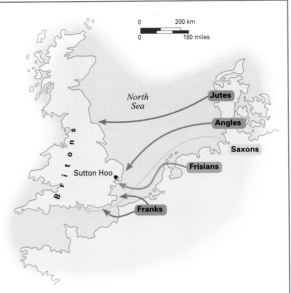

▲ The people known as the Anglo-Saxons were in fact five different peoples – the Franks who came from northern France, the Frisians and Saxons from Germany, and the Angles and Jutes from Denmark.

Towns and kingdoms

The Anglo-Saxon immigrants to Britain gradually began to take over more land and to build farms, villages and towns. In 200 years, from about 450 to 650, they moved further west and established kingdoms. Some Anglo-Saxon place names survive, such as East Anglia, the kingdom of the East Angles. Other Anglo-Saxon names are still in use today. A *ford* is a crossing, as in Bradford, for example. *Ton* meant farm or village and there are a lot of place names in Britain ending in -*ton*.

Alfred is the most famous of the Anglo-Saxon kings. He ruled in southern England in the 9th century, and during his reign the Anglo-Saxon Chronicles, an important record of events in the kingdom, were begun. Alfred was also responsible for founding a number of new

• From the middle of the 6th century Irish monks began to convert the people of the north of Britain to Christianity. In 597 the Pope sent Augustine, a monk in Rome, to convert the people of southern Britain. There had been some Christian communities in Britain since Roman times, but many more people now became Christians. Churches were built – most of wood but some of stone – and a few can still be seen today.

fortified towns, called *burhs*. These towns were protected by strong banks so that the townspeople and those who lived in the countryside around could take refuge from the new invaders, the Vikings. Canute and his Viking army conquered all England eventually, and in 1016 Canute was accepted as king. From 1042 Anglo-Saxon kings again ruled England. But in 1066 they were defeated by William the Conqueror, who put England under Norman rule.

Anglo–Saxon clothes and runes

From the small fragments of cloth found in graves, archaeologists have worked out that women often wore long, flowing gowns fastened at the shoulders with big brooches. On their belts they might have hung a purse. Jewellery such as brooches, necklaces, pins and bracelets has been found too. Men usually wore short tunics over leggings, and cloaks for warmth. Some men were buried with a shield and sword.

Before Christianity introduced Latin to the Anglo-Saxons they used an alphabet with 33 special letters called *runes*. It was often used to inscribe pots, metal jewellery or special objects made of bone.

◄ This is a modern reconstruction of an Anglo-Saxon wooden house. Anglo-Saxon villagers kept sheep, cattle and pigs. They hunted deer and ate fish and wild birds.

Archaeology

Archaeology is the study of history based on physical evidence. Archaeologists locate, excavate and interpret this evidence to tell us things about the past we might otherwise never know.

Sometimes the remains of the past are so big they can easily be seen, like the great Inca city of Macchu Picchu in Peru. More often, however, archaeologists must seek clues more carefully. To do this they may use hundreds of photographs taken from aeroplanes every year. Archaeological sites may be visible from the air, or crops may grow in different ways if their roots grow over a buried wall or a filled-in ditch.

Excavation

Once a site is discovered, it is carefully measured and detailed records (drawings, photographs and notes) are made. Any surface remains are gathered up, and their position at the site plotted.

Most full-scale excavations today are 'rescue excavations'. These are carried out because the sites are to be disturbed by new roads, buildings or deep ploughing. Excavation of the site means that the archaeologists must destroy most of it in order to understand it.

Interpretation

After an excavation, specialists examine the records and write a report. Many people, including experts in identifying and dating different types of animal bone, fragments of pottery, or

▲ Archaeologists at a burial site in a cave near the Pyramid of the Sun in Teotihuacán, Mexico.

seeds from plants, are needed to put together the 'story' of the site. However, even using the most up-to-date scientific methods it is a difficult job to reconstruct a full picture of the past because not everything will have survived.

find out more
Ancient world
Anglo-Saxons
Aztecs
Celts
Egyptians, ancient
Greeks, ancient
Incas
Maya
Prehistoric people
Romans
Vikings

Armour

Warriors have worn armour to protect themselves in battle for thousands of years. Bullet-proof vests and riot gear are modern forms of armour.

The ancient Greeks wore linen or leather shirts with metal plates sewn on to protect the heart and shoulders. The hoplites (armed foot-soldiers) wore a breastplate of bronze shaped to fit. Roman foot-soldiers and cavalry wore armour of iron hoops protecting the back as well as the front of the body. Romans also used mail, at first made of small metal plates sewn on a leather jerkin, overlapping like tiles on a roof. Later it was made of metal links, known as chain-armour.

In the early Middle Ages, European soldiers wore chain-mail armour. From about 1330 knights wore heavy armour of jointed steel plates. After the development of guns, armour was gradually reduced to a cuirass (breast plate) and helmet. By the 20th century only the helmet remained. From the 1940s a new kind of body armour made of nylon, other plastics and glass fibres came into use.

▼ Some different types of armour.

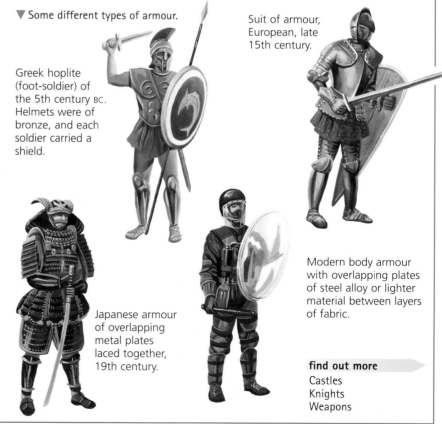

Greek hoplite (foot-soldier) of the 5th century BC. Helmets were of bronze, and each soldier carried a shield.

Suit of armour, European, late 15th century.

Japanese armour of overlapping metal plates laced together, 19th century.

Modern body armour with overlapping plates of steel alloy or lighter material between layers of fabric.

find out more
Castles
Knights
Weapons

Australia

The first inhabitants of Australia were the Aborigines. They probably arrived at least 45,000 years ago from Asia, travelling from island to island in dugout canoes. They spread over the country in large family groups known as tribes.

Spanish and Portuguese seafarers first sailed close to Australia's shores in the 17th century. The first European to sail right around Australia was Abel Tasman, a Dutchman. In 1642 he discovered the island that is now named after him, Tasmania. These early voyagers thought that the country was too barren to settle.

In 1770 the British explorer Captain James Cook landed on the more fertile east coast. He named the land New South Wales and claimed it for Britain. The first settlers were convicts and soldiers who were sent by Britain in 1788.

Settlement

During the 19th century more settlers arrived to start farms or make their fortune in the Australian gold fields. They fought with the Aborigines and slowly occupied more and more land. At first they found it hard to make a living. They did not share the Aborigines' knowledge of the land.

From 1855 Australia gradually obtained greater independence from British rule until, in 1901, it became a self-governing country.

Australia in the 20th century

Australia continued to have close links with Britain. Australian troops helped Britain to fight in World Wars I and II, and the British Queen is also the Queen of Australia. Since World War II

find out more
Cook, James

▲ These Aboriginal rangers in Queensland are sitting underneath ancient cave paintings, which were painted by their ancestors many thousands of years ago. Some Aboriginal sites with rock paintings date back between 40 and 60 thousand years.

• Aborigines were not allowed to vote in Australia until 1966. After years of campaigning, laws which were intended to wipe out their culture have been reversed. Some sacred sites are being returned to their original owners and Aboriginal people now have a voice in running their own affairs.

Australia has also strengthened its ties with the United States. In the 1960s it sent troops to help the USA fight the Vietnam War. It has also increased its contact with Asian countries, particularly in trade and tourism. Immigrants have come from all over the world, changing Australia from a country of British origins to one with a varied mix of races and cultures. Many Australians now think that the Queen should be replaced as head of state by a president elected by the Australian people.

▼ This print shows Sydney Harbour (Port Jackson) and the surrounding land as they were in 1823. Sydney harbour is one of the best natural harbours in the world.

Austrian empire

Today Austria is only a small country, but in the past it ruled a great European empire. This empire lasted from the Middle Ages until the end of World War I in 1918.

For over 600 years the powerful Habsburg family ruled Austria. For much of that time the Habsburgs also ruled the Holy Roman Empire. During the religious wars of the Reformation the Austrians fought on the Catholic side. They also fought against the Ottoman Turks. They successfully stopped the Turks extending their empire across Europe, and they took Hungary from them.

By the 19th century the Austrian empire covered much of central Europe. It included many different peoples speaking many different languages. Many of these peoples did not like being ruled by the German-speaking Austrians, and there was a lot of unrest.

The end of empire

In 1914 a Serb assassinated the son of the Austrian emperor in the Bosnian capital, Sarajevo. This led to the outbreak of World War I. During the war Austria sided with Germany and was defeated. Afterwards, the peoples of the empire gained their own independent countries, and Austria itself became a small republic.

◀ Emperor Franz Josef ruled the Austrian empire from 1848 to 1916. In 1867 the Austrians allowed Hungary, which was part of the empire, to have its own parliament. The empire then became known as the Austro-Hungarian empire, or Austria–Hungary.

• For centuries Austria was the most powerful German-speaking state in Europe. But in 1866 Prussia defeated Austria, and five years later the king of Prussia became emperor of a strong and united Germany.

find out more
Germany
Holy Roman Empire
Ottoman empire
Reformation
World War I

Aztecs

find out more
Maya
North America
Spain

The Aztecs were a people who created an ancient civilization in the Valley of Mexico in the 14th century.

When the Aztecs came to the Valley of Mexico in about 1345, they built a huge city on an island in Lake Texcoco. They called it Tenochtitlán (now Mexico City) and it became the capital of the Aztec empire. There were canals instead of streets, and raised causeways crossed the lake. Feathers, tools and cacao beans were traded in place of money.

Daily life

Most Aztecs lived in small houses made of mud bricks. Men and boys worked as farmers in the fields. Women and girls looked after the home,

▲ The Aztecs worshipped many gods. This turquoise mask with eyes and teeth of white shell is thought to represent Quetzalcóatl, the god of learning and priesthood.

capital city
area of Aztec influence
territory paying tribute to Aztecs

0   200 km
0   150 miles

TARASCAN STATE
Tenochtitlán TLAXCALA
TEOTITLÁN
Gulf of Mexico
XICALANCO
YOPITZINCO
MIXTEC STATES
XOCONOCHCO
PACIFIC OCEAN
MAYAN STATES

▲ At its height, the Aztec empire dominated much of the area that is now Mexico.

ground corn (maize) to make pancakes, and spun and wove cotton cloth.

The emperor had all the power. Below him were high-ranking soldiers, priests and rich merchants. The ordinary people did not have much freedom or say in government. Below them were the slaves.

Conquest and destruction

In 1519 the Spanish conqueror Hernán Cortés arrived at Tenochtitlán. He captured the Aztec emperor, Montezuma II. The Aztecs rebelled, but after fierce fighting they were defeated by the heavily armoured Spaniards. The Spanish then ruled Mexico. They destroyed the temples and the great city of Tenochtitlán.

Balkans

The south-eastern corner of Europe, known as the Balkans, is one of the great crossroads of the world. In the past many different races, religions and cultures met here, in peace and war.

The complex history of the area explains why Greece, Romania, Bulgaria, Serbia, Croatia, Bosnia and the other modern Balkan states are so different from each other, and why the region has been so troubled.

The Ottoman empire

For hundreds of years the Balkans were part of the Muslim Ottoman empire. From the 1820s, the Balkan peoples began to rebel and set up their own countries. Greece became independent in 1831, Romania in 1861, Serbia and Bulgaria in 1878, and Albania in 1912.

The Ottoman empire was abolished after World War I. A new kingdom of Yugoslavia was formed, home to Serbs, Bosnians, Croats and other peoples, both Christian and Muslim.

Civil war

After World War II the communist leader President Tito set up a new republic of Yugoslavia. His strict rule held the country together and for a time it prospered. However, after Tito's death in 1980 the old racial and religious squabbles began again.

As the Serbs seemed to be trying to take over the whole country, a bloody civil war broke out in 1991. Slovenia, Croatia, Bosnia and Herzegovina, and Macedonia became independent states. A ceasefire was arranged in 1995, but fighting broke out again in 1999, in Kosovo in southern Yugoslavia.

◀ The Balkan countries after the ceasefire in 1995.

● Josip Broz (1892–1980), popularly known as Marshal Tito, made his name during World War II as a guerrilla leader fighting the Nazis. As president of Yugoslavia after the war, he steered a clever middle path between Soviet communism and Western democracy.

◆ capital city

| 0 | 400 km |
| 0 | 200 miles |

find out more
Europe
Ottoman empire
United Nations

Black Death

In the middle of the 14th century, about one-third of the people of Europe died in the Black Death. The Black Death was the first great outbreak of the disease known as bubonic plague.

People who caught the plague developed large black swellings under their arms and in their groin. They got a raging fever and usually died within a few days. Doctors could do nothing to help them.

March of death

The plague spread from northern India to China and west to Constantinople (Istanbul). From there it passed into Europe. It reached England in 1348, and Moscow three years later. Some areas escaped completely, but in others whole communities perished and villages were deserted. About 25 million people died. There were several more outbreaks of the plague over the next few hundred years. The last plague in Britain was in 1665.

◀ Death became a popular subject for artists for many years after the Black Death.

Punishment from God?

The plague terrified medieval people because it was mysterious as well as deadly. Some people said it was God's punishment for wicked behaviour. They thought that the disease was carried in infected air. In fact it was carried by fleas that live on rats. And in the often filthy living conditions of the Middle Ages it spread rapidly.

Not all the effects of the Black Death were bad. Life actually got better for many of the survivors. The massive decrease in Europe's population meant that there were fewer peasants to work the land, so landowners were forced to pay higher wages.

● The Black Death was brought into Europe by Italian ships trading in the Black Sea. Hidden in the cargoes of grain that these ships were carrying were the rats that carried the disease.

find out more
Medieval England
Middle Ages

Britain since 1900

During the 20th century Britain lost its position as the world's most powerful country. But society became fairer, and despite two world wars and the Great Depression, the average family's standard of living rose sharply.

These changes were well under way in the period before World War I. Suffragettes campaigned for votes for women and trade unions called strikes for better pay and conditions. The Liberal government introduced old-age pensions. By 1914 British industry had been overtaken by the USA and Germany.

Between the wars

World War I (1914–1918) cost almost a million British lives and left Britain with huge debts. It also speeded up the rate of change. In 1918 women over 30 got the vote in national elections. In 1921 Ireland was divided between the Catholic Irish Free State and Protestant

▶ In the 1960s, 'Swinging Britain' was the cultural centre of the world. This trend was led by fashion designers like Mary Quant and bands like the Beatles, which gave British 'pop' a huge international following.

Ulster, which remained in the United Kingdom.

Times were tough for the traditional industries – coalmining, iron and steel, and shipbuilding – and unemployment remained high. Hard-pressed workers resorted to strikes. The biggest of these was the nine-day General Strike of 1926. The Great Depression (from 1929 onwards) deepened the misery, and by 1932 unemployment stood at 2.7 million.

Nevertheless, the middle class grew, suburbs spread, and people were buying more things. Politics changed, too. The Liberals lost popularity to the Labour Party, although in 1931 a coalition (all-party) National Government was formed to deal with the problems of the Great Depression.

War and welfare

In 1939 Britain was at war again. Enemy German planes regularly bombed London and other cities. Winston Churchill's coalition government rationed food and other necessities. With most men aged between 18 and 50 in the forces or doing war work, women kept the country going.

After World War II ended in 1945, a Labour government introduced the 'Welfare State' to help poorer families. Its reforms included better unemployment pay and pensions, child allowances and setting up the National Health Service. All children under 16 had free education. The government also took over ('nationalized') several large industries, including coalmining and railways.

The 50s and 60s

The British empire was broken up between 1947 and 1970 as former colonies became independent. Most joined the Commonwealth of Nations, whose head is the British monarch. Thousands of immigrants came to Britain, creating a multicultural society, and racism was officially made illegal. ◗

▼ A poor family in a slum house before World War I. Millions of homes had no bathrooms and only an outside toilet.

The country prospered. Slums were cleared, and most homes now had bathrooms, fridges and televisions. Millions of new cars began to clog up the roads. Harold Macmillan's Conservatives won the 1959 election with the slogan 'You've never had it so good'.

Towards the millennium

The 1970s were plagued by inflation, unemployment and strikes. Rising oil prices made matters worse, and by 1982 unemployment was over 3 million. The discovery of oil fields beneath the North Sea and joining the European Economic Community (now the European Union) in 1973 brought some relief. Margaret Thatcher's Conservative government (1979–1990) curbed the power of trade unions, cut government

▶ The Channel Tunnel was more than just a great feat of engineering. It was a symbol of Britain's willingness to work more closely with Europe.

spending and sold off many nationalized industries. Inflation came under control but unemployment remained high. Average living standards went on rising, but the gap between rich and poor grew.

Terrorism caused over 3000 deaths in Northern Ireland between 1968 and 1994. The Welsh and Scots wanted greater independence, and environmental pollution became a major issue. Violent crime increased, divorce rates rose, and there was a decline in organized religion.

Britain seemed unsure about where it stood in the world. It could field only small forces for the Falklands and Gulf Wars

(1982 and 1991) and found the European Union difficult to work with. In 1997 Tony Blair led a Labour government to power. At this time, Britain began to co-operate with the rest of Europe, inflation was low, and steps were being taken to tackle poverty, crime and pollution.

find out more
Churchill, Winston
Ireland
Scotland
Twentieth-century
  history
Victorian Britain
Wales
World War I
World War II

Buddhists

The Buddhist religion began between the 6th and 5th centuries BC. An Indian prince called Siddhartha Gautama found a way of life that he believed could make all beings peaceful and happy. He became known as Buddha, the 'enlightened one', and today he has followers all over the world.

The Buddha taught four 'noble truths':
1 Life can never be perfect, because there will always be suffering. 2 Suffering is caused by our greed or selfishness.
3 Suffering can only end when we no longer want anything for ourselves. 4 There is a way of life, or path, that can lead to enlightenment, a state of inner peace called *nirvana*.

Buddha himself began the spread of Buddhism by sending monks out to teach people in their own languages. First, Buddhism spread over India, then along the Silk Road to China, Korea and Japan. Although it almost died out in India, it established itself in Sri Lanka, South-east Asia and Tibet. Tibetans still look on the Buddhist monk Dalai Lama as the rightful ruler of their country, even though he lives in exile in India because Tibet is currently under Chinese control.

Over the centuries two main forms of Buddhism have developed. In Theravada Buddhism the rituals are few and simple. In Mahayana Buddhism the rituals are much more elaborate. In the 20th century Buddhism also started to grow in Western countries.

▶ Although Buddhists do not think of the Buddha as a god, they keep statues of him in their houses to inspire them to try to follow his teachings.

find out more
India
Monasteries

Byzantine empire

For over 1000 years, the city of Byzantium was the centre of the eastern Roman empire, the Byzantine empire, and it became one of the largest and richest cities in the world.

Byzantium (now the city of Istanbul in Turkey) was an ancient Greek town which was easy to defend because there was sea on three sides. Constantine the Great, the first Christian emperor of Rome, made it the capital of the whole empire instead of Rome, and in AD 330 he changed its name to Constantinople.

Gains and losses

While the western Roman empire was crumbling, the eastern empire stayed strong. In the 6th century the Byzantine emperor Justinian won back parts of Italy, Spain and North Africa. But from the 7th century the empire was continually being attacked. After attempts by Slavonic tribes and Muslim Arabs failed, Turks from the east succeeded in occupying Palestine in 1071. The emperor appealed to the Christians of western Europe for military help in 1099. The result was the Crusades. The Byzantine empire lasted another 250 years. Finally the Turks captured Constantinople in 1453 and made it the capital of the Ottoman empire.

• In the 6th century, Byzantine emperor Justinian's most lasting achievement was a Code of Roman Law. He had all the laws that had been made over 1000 years put into a single legal system. This is still the basis of the legal system in France, Italy, Scotland and many other countries.

find out more
Christians
Crusades
Dark Ages
Holy Roman Empire
Ottoman empire
Romans

▼ The greatest of all the Byzantine churches was the cathedral of Saint Sophia in Istanbul. The walls are covered in glowing mosaic pictures of stories from the Bible and of famous Byzantine figures. This beautiful mosaic shows Empress Zoe, the most powerful woman in the Byzantine empire.

Caesar, Julius

Born 100 BC in Italy
Murdered 44 BC
aged 55

find out more
Celts
Cleopatra
Romans

Julius Caesar was a powerful Roman general with great ambitions. He used his vast army to win a civil war against his political rivals and make himself the sole ruler of the mighty Roman empire.

Julius Caesar was born into an important Roman family and soon became a successful politician. He served his time in the army and then held various public offices. In 60 BC he was elected to serve for one year as consul, the highest position in Rome. He was now in charge of the state's administration and the armed forces, although he held power jointly with another consul. He then governed provinces in northern Italy and Gaul (part of modern France).

◄ This painting by Lionel Noel Royer from 1899 uses accounts from Caesar's time to reconstruct a scene in which Vercingetorix, who led a doomed rebellion against Roman rule, surrenders to Caesar.

From there he conquered a vast new area in Gaul and Germany and invaded Britain twice, in 55 and 54 BC.

Caesar was now a very powerful leader with a huge army under his control. He decided not to disband his troops, as he should have done by law, and marched into Italy in 49 BC. Caesar had declared war on the Roman state, and this meant civil war. Pompey the Great fought against Caesar. The war lasted until Caesar's victory in 45 BC, and the next year he was appointed 'dictator for life', making him the sole ruler. However, not everyone wanted to be ruled by one man, and on the day called the Ides of March (15 March) in 44 BC, Caesar was stabbed to death outside the building where the senate (parliament) of Rome met.

Canada

The original Canadians emigrated from Asia during the Ice Age at least 25,000 years ago. Many bands of people crossed what is now the Bering Sea, when sea levels were lower. The Inuit of Canada, whom Europeans once called Eskimos, arrived 4000 years ago along the Arctic coast.

The Native Americans here have many distinct language and cultural groups. The Haida of the west coast are known for their totem poles; the Ojibwa (also called the Chippewa) perfected the birch-bark canoe; and the Cree invented the toboggan.

European settlement

In 1497 John Cabot, an Italian navigator who had settled in England, landed in Nova Scotia. He explored the St Lawrence estuary and claimed the area for the king of England. British colonists settled in the warmer lands to the south. In the 17th century the French sent 10,000 settlers to the St Lawrence River to farm and trade for fur. The Native Americans helped the French fur traders and became their partners.

In the 18th century the French and English fought over these valuable lands. The British gained control after the capture of the city of Québec in 1759, although the French were given rights of language and education. When the USA became independent, thousands of Britain's supporters fled to Canada, including some slaves. Canada outlawed slavery in 1834 and runaway slaves continued to escape to Canada from the USA for almost 30 years.

Canadians feared that the USA might try to take them over. As a result, several colonies formed the Dominion of Canada in 1867. Each colony became a province. The new country purchased land and planned a cross-continental railroad. As the number of settlers increased and moved westwards, new provinces were founded.

Modern Canada

At first most immigrants to Canada came from Britain, but settlers from eastern and northern Europe followed. In the 1960s many people from Italy, Greece and Portugal arrived to do construction work, but started their own businesses. Today most immigrants are from Asia and the Caribbean. Canada gradually became a fully independent country, but it kept its links with Britain. Canadians fought on Britain's side in World Wars I and II, and the British Queen is still Canada's formal head of state.

Canada is a peaceful and wealthy country, but there have been some difficulties among its various peoples. Many French-speaking Canadians, most of whom live in Québec Province, want Québec to leave Canada and become an independent country. Some people in the western provinces, where farming is important, feel that the more industrial eastern provinces control the country and ignore their needs. There have also been campaigns by Native Americans to recover their traditional lands, which were taken from them by the Europeans in the 19th century. Despite these internal problems, Canada has played an important part in world affairs, and Canadian troops have served with United Nations peace-keeping forces in many parts of the world.

▲ A poster encouraging British people to migrate to Canada in 1914.

find out more
France
Native Americans
North America
United States of America

▼ Upper Fort Garry, Hudson Bay, on the east coast of Canada, in 1845. Hudson Bay was discovered by the English explorer Henry Hudson in 1610. It became the site of the company that dominated the early economy of Canada.

Caribbean

Five hundred years ago the Caribbean islands were home for two groups of Native Americans, the Arawaks and the Caribs. Today nearly all Caribbean people are descended from people who have come there since 1492 – Europeans, Africans, Indians and Indonesians. Many of them are of mixed race.

Up to 50 Arawak or Carib families lived with their chief in a village. Every few years they moved their thatched huts and their sleeping hammocks to a new place for farming. The Arawaks lived mostly in the western islands. The Caribs lived on the South American mainland and in the eastern Caribbean.

European empires

In 1492 Christopher Columbus sailed into the Caribbean from Spain. He hoped he had sailed around the world to the East Indian islands. Other explorers recognized that these were

◀ Toussaint l'Ouverture was the most famous leader of the black armies who fought against the French in St Dominique. In 1804, renamed Haiti, the island became the first independent black country in the Caribbean.

different islands, which they named the West Indies. The Spanish built up an empire in the Caribbean and the Americas. Many Arawaks died in fighting or from European diseases.

French, Dutch and English sailors began to raid the Spanish empire and captured many islands, especially in the Caribbean. There were many wars between the settlers and the Caribs. Today, only a few people on the smaller islands have Carib ancestors.

Slave life

Over a period of about 200 years, about 5 million men, women and children were brought from West Africa and sold as slaves to sugar and tobacco plantations.

As time went on, the African traditions they brought with them combined with the ways of the Europeans. Many Caribbean people today speak Creole languages with French or English words and mainly African grammar. Music and dance forms combine African and Caribbean traditions.

Slavery did not completely end in British colonies until 1838. Slavery lasted in the French islands (Martinique and Guadeloupe) until 1848, and in the Spanish islands (Cuba and Puerto Rico) until 1886. After slavery was abolished the British and Dutch hired workers from India and Indonesia to work on plantations in Trinidad, Guyana and Suriname, where their descendants are known as 'East Indians'.

Independence

Although most ex-slaves left the plantations to find work or set up businesses on their own, Europeans kept the best land and did little to see that black people had jobs, schools or health care. Some people had to emigrate to find work. Many West Indians went to the USA, Canada or Europe.

In the 1920s and 1930s, most people in the Caribbean were still desperately poor. Trade unions and political parties were formed to press for better conditions and, later, for independence. Jamaica, and Trinidad and Tobago, achieved independence in 1962. Suriname became independent in 1975. Most of the former British colonies are now independent countries, but the French islands are governed as if they were districts of France. Puerto Rico, once a Spanish colony, is linked to the USA.

▲ Many Caribbeans migrated to Britain from the late 1940s in search of work.

• Marcus Garvey, a black rights campaigner from Jamaica, tried to bring together the people who had left the Caribbean. He wanted to unite them as members of a single nation with its roots in Africa. In 1914 he started his Universal Negro Improvement Association and he inspired many black people to work towards independence.

find out more
Africa
Columbus, Christopher
Native Americans
Slaves
South America

Castles

Castles are strong buildings, or groups of buildings, that were designed to protect the people who lived in them from attack. They were usually the homes of chieftains, kings or knights.

• The word 'castle' comes from the Latin *castellum*, which means 'a little fort'. The word 'fort' comes from the French word for 'strong'. Forts are usually built as soldiers' headquarters. The Romans built forts for their armies and strong walls to protect their towns.

find out more
Crusades
Knights
Middle Ages
Normans
Weapons

Most castles date from the Middle Ages and were built in Europe. Asian countries such as China, India and Thailand have their own strongholds, but these are usually known as *forts*. They are often not strong in themselves but are protected by strong walls.

The first true castles were built in 10th-century France. Many started as a simple wooden tower (*keep*), built on a high mound (*motte*) and encircled by a wall made of earth or wood. There was sometimes a surrounding ditch filled with water, called a *moat*.

Builders often put up fences round the foot of the mound. The area between the fence and the wall formed a yard known as a ward or bailey. Such castles are called *motte-and-bailey* castles.

Motte-and-bailey castles were very popular with the Normans, and during the 11th century they became common all over western Europe. In many places builders remade the keeps and outer walls in stone. This was to stop attackers from setting fire to them. Baileys became bigger too, so that more buildings could be added.

Builders constantly thought of ways to make their castles safer from attack. After 1100 European builders got many ideas from the crusaders, who had seen the mighty fortresses of their Arab enemies. They made the outer walls much thicker, usually with a second wall inside. Along the top was a walkway for the soldiers to

patrol. A wall called a *battlement* ran along the walkway. It protected the patrols, but it also had openings in it so that attackers could be fired upon. Towers guarded each section of the wall. The *drawbridge* at the main gateway was the first thing to be raised in case of attack. Stables, gardens, kitchens and a chapel were often built inside the bailey.

Enemy attempts to capture castles were called *sieges*. It was possible to fire arrows at the attackers through narrow slits in the walls or through the gaps in the battlements. If they came closer, the defenders could drop heavy objects on them or pour hot oil through holes beneath the battlements.

The arrival of gunpowder in Europe in the 15th century meant that castles could be conquered much more easily. They were still built, but not to stand up to sieges.

▶ A cut-away illustration of a medieval European castle. Inside the keep were rooms for eating and sleeping, and storerooms for keeping supplies. The great walls around the castle protected the people inside from attack. Inside the walls was the yard or bailey, which often had gardens for growing food and stables for keeping animals.

keep
lord's living quarters
great hall
guardroom
storerooms
kitchen
tower
outer walls and battlements
well
orchard
guards
church
moat
dungeon
drawbridge

Celts

The Celts are an ancient European people. They are known as a fierce and warlike people, but this may be because they left no written records and the Greeks and Romans who wrote about them were, for most of the time, their enemies.

Many Europeans are descended from the Celts, and Celtic place names (such as London and Paris) and river names (such as Rhine, Danube and Thames) are still used today.

Conquest and defeat in Europe

The Celts' first homeland was probably in what is now southern Germany and the Czech Republic. They were warriors, farmers and traders, who used iron weapons to conquer more lands, and iron tools to farm them. By 400 BC Celtic tribes were settled in the British Isles, Spain, France and Italy. Fellow Celts were soon advancing into the Balkans, and in about 276 BC a Celtic people even moved into Asia Minor (now Turkey). Their opponents found the Celtic warriors terrifying. To scare their enemies in battle, Celtic warriors combed their hair to make it stand on end, often tattooed or decorated their bodies, and rushed shouting into battle.

It must have seemed for a while that the Celts would make all Europe their own. But they showed little interest in creating an empire, or in making a union of all their territories. From about 200 BC, the Celts rapidly lost ground: to the Germans in the north, the Dacians in the east and the Romans in the south.

Celtic Britain

Celtic-speaking people first came to Britain in about 700 BC and tribes of invaders kept on coming until the 1st century BC. Each tribe had its own rulers and quite possibly its own gods. For this reason the tribes often fought each other, and did not join forces against the successful Roman invaders who came after AD 43.

After the Roman occupation, the new Anglo-Saxon settlers edged the Celts out too. Celtic culture did linger on in Cornwall and in the highlands of Wales

▶ High crosses were usually gifts from powerful chiefs and kings. Many were built in the 9th and 10th centuries at important Christian centres. The coils and spirals in this design are typical of the work of the Celtic craftspeople; no one knows whether they had any special meaning.

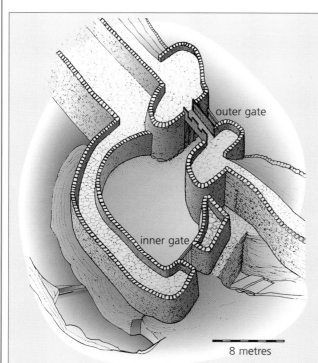

Hillforts

Celtic people built hillforts as a strong defence against enemy tribes and wild animals. They chose hills which had their own defences, such as cliff edges. Then they built huge banks of earth all around by digging out deep ditches. Some hillforts have steep stone walls in front of these banks of earth. The entrances made enemies twist and turn between high walls, leaving them open to attack from swords, spears or slings. But even the sling-throwers able to kill an enemy at 60 metres away were no match for the giant catapults of the Roman artillery and the Celts were forced out of their hilltop towns.

◀ The entrance to the hillfort of Crickley Hill in Gloucestershire, England. An enemy would have to break through the outer gate, but would then be trapped in the slingers' crossfire in front of the inner gate.

outer gate

inner gate

8 metres

• Celtic myths and legends were passed on by word of mouth. Many people in Cornwall, Ireland, Scotland and Wales today continue to tell them. The stories are about giants like Ysbadaden, who propped his eyelids open with pitchforks; wizards like Merlin, who helped King Arthur; and warriors like Geraint of Cornwall or Gawain of Wales.

and Scotland. Ireland was never invaded by the Romans or Saxons. It remained a Celtic country until the Vikings came in the 9th century AD. So the Irish people went on speaking their Celtic or 'Goidelic' language.

Celtic society and beliefs

The Celts had a carefully organized society with laws made by nobles who were leaders – princes or chiefs – of their own tribes or clans. They lived not only in hillforts, but also on farms and in small 'villages' made up of five or six families. As well as vegetables, they grew wheat and barley to make bread; the barley was also used to make beer. They reared cows, goats, horses, pigs and sheep, and used dogs for hunting wild boar. They liked to wear multi-coloured and embroidered clothes finished off with patterned bronze or gold jewellery.

Celtic people worshipped dozens of gods and spirits, and the Sun and Moon. They made offerings to please their gods and their Druids made both animal and human sacrifices.

Druids were the priests of the Celtic peoples who lived in Gaul (now mainly France) and Britain in the 1st century BC. Druids could be male or female and they acted as chiefs and judges as well as priests. 'Druid' comes from the Greek word for oak, *drus*. Druids believed that the oak tree was sacred and they held important religious ceremonies in oak groves.

• The Celtic warrior-chief King Arthur is the hero of many Celtic myths and legends. The stories say he ruled all Britain and conquered most of western Europe. His 12 most trusted warriors were called the Knights of the Round Table.

◀ This Celtic silver cauldron was found in Denmark, but was probably made in south-eastern Europe. The detailed scenes on it show gods and goddesses, bulls and bullfights, processions of warriors, and sacrifices.

find out more
Anglo-Saxons
Ireland
Romans
Scotland
Wales

Charlemagne

Born about 742 probably in Aachen, now in Germany
Died 814 aged 72

Charlemagne was a soldier and conqueror who became the greatest ruler of the early Middle Ages. He is regarded as one of the main founders of Western civilization.

• Charlemagne built magnificent palaces in Aix-la-Chapelle (Aachen) and in other parts of his kingdom, such as Zürich, Paris and Frankfurt. His court became a centre of art and learning as he encouraged artists, musicians, writers and scholars.

find out more
Byzantine empire
Dark Ages
Holy Roman Empire

Charles (later called Charlemagne) was the eldest son of Pepin, king of the Franks. The Franks had invaded part of the Roman empire and settled in what is now France and Germany. When King Pepin died in 768, he divided his kingdom between his two sons, Charles and Carloman. Three years later Carloman died, and Charles became the sole ruler.

Charles's aim as king was to enlarge the kingdom he had inherited and at the same time to spread Christianity among

the people he conquered. During his long reign of over 40 years he organized about 60 military campaigns. His empire extended to include what is now France, most of Germany, and

parts of Hungary, the Czech Republic, Slovakia, Italy, Spain and the Balkan countries.

His conquests earned him the name Charlemagne ('Charles the Great'). Pope Leo III asked him to take over part of Italy, and in 800 he was crowned emperor of what was later to become known as the Holy Roman Empire. After Charlemagne's death, his mighty empire fell apart.

◀ Charlemagne was both the ruler of much of Europe and the head of the Church within his empire. This engraving by Hieronymus Wierix shows him in both of these roles: he is standing astride the lands of his empire while wearing a bishop's hat.

China

Chinese civilization is one of the oldest in the world. From at least 2000 BC until the 20th century China was ruled by a series of 'dynasties', each named after the family of the ruling emperor.

Change came in the form of a revolution in 1911, when China became a republic. In 1949, after a long civil war, the Communist Party took power and China became a communist state.

The early dynasties

The first four dynasties that we know much about were the Shang, Zhou, Qin and Han who, between them, ruled from about 1500 BC to AD 220. During their rule China became united as a single country and the Great Wall was built – to keep out 'barbarians' from the north. Irrigated rice-growing began, cities were built and a writing system developed.

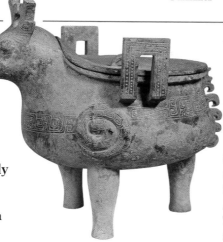

◀ A bronze tripod from the 7th century BC, made in the shape of a deer. People of the Shang and Zhou dynasties used such pots for cooking and storing food and drink used in religious ceremonies.

During the Han dynasty merchants from Arabia and Asia began to trade between China and the Roman empire, along the route called the Silk Road. At this time there were 59 million people in China, more than all the people in the Roman empire.

The Han emperors needed hundreds of thousands of officials to rule so many people. Young men who wanted to become officials had to pass difficult exams. They studied the teachings of Confucius, a philosopher who had lived in the 5th and 6th centuries BC.

Confucius taught how people could live in harmony, and how the country should be ruled. Another group of teachers, the Taoists, taught people to live simply, in harmony with nature. A third religion, Buddhism, was introduced to China from India in Han times.

The later dynasties

During the Tang and Song dynasties (618–1279) China governed much of central and South-east Asia. The arts flourished, Chinese technology was far in advance of anything in Europe, and there were many cities in China with populations of over 1 million people.

In 1279 China was conquered by the Mongols, who swept over the Great Wall and set up the Yuan dynasty (1279–1368). The Italian

Dynasties	Starting date
Xia	about 2000 BC
Shang	about 1500 BC
Zhou	about 1030 BC
Qin	221 BC
Han	206 BC
Time of the three kingdoms	AD 220
Sui	581
Tang	618
Five dynasties	907
Song	960
Yuan	1279
Ming	1368
Qing (Manzhou)	1644
Nationalist Republic	1912
People's Republic	1949

Chinese inventions
1st century AD
Magnetic compass
Ship's stern rudder
Canal locks
Seismograph
2nd century
Paper
3rd century
Wheelbarrow
5th century
Horse-collar harness
6th century
Suspension bridge
9th century
Gunpowder
11th century
Movable-type printing
Mechanical clock

◀ The 2700-km Great Wall of China was built between 221 and 210 BC. It was extended 400 years later, then rebuilt in the 15th and 16th centuries. It is the only man-made object that can be seen from space.

merchant Marco Polo visited the Chinese emperor Kublai Khan at this time.

In 1368 the Yuan were defeated by the Chinese Ming dynasty. Beijing was laid out by the Ming emperors. At the centre was a sacred palace, the Forbidden City, where China's emperors continued to live until 1911. The Ming dynasty was overthrown in 1644 by the last dynasty, the Qing, from Manchuria in the north-east.

When Portuguese explorers reached China by boat in 1517, they found a powerful, well-organized, sophisticated society, but one that was rigid and unwilling to change. By the 19th century, China's power had declined. Europeans trading with China found excuses to seize Chinese ports. This was how the British took control of Hong Kong in 1842.

By 1900 a number of Western-educated Chinese were worried that their country might be divided up between the Europeans and made into colonies. In 1911, led by Sun Yixian (Sun Yat-sen), they organized a revolution that overthrew the Qing (Manzhou) emperor, Pu Yi, and made China a republic.

Mao and after

Sun Yixian's democratic government quickly collapsed. After a period of unrest and a long civil war, General Jiang Jieshi (Chiang Kai-shek), came to power at the head of a nationalist government. His most serious rivals were the communists, led by Mao Zedong.

In 1937 Japan attacked China, and until 1945 the Chinese were united against the Japanese invaders. But after Japan's defeat, civil war broke out. Mao emerged victorious in 1949, and set up the communist People's Republic of China. Jiang Jieshi fled to Taiwan, where he headed a pro-Western government.

For 30 years Mao was the most powerful figure in China. Under communism education, health and the rights of women

▲ In 1900 the ordinary Chinese tried to drive out the European 'foreign devils' from their country. The Boxer rebellion, as it was known, was crushed by an army of European soldiers.

improved a lot. But private businesses were not permitted, and agriculture and industry made unsteady progress. After Mao's death in 1979, the new leaders began to allow some private enterprise, and with help from abroad the economy boomed. But opposition to the government was still not allowed, and some countries refused to trade with China because of this. However, relations with other countries have gradually improved, industries have done well and the economy has grown. In 1997 Hong Kong, a British colony since 1842, was returned to China.

• In 1989 many democracy campaigners were killed during a demonstration in Tiananmen Square in Beijing. There was an international outcry over this massacre.

• After 200 years of Chinese rule, Tibet became independent in 1912. The Chinese re-took Tibet in 1951, drove out the Dalai Lama (the traditional ruler) and tried to force Chinese communist ways on the Buddhist people.

find out more
Buddhists
Explorers
Mao Zedong
Mongol empire
Writing

▶ A painting showing Mao Zedong giving a speech to his troops during the civil war.

Christians

The Christian religion began with the life and teachings of Jesus, a Jew who lived in Palestine from about the year 4 BC to AD 29. Within a hundred years of his death, missionaries had taken Christian teachings to many countries around the Mediterranean Sea. There are now Christians all over the world.

▲ An icon (picture) of Jesus from the cathedral of Saint Sophia, Istanbul, Turkey.

● At the time Jesus was born, the Romans dated years from the legendary foundation of Rome. About 500 years after Jesus lived, Christian scholars worked out a new system counting from what they thought was the year of his birth. Their calculations were wrong. Later historians realized that Jesus was born four years earlier. BC means 'before Christ' and AD means after Christ was born. (AD is short for *anno domini*, which means 'in the year of our Lord'.)

● Heretics were Christians who disagreed with Church leaders over matters of religion, choosing for themselves what to believe. Something a heretic believes which does not agree with the Church's teaching is called a 'heresy'.

find out more
Byzantine empire
Crusades
Dark Ages
Holy Roman Empire
Middle Ages
Monasteries
Muslims
Ottoman empire
Reformation
Renaissance
Romans

Jesus taught his followers to love both God and their neighbours. They came to believe that he was the Messiah or Christ (a king whom the Jewish people believed was coming to save them). The ruling Roman government in Palestine felt threatened and had him arrested and sentenced to death by crucifixion (being nailed to a cross). Christians believe that on the third day after his death Jesus rose from the dead.

Christianity in the Roman empire

Jesus chose 12 men from among his followers to carry on his teaching. They were called apostles, meaning 'those who are sent out'. In the Bible, the Acts of the Apostles tells the story of the spread of Christianity from Palestine, through parts of Greece and other Mediterranean lands to Rome. One of the first Christian missionaries to reach Rome was St Paul, who was put to death for his beliefs. Gradually Christianity spread throughout the Roman empire. But many early Christians were still harassed and persecuted for their beliefs. Some were even killed for the amusement of the Roman crowds. The first emperor to accept the teachings of Christ publicly was Constantine. In AD 313 he allowed Christianity to be recognized, and persecution ended.

The Church in the Middle Ages

When the Roman empire collapsed in western Europe in the 5th century, Christianity survived in some places. Over the next few centuries Christianity spread again through Europe, and the Church became a powerful force. It owned large amounts of land and other riches. Most teaching was carried out by priests, monks and nuns, and this helped to maintain the power and authority of the Church. The Pope himself, the head of the Church in Rome, was also a kind of prince, ruling a large part of Italy.

In the 11th century the Western and Eastern Churches split. Rome continued to be the headquarters of the Christian Church in the West (the Roman Catholic Church). The capital of the Byzantine empire, Constantinople (modern Istanbul), became the centre of the Eastern Orthodox Churches. By the 13th century even the most remote parts of Europe had been converted to Christianity.

However, some areas were lost to Christianity. In the 7th century the Arabs conquered most of the Middle East, North Africa, Spain and Portugal, bringing with them the Muslim religion. The crusaders of the Middle Ages tried unsuccessfully to reconquer parts of the Middle East for Christianity. The Spanish and Portuguese did eventually defeat the last Muslims in their lands in 1492. Meanwhile, the Ottoman Turks had taken over the Byzantine empire, and brought the Muslim religion into south-eastern Europe. For many centuries the Christians fought to keep back the Turks.

▲ This 15th-century illustration shows St Paul being converted to Christianity. St Paul had a great influence on Christian teaching.

Christianity since the Reformation

There was another major split in the Church in the 16th century. During this period, called the Reformation, many people thought that the Catholic Church had become too rich and too powerful. These people, known as Protestants, formed new churches, and felt that they were returning to beliefs and a way of life closer to that of the Bible. Many wars followed between Protestants and Catholics. At around the same time, Europeans began to colonize different parts of the world, taking Christianity with them.

Churchill, Winston

Born 1874 at Blenheim Palace, Oxfordshire, England **Died** 1965 aged 90

• 'Never in the field of human conflict was so much owed by so many to so few.' Winston Churchill on the skill and courage of British airmen during the Battle of Britain, 1940.

find out more
Britain since 1900
World War II

Winston Churchill was the prime minister of Britain during most of World War II. His strong leadership helped steer the country to victory in 1945.

Winston Churchill was the grandson of the seventh Duke of Marlborough. His political career started in 1900 when he was elected to Parliament as a Conservative. However, in 1904 he fell out with his party and joined the Liberals, and he held several posts while they were in government. Before and during World War I he served as head of the Admiralty, but he resigned from government to command troops in France for a time. After serving again as a Liberal minister after the war, he returned to the Conservative Party, and was Chancellor of the Exchequer from 1924 to 1929.

Churchill did not hold a government post during the 1930s. He warned that there was a danger of another world war, but many people ignored him. However, when World War II did break out, he was put in charge of the Admiralty once again. Then, when German armies were overrunning Europe in May 1940, King George VI asked him to be prime minister and lead a coalition government of all parties. His courage and speeches inspired people to withstand air raids and military defeats, and carry on to victory.

Churchill remained prime minister until the 1945 general election brought Labour to power, just before the end of the war. He was prime minister again from 1951 to 1955, before giving up politics in 1964.

▼ Churchill on his way to the House of Commons in London on 8 May 1945. This was VE Day, the day on which the Allies celebrated their victory against Hitler's forces in Europe.

Cities

When people began to grow crops and raise animals from about 9000 BC, they started to settle in villages. Some of these villages grew into towns. The first cities were built in Mesopotamia (modern Iraq) around 4000 BC.

Over the next 3000 years people began to build cities in other parts of the Middle East, and also in eastern China, the Indus valley (in modern Pakistan and India), Central America, and Peru. The cities grew up in places where it was possible to produce a lot of food. They were usually near rivers, which offered good soils and a plentiful supply of water.

With the cities came the earliest civilizations. If there was plenty of food, not everybody had to work on the land. Instead, some people became craftspeople, merchants or priests. Those who owned the land became powerful rulers, and employed soldiers and administrators. People developed writing systems to help run the new city-states.

Later on cities often grew up around centres of trade. They were usually built by a large river or where there was a good natural harbour. Cities also got bigger. In the 18th century new farming methods meant that fewer people were needed to work the land. More and more people were forced to move to the towns and cities. There they found jobs in the new factories that sprung up in the Industrial Revolution. Today most people in the developed countries live in cities.

• One of the oldest cities is Jericho, on the west bank of the River Jordan. People have lived there since 9000 BC.

• Rome in the 2nd century AD became the first city to have a population of 1 million. By the 13th century there were several cities in China with more than a million people. London did not reach this size until 1800.

find out more
Agricultural Revolution
Ancient world
Government
Industrial Revolution
Transport

◀ The remains of Angkor Wat, a magnificient 12th-century temple in Angkor. Angkor was the capital of the Khmer empire in Cambodia until the 15th century.

Cold War

The Cold War was a long period of tension between the Soviet Union (the USSR) and its allies on the one side, and the United States of America (USA) and its allies on the other. It began in 1945 and lasted until the collapse of the USSR in 1991.

This period was called the Cold War because there was no actual fighting between the USSR and the USA. However, the Cold War created barriers between people, for example between eastern and western Europe. It also led to wars in which one side fought the allies of the other.

Two world views

The USA and the USSR had very different ideas about how the world should be run. The USA and its allies are democracies and favour private businesses (capitalism). The USSR and its allies had communist governments. This means that they believed that everything should be owned by the people. In fact it was the governments that had all the power.

Europe divided

When Germany was defeated at the end of World War II the Soviet army occupied most of eastern Europe, which it had freed from German control. The Soviets set up communist governments in the countries of eastern Europe, and also in the eastern half of Germany. It was said that an 'Iron Curtain' had fallen across Europe. The Americans feared that the Soviets wanted to spread communism to every part of the world, and decided that they would stop them.

Korea and Vietnam

Korea had been ruled by the Japanese for many years, but when Japan was defeated in 1945 the country was divided between communist North Korea and capitalist South Korea. In 1950 the North Koreans invaded the South. The United Nations sent troops, led by the USA, to help the South. The communist Chinese also joined the fighting on the side of the North. Neither side managed to win the war, which ended in 1953.

Vietnam was also divided in the same way in 1954, after fighting for its independence

from France. Communist North Vietnam attacked the capitalist South, and in the 1960s the USA sent its armed forces to fight the communists. Many people in the USA were against the war, and the USA stopped fighting in 1973. Two years later the North defeated the South and reunited the country.

Nuclear weapons

Both the USA and the USSR had enough nuclear weapons to destroy each other completely. This is one of the reasons the two countries never went to war. In 1962 the USSR took nuclear missiles to Cuba, its ally in the Caribbean, near to the USA.

The Americans threatened to use nuclear weapons if the missiles were not removed. Eventually the USSR agreed to take them away. After that the two sides started to talk about reducing the numbers and types of nuclear weapons on both sides. ♦

▲ ENIAC, one of the first electronic computers, was completed in 1946. It was used by the US armed forces to work out the best way to fire shells from guns. During the Cold War the USA spent more and more money developing its military technology. In the end the USSR was not rich enough to keep up.

◄ The test explosion of a nuclear weapon in 1953. Both the USA and the USSR had enough nuclear weapons to destroy the world several times over. Since the end of the Cold War, both sides have got rid of many of these weapons.

Other conflicts

Both sides interfered in the affairs of other countries during the Cold War. The USA helped to overthrow several governments that it believed were too friendly towards the Soviet Union. It also supported several anti-communist governments that were undemocratic and cruel to their own people.

The USSR sometimes behaved in a similar way. When some of the countries of eastern Europe tried to free themselves from the USSR, the Soviets sent in tanks. This happened in Hungary in 1956 and in Czechoslovakia in 1968. In 1979 the USSR invaded Afghanistan. Relations between the USA and the USSR became very bad for a few years. There was fighting in several places in Africa and Central America.

The end

In 1985 Mikhail Gorbachev became the new leader of the USSR. Gorbachev realized that the USSR was not wealthy enough to win the Cold War. He also realized that reform was needed in the USSR and its allies, otherwise their economies would collapse. He made more treaties with the USA to reduce the numbers of weapons held by both countries.

He also encouraged greater democracy.

In 1989 and 1990 the peoples of eastern Europe got rid of their communist governments and became democracies. In 1991 the 15 republics that made up the Soviet Union declared themselves independent. Russia was the largest of these republics. The USSR itself collapsed, and the Cold War was over.

◄ Contra rebels who fought the Sandinista government in Nicaragua in the 1980s. The USA supported the Contras, because they thought the Sandinista government was too friendly to the Soviet Union.

find out more
China
Communists
Europe
Germany
Government
Kennedy, J. F.
Peace movement
Russia
Stalin, Joseph
United States of
  America
Vietnam War
World War II

Born 1451 in Genoa, Italy
Died 1506 aged 54

find out more
Caribbean
Explorers
South America

▼ This statue of Columbus is from Cartagena in Italy.

Columbus,
Christopher

Christopher Columbus is one of the most famous explorers and navigators of all time. He came across the Americas while trying to find a westward route from Europe to the Far East.

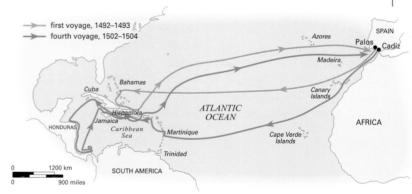

first voyage, 1492–1493
fourth voyage, 1502–1504

SPAIN
Azores
Palos   Cadiz
Madeira
Bahamas
Cuba
Canary
Islands
ATLANTIC
OCEAN
Hispaniola
Jamaica
HONDURAS
Caribbean
Sea
Martinique
Cape Verde
Islands
AFRICA
Trinidad
SOUTH AMERICA

0   1200 km
0   900 miles

On 3 August 1492 Columbus, funded by the king and queen of Spain, set sail with three small ships, *Santa Maria*, *Niña* and *Pinta*, and about 90 men. After 9 weeks they sighted land. It was, in fact, one of the Bahamian islands, but Columbus was convinced it was the Indies and that he was very near Japan. He thought the local people were 'Indians', which is why Native Americans are sometimes so called.

Columbus returned to Spain a hero, and was given the titles of Admiral of the Ocean Sea and Viceroy of the Indies. This meant that he could set up and govern colonies in the new land. He went on a second voyage in 1493, when he visited Jamaica, and a third trip in 1498, when he set foot on mainland South America.

Although he was a good explorer, Columbus was not a good governor. Complaints were

▲ This map shows two of Columbus's voyages across the Atlantic Ocean.

made about his harsh rule, and he was arrested and sent back to Spain. However, he was soon pardoned, and in 1502 he was allowed to make one more voyage. He died in 1506, still believing he had reached the Far East. He never realized that he had, in fact, found a land that no European at the time knew existed.

Communications

find out more
Transport
Writing

▼ The inventor of the telephone, Alexander Graham Bell, making the first phone call from New York to Chicago in 1892.

About 5000 years ago people used writing for the first time. They communicated over long distances with written messages carried by runners or messengers travelling on horseback.

Until the 15th century, written documents were made and copied by hand. But when the first practical printing system in Europe was invented in the 15th century, books and pamphlets could be produced in large numbers. This meant that ideas and education could be shared among many more people.

In the 19th century new inventions produced another revolution in communications. Railways greatly increased the speed at which letters could be delivered. The telegraph sent messages along electric wires, coded as long and short bleeps. The telephone meant that people could actually speak to each other over long distances. And finally the invention of radio in the 20th century led to mass communications through radio and television broadcasts.

Another communications revolution took place at the end of the 20th century. People can now talk to each other from opposite sides of the world using a phone they carry around with them. The combination of telephone and computer technology has also led to electronic mail (email) and the Internet, by which people can obtain information from computer databases all round the world.

Key dates

1450 Johann Gutenberg invents first practical printing system
1837 Invention of the telegraph
1840 Stamps first used on letters
1876 Alexander Graham Bell invents the telephone
1895 Guglielmo Marconi makes first long-distance radio transmission
1920 First regular public radio broadcasting
1926 John Logie Baird invents television
1962 Telstar, the first communications satellite, launched into space
1983 Creation of the Internet

Communists

'Workers of all countries, unite!' So wrote Karl Marx and Friedrich Engels, who together were the founders of modern communism. Communism is a political theory. It calls for a society in which all property and businesses are owned by the people, and in which each person is paid according to their needs, whatever their abilities are.

Marx, a German political writer living in London, England, developed the ideas on which communism is based in his influential book *Capital* (1867–1894). In it, he claimed that one day workers would rise in revolution, destroy the rich and set up communism across the world.

▶ Fidel Castro, communist leader of Cuba since 1959, speaking in front of a poster of Che Guevara, who fought with Castro to overthrow the Cuban dictator Batista.

However, communist revolutions did not come about in rich, industrial states, but in underdeveloped countries, such as Russia and China. Under communism people were better educated, and unemployment and extreme poverty were eliminated. But, as Marx had wanted, communist states were dictatorships. In Stalin's Russia and Mao Zedong's China everything was controlled by the Communist Party. This led to much corruption and cruelty. By the 1990s most communist governments, including those in Poland and the former Soviet Union, had collapsed.

Some of the communists' ideals live on in *socialism*, a moderate version of communism. This rejects revolution and dictatorship, but accepts the need for justice and equal opportunities for all.

find out more
China
Cold war
Mao Zedong
Russia
Stalin, Joseph

Cook, James

James Cook was a sailor and navigator who explored and mapped the Pacific Ocean and its islands. He claimed Australia and New Zealand for the British empire.

James Cook was 18 before he first worked on sailing ships. Nearly 10 years later, with England on the brink of war with France, Cook joined the Royal Navy as a seaman. He soon won promotion and was entrusted with the navigation of a ship.

In 1768 he was given command of the ship *Endeavour*. His main task was to take some astronomers to the Pacific island of Tahiti, but he was also given secret orders to search for the Great Southern Continent which people believed existed.

On that voyage around the world from 1768 to 1771, Cook explored and charted the coast of New Zealand and the eastern coast of Australia. The following year he sailed south of the Antarctic Circle, before cruising the Pacific Ocean to visit and chart many of the islands.

Cook was promoted to captain before going on a trip to find a possible sea route running north of Canada from the Pacific. He was the first European to visit the Sandwich Islands (Hawaii), and he passed through the Bering Strait between Alaska and Siberia into the Arctic Ocean. He was then forced to stop and turn round by a thick pack of ice. He returned to Hawaii to pick up food and water, but was killed by islanders in a scuffle on shore.

Born 1728 in Yorkshire, England
Died 1779 aged 50

find out more
Australia
Explorers
Georgian Britain
New Zealand

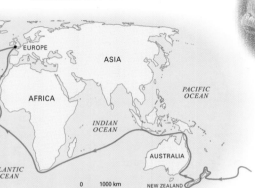

◀▲ James Cook sailed around the world on his first voyage. He sailed his small ships over a wider area of unknown seas than any other explorer.

Crimean War

The Crimean War, which lasted from 1854 to 1856, was a quarrel about power. As the Ottoman (Turkish) empire declined, Russia began to expand into areas that had been Turkish. British, French, Italian and Turkish troops fought the Russians over who was to hold power in the eastern Mediterranean.

Britain and France decided to attack the Crimea in south Russia (now part of Ukraine). They wanted to capture Sebastopol, Russia's important port on the Black Sea. Neither side had fought a war for 40 years, and there was chaos.

The British army travelled in filthy ships, and many soldiers died of cholera before they even reached the Crimea. Nearly 500 men and horses died needlessly in the 'Charge of the Light Brigade' at the battle of Balaclava, because a mistaken order sent them charging down a narrow valley into a death-trap of Russian guns.

When winter came, there were not enough tents, so soldiers had no shelter. The British wounded had no proper care, and suffered terribly. Reports of the appalling conditions appeared in the newspapers in Britain, and things began to change for the better. The British and French finally captured Sebastopol, mainly because the Russians were also very disorganized. But the war settled nothing between the countries that fought each other.

◀ Florence Nightingale working as a nurse during the Crimean War. She set up proper hospitals for the wounded, and became one of the founders of modern nursing.

find out more
Balkans
Ottoman empire
Russia
Victorian Britain

Cromwell, Oliver

Oliver Cromwell became the leader of the troops fighting on the side of Parliament against the king during the English Civil War. Cromwell and his men never lost a battle, and his victories made him the most powerful man in England.

Cromwell was 41 when he first joined the English Parliament in 1640, and he was a strong supporter of Parliament's powers. When the English Civil War began, he trained his own cavalry, nicknamed 'Ironsides' because they were such good fighters. They joined Parliament's victorious 'New Model Army', which Cromwell later commanded.

After winning the war, Cromwell and other army leaders tried to make a deal with Charles I, but the king broke his promises. Charles was put on trial for bringing war to his people and publicly beheaded. It is said that Cromwell came on his own to look at the dead king, and muttered sadly: 'Cruel necessity'.

Cromwell was determined to defend the new 'Commonwealth' (republic) of England. He distrusted the Irish, and carried out a ruthless conquest of Ireland. When the Scots tried to help the young Charles II, he defeated them too.

Cromwell became 'Lord Protector' in 1653. He tried to rule with Parliament, although he also used his army to enforce what he thought right. He allowed more religious freedom than usual (except in Catholic Ireland), and won a high reputation abroad. When Parliament offered him the crown, he refused it. But when he died, his funeral was as grand as any king's.

Born 1599 in Huntingdon, England
Died 1658 aged 59

▼ Oliver Cromwell with his soldiers, following his victory in the battle of Marston Moor in 1644.

find out more
Stuart Britain

Crusades

Crusades were wars waged by the knights of Europe against non-Christian peoples in the Middle Ages. The best-known crusades were against the Muslims of the Middle East between 1096 and 1291.

The crusaders wanted to help the Christian emperor of Constantinople in his wars with the Muslim Turks. They also wanted to seize the holy city of Jerusalem, and to protect Christian pilgrims who went there. But perhaps they were keenest of all to win lands, fame and fortune.

The four crusades

Pope Urban II called for the first crusade in 1095. From then until 1291 thousands of ordinary men and women fought alongside knights in a series of wars which were part of four different crusades.

By 1100 the crusaders had won and there was a Christian king in Jerusalem. However, in 1187 Saladin, the Muslim sultan of Egypt, recaptured the city. Attempts to reclaim it, made by England's Richard I ('the Lionheart') and the French king Philip II, failed.

In 1204 the fourth and final crusade took Constantinople rather than Jerusalem. Crusaders looted the city, which they held until 1261. By 1291 all other remaining Christian strongholds had fallen to the Muslims.

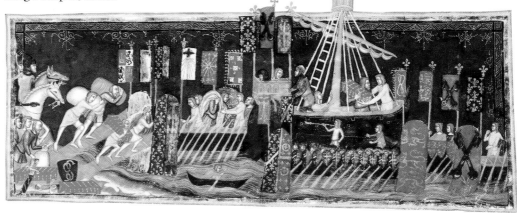
▼ This medieval French illustration shows crusaders loading their ship with supplies before setting out on the journey to Jerusalem.

• 'Crusade' comes from the Latin word *crux*, which means 'cross'. The first crusaders had the Christian cross sewn onto their clothes.

find out more
Byzantine empire
Knights
Middle Ages

Dark Ages

When we say the 'Dark Ages' we are talking about the centuries following the collapse of the Roman empire in western Europe. When people began to study history seriously, about 200 years ago, they could not find out much about these times because there were few written records or large archaeological remains. That is why they called it the 'Dark Ages'.

Today we know a great deal more about these centuries. Instead of talking about the Dark Ages, historians now usually call this period the 'early Middle Ages'.

Great migrations

The frontiers of the Roman empire were inhabited by tribes who did not accept the Roman way of life. The Romans called them 'barbarians'. In the north lived Germanic peoples, such as the Angles, Saxons, Jutes, Burgundians and Franks. Other Germanic groups – Vandals and Goths – lived further east. In the 4th century AD a new and warlike people arrived from Asia – the Huns. The Huns began to push the Germanic tribes out of their homelands.

By the 5th century AD, the Roman empire was beginning to crumble. The Germanic tribes invaded Roman territories. Angles, Saxons and Jutes swept into Britain. The Huns entered northern Italy. Franks and Burgundians moved into France, and Goths pushed south into Greece, southern Italy and Spain. In AD 410 they captured the city of Rome itself. The Vandals careered through Germany, France and Spain, and ended up in North Africa.

The main barbarian kingdoms of Europe at the beginning of the 6th century AD.

Barbarian kingdoms

By about AD 500 the Roman empire in the west had broken up into a number of small barbarian kingdoms. In the east it survived as the Byzantine empire.

The new kingdoms fought each other for territory. In the 6th century the Byzantine empire won many victories and conquered most of Italy. But this success did not last long. In the 7th century a new power swept out of the Middle East. These were the Arabs, who went on to conquer North Africa, Spain, Portugal and southern Italy.

A new civilization

In western Europe the Roman way of life had gone for ever. But a new civilization grew up in its place. Although parts of Europe were in turmoil, in other areas, such as England and France, the countries of modern Europe began to emerge. The more able kings worked hard to maintain law and order. In some places they set up orders of knights to defend their lands. This was the beginning of the medieval feudal system. One of the greatest of these kings was the 8th-century Frankish king, Charlemagne. Charlemagne carved out a great empire that included France, Germany and Italy, but his empire broke up after his death.

The Christian religion was at the heart of the new civilization. After the fall of the western Roman empire Christianity only survived in some places. But missionaries from Ireland and Rome gradually spread the Christian gospel round Europe. Christianity and learning in the Dark Ages was based in the monasteries.

find out more
Anglo-Saxons
Byzantine empire
Charlemagne
Christians
Holy Roman Empire
Middle Ages
Middle East
Muslims
Romans
Vikings

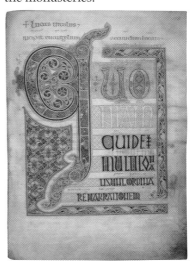

A page from the Lindisfarne Gospels. This beautifully decorated manuscript was made in the late 7th century in the monastery of Lindisfarne, north-east England.

Egyptians, ancient

Egypt became a single kingdom in about 3100 BC. This makes it one of the oldest states in the world. The ancient Egyptians conquered other countries and established a vast empire. They became famous for their great buildings, their statues and their ability to farm a land which was largely desert.

- The Egyptian empire came to an end in 30 BC when the Romans invaded and Egypt became part of the Roman empire.

- The Egyptians were good at engineering. They built special 'Nilometers' to measure the height of the flood waters in July, to work out how much water they could use when ploughing began in October.

▼ Tutankhamun (about 1370–1352 BC) is one of the best known of all the Egyptian kings. His fame is based mainly on the amazing treasures found inside his tomb when it was discovered in 1922. These include a solid gold coffin, a throne, jewellery, weapons, chariots and this beautiful gold funeral mask, which shows what the young king actually looked like.

Egypt could never have become a prosperous and powerful country without the River Nile. Each year the Nile floods the land, bringing water to a country which has very little rainfall. The river also washes fertile mud onto the soil. The Egyptians were able to grow corn for bread, and lettuces, onions, peas, cucumbers and other vegetables. Once the crops were growing, the Egyptians were able to water the soil by digging irrigation channels from the Nile. The Egyptians regarded the River Nile as a god, called Hapy, who was generous to them. He was not always reliable though, and there were years of drought and sometimes floods.

The king and the government

The rulers of Egypt were called *pharaohs*. The pharaoh was a king but was also thought to be a god after death. He was the High Priest of the Egyptians, the chief judge and also the commander-in-chief of the army. The king usually married his own sister and their son would become the next pharaoh.

A large number of officials, appointed by the king, ran the government. Some would have been relatives of the king. These officials looked after government departments such as the treasury, the civil service, the foreign office and the public records.

Ordinary Egyptians

A lot of ordinary Egyptians worked on the land as farmers. People not only planted crops but kept animals such as cows, sheep, goats and pigs. They also hunted animals such as deer, and trapped birds and fished, sometimes just for sport.

There were also a large number of special jobs to be done. Some Egyptians were fishermen, or boat-owners moving goods up and down the Nile. Builders were needed for the towns, palaces and the tombs. Craftspeople were trained to be tomb-painters or statue sculptors, or to make objects such as furniture

▲ This painting comes from a tomb in Thebes. It shows the nobleman Nebamun as a hunter throwing a stick at birds. Notice the great variety of birds in the air and fishes in the River Nile below his boat of reeds.

and jewellery. Some Egyptians were good engineers.

Pyramids and other buildings

Very important buildings, such as pyramids and temples to the gods, were built of stone cut from quarries. All the other buildings (people's houses, palaces and government buildings) were made of mud bricks. Earth was mixed with straw and water and put into wooden moulds. Once it had dried hard in the sun it could be used as a

▼ This map of ancient Egypt shows how all the major settlements were along the banks of the life-giving Nile.

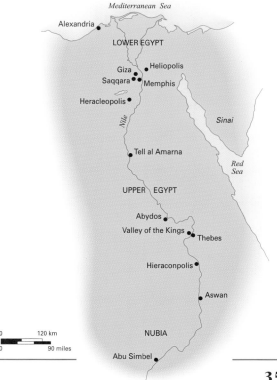

Mediterranean Sea

Alexandria

LOWER EGYPT

Giza • • Heliopolis
Saqqara • • Memphis
Heracleopolis •

Nile

Sinai

Tell al Amarna

Red Sea

UPPER EGYPT

Abydos
Valley of the Kings • • Thebes

Hieraconpolis

Aswan

NUBIA

0   120 km
0   90 miles

Abu Simbel

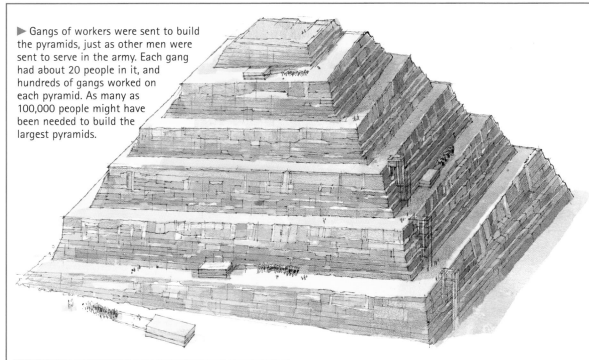

▶ Gangs of workers were sent to build the pyramids, just as other men were sent to serve in the army. Each gang had about 20 people in it, and hundreds of gangs worked on each pyramid. As many as 100,000 people might have been needed to build the largest pyramids.

• The ancient Egyptians are famous for using a kind of reed called papyrus to make writing materials. They used papyrus to write on and for painting pictures. They used pictures (called hieroglyphs) for their writing, which we can translate today.

▼ Animal mummies, like this cat mummy from Abydos, were found in tombs. To mummify a human or animal body, specialist workers removed the liver, lungs and other organs, then dried out the rest of the body using a type of salt. After about 70 days, when the body was completely dry, it was wrapped in linen bandages and sealed inside a coffin.

Egyptian gods and goddesses
The Egyptians worshipped over 750 gods. The gods ruled the upper world where humans lived, and the underworld where souls went after death.

Four Egyptian gods
Ra Egyptians believed that the world was brought to life by Ra (right), the Sun-god. Every day Ra sailed through the sky, bringing light to the world. Every evening he began a night-long voyage through the caves and tunnels of the underworld.

Osiris and Isis Osiris (second from right) and Isis (second from left) were the king and queen of all humans. Their brother, Set, the storm-god, murdered Osiris, cut his body into 14 pieces and floated them down the Nile. Osiris went to the underworld, where he became ruler of the dead. On each anniversary of his death, Isis wept for him and her tears caused the yearly Nile floods.

Anubis Ancient Egyptians believed that when a body died, the ka, or spirit-self, lived on. Jackal-headed Anubis (left), god of tombs, weighed each ka's heart against the Feather of Truth on a pair of scales. Wicked kas were handed over to the Eater of Corpses. Good kas were led to Osiris, who gave them eternal happiness.

building brick. Bricks lasted for a long time because the climate in Egypt is dry and hot.

The pharaohs and other important people of ancient Egypt were buried in fine tombs from the earliest times. In about 2686 BC a new type of tomb was built for the Pharaoh Zoser at Saqqara. It is called a step pyramid because it was built as a series of steps or platforms. Later, engineers worked out how to build smooth-sided pyramids of enormous height. Later still, tombs cut into rock were used as burial places. The most famous is that of Tutankhamun, in the Valley of the Kings at Thebes.

In pyramids the actual burial place was reached by a long passage carefully blocked and hidden from tomb-robbers. Pyramids were built close to the Nile so that stone blocks could be brought to the site by boat and moved on sledges. The body of the pharaoh also arrived by boat.

The afterlife
The Egyptians were very religious and believed that gods played a great part in their lives. They also believed that there was life after death. They thought that the dead person made a journey to the next world and continued to live the same sort of life there. The king would still be a king; a farm labourer would still be a farm labourer. To help in this journey, the rich were given a painted tomb with a variety of their possessions. The Egyptians also tried to preserve the body of a dead person in a life-like way using a special technique called mummification.

find out more
Alexander the Great
Ancient world
Egypt
Middle East
Romans
Writing

Elizabeth I

Elizabeth I was the queen of England from 1558 to 1603. During her reign England became more powerful and prosperous, and literature and the other arts flourished.

Elizabeth's early life was not easy. Her father, Henry VIII, did not want a daughter, and when she was 2 years old, her mother, Anne Boleyn, was executed. She was in great danger during her Catholic sister Mary's reign because she was a Protestant: when she was 21, she was imprisoned in the Tower of London for allegedly plotting against Mary. Not surprisingly, the 25-year-old woman who became queen in 1558 had learnt to hide her feelings. She was also cautious, clever and quick-witted.

Elizabeth was a strong-willed woman. In 1559 she changed the country's religion from Catholicism to Protestantism, even though this created many problems for herself and her people, particularly the Catholics. She often put off difficult decisions. Although Mary Queen of Scots was a great threat because Catholics thought she should be queen, Elizabeth took 19 years to agree to her execution.

Elizabeth hated spending money. She avoided an expensive war with Philip II of Spain for as long as possible, although she secretly encouraged the attack and plunder of Spanish ships. When the Spanish Armada set out to invade England, Elizabeth was an inspiring war leader and yet, after the victory, she did not pay the English sailors who had done the fighting.

Elizabeth was a woman in a world of powerful men. Everyone expected her to marry, and she once promised Parliament she would marry 'as soon as I can conveniently' – but it never proved to be convenient.

Born 1533 in London, England
Died 1603 aged 69

find out more
Henry VIII
Mary, Queen of Scots
Reformation
Tudor England

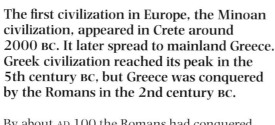

◄ When she was older, Elizabeth I wore thick white make-up and a red wig (she may have lost her hair when she had smallpox). She took great care to ensure that she looked like an impressive queen in all her portraits. This one was painted to celebrate the English victory over the Spanish Armada in 1588.

Europe

The first civilization in Europe, the Minoan civilization, appeared in Crete around 2000 BC. It later spread to mainland Greece. Greek civilization reached its peak in the 5th century BC, but Greece was conquered by the Romans in the 2nd century BC.

By about AD 100 the Romans had conquered many of the lands that now make up the countries of modern Europe, including Spain, France and Britain. But their empire did not extend beyond the River Rhine. Across this frontier were Germanic tribes whom the Romans called 'barbarians'. The Roman empire eventually became Christian, and split into a western and an eastern half (the Byzantine empire).

Dark Ages

As the Roman empire declined, many tribes moved into western Europe. These peoples gradually came to accept the power of the Church and, throughout Christendom, Latin became the official language of Church services, of governments, and of lawyers and scholars.

Muslim invaders

The followers of the prophet Muhammad, known as Muslims, conquered North Africa and the Middle East after his death in AD 632. In the 8th century they invaded Spain and France. Charles Martel drove the Muslims out of France. But Muslim Moors from North Africa settled in Spain, and for hundreds of years southern Spain was Islamic. The Muslims ruled Granada until 1492. In the 15th century the Muslim Ottomans took Constantinople.

Nation states emerge

Gradually, during the Middle Ages, people in western Europe who spoke different languages began to divide into separate nations. The first strong, united country was Francia (France), ruled over by Charlemagne (Charles the Great). England became a united country even before the Norman invasion of 1066.

Later Spain, Portugal, Sweden and other countries gradually established themselves. Many

◄ The Venus de Milo is one of the most famous statues of the ancient Greeks. Greek art, literature and philosophy have had a great influence on European culture.

Europe

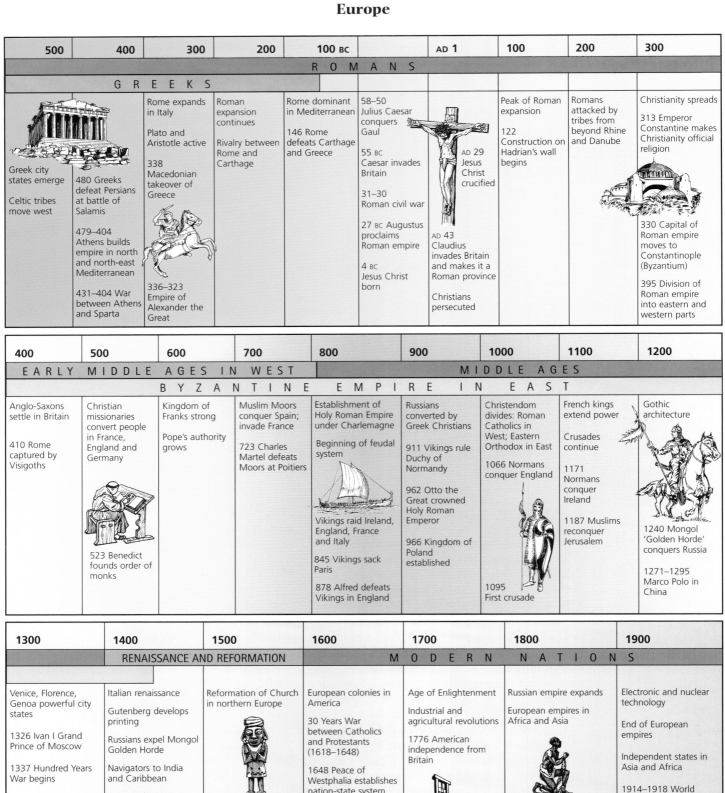

500	400	300	200	100 BC		AD 1	100	200	300
R O M A N S									
G R E E K S									

Greek city states emerge

Celtic tribes move west

480 Greeks defeat Persians at battle of Salamis

479–404 Athens builds empire in north and north-east Mediterranean

431–404 War between Athens and Sparta

Rome expands in Italy

Plato and Aristotle active

338 Macedonian takeover of Greece

336–323 Empire of Alexander the Great

Roman expansion continues

Rivalry between Rome and Carthage

Rome dominant in Mediterranean

146 Rome defeats Carthage and Greece

58–50 Julius Caesar conquers Gaul

55 BC Caesar invades Britain

31–30 Roman civil war

27 BC Augustus proclaims Roman empire

4 BC Jesus Christ born

AD 29 Jesus Christ crucified

AD 43 Claudius invades Britain and makes it a Roman province

Christians persecuted

Peak of Roman expansion

122 Construction on Hadrian's wall begins

Romans attacked by tribes from beyond Rhine and Danube

Christianity spreads

313 Emperor Constantine makes Christianity official religion

330 Capital of Roman empire moves to Constantinople (Byzantium)

395 Division of Roman empire into eastern and western parts

400	500	600	700	800	900	1000	1100	1200
E A R L Y M I D D L E A G E S I N W E S T				**M I D D L E A G E S**				
B Y Z A N T I N E E M P I R E I N E A S T								

Anglo-Saxons settle in Britain

410 Rome captured by Visigoths

Christian missionaries convert people in France, England and Germany

523 Benedict founds order of monks

Kingdom of Franks strong

Pope's authority grows

Muslim Moors conquer Spain; invade France

723 Charles Martel defeats Moors at Poitiers

Establishment of Holy Roman Empire under Charlemagne

Beginning of feudal system

Vikings raid Ireland, England, France and Italy

845 Vikings sack Paris

878 Alfred defeats Vikings in England

Russians converted by Greek Christians

911 Vikings rule Duchy of Normandy

962 Otto the Great crowned Holy Roman Emperor

966 Kingdom of Poland established

Christendom divides: Roman Catholics in West; Eastern Orthodox in East

1066 Normans conquer England

1095 First crusade

French kings extend power

Crusades continue

1171 Normans conquer Ireland

1187 Muslims reconquer Jerusalem

Gothic architecture

1240 Mongol 'Golden Horde' conquers Russia

1271–1295 Marco Polo in China

1300	1400	1500	1600	1700	1800	1900
RENAISSANCE AND REFORMATION			**M O D E R N N A T I O N S**			

Venice, Florence, Genoa powerful city states

1326 Ivan I Grand Prince of Moscow

1337 Hundred Years War begins

1347 Black Death

Italian renaissance

Gutenberg develops printing

Russians expel Mongol Golden Horde

Navigators to India and Caribbean

1453 Turks capture Constantinople

1492 Columbus sails to Caribbean

Reformation of Church in northern Europe

Spanish conquer Aztecs and Incas

English–Spanish naval struggle

1526 Turks besiege Vienna

1588 English defeat Spanish Armada

European colonies in America

30 Years War between Catholics and Protestants (1618–1648)

1648 Peace of Westphalia establishes nation-state system

1642–1649 English Civil War

Age of Enlightenment

Industrial and agricultural revolutions

1776 American independence from Britain

1789 French Revolution

Russian empire expands

European empires in Africa and Asia

Abolition of slavery and serfdom in British, French and Russian empires

1815 Napoleonic wars end at battle of Waterloo

1861 Unification of Italy

1870 Unification of Germany

Electronic and nuclear technology

End of European empires

Independent states in Asia and Africa

1914–1918 World War I

1917–1991 Soviet Union

1939–1945 World War II

1957 European Union formed

▲ For many centuries European monarchs believed that God had given them the right to rule over their peoples. This painting is of Henry VI, who was king of England in the 15th century.

German-speaking people were ruled by the emperor of Austria, who for centuries used the title Holy Roman Emperor. Italian-speaking people did not unite until 1860.

Renaissance and Reformation

Between the 14th and 17th centuries great advances took place in learning and the arts. Italian artists, sculptors and architects led a 'rebirth' (Renaissance) of interest in the styles and ideas of the ancient Romans. Their enthusiasm spread all over Europe. Printing made it possible for books and pamphlets to be produced, and more people learnt to read.

Many people wanted to read the Bible in their own language and, for this and other reasons, they split from the Roman Catholic Church. This 'Reformation' created Protestant Churches, which became powerful in northern Europe. Terrible wars between Catholics and Protestants followed.

France and Britain

After these religious wars, France emerged again as the strongest country in Europe. For a century, from about 1660, France was the centre of European civilization. But Britain began to challenge her power overseas. In the Seven Years War from 1756 to 1763 Britain defeated France in India and Canada. The new inventions of the Industrial Revolution were also helping to make Britain economically powerful. In 1789 the French Revolution took place and France became a republic.

The Napoleonic wars

After the Revolution, the French general Napoleon came to power. He wanted France to rule all Europe. And between 1803 and 1812 his armies entered Germany, Austria, Italy, the Netherlands, Prussia, Poland, Spain and Russia. He was finally defeated in 1815.

Colonies and wars

The influence of Europe spread throughout the world. During the 19th century most western European countries took over as many colonies as they could. Britain and France built the biggest empires. Rivalry between the European nations led to war between France and Germany in 1870–1871 and then to the two great world wars of 1914–1918 and 1939–1945.

The 20th century

In World War II Britain, the USA, the USSR and their allies defeated the Axis powers of Germany, Italy and Japan. After this war the USSR dominated the countries of central and eastern Europe for over 40 years. While the eastern European countries were ruled by communist governments, western Europe grew prosperous. The new European Community strengthened western Europe still further.

In 1989 the communist governments lost power in Poland, Hungary, East Germany and Czechoslovakia. The USSR collapsed and East Germany united with West Germany in 1990.

In 1993 the European Community became the European Union (EU) and greater economic, political and military co-operation developed within Europe. The EU expanded in 1995, when Austria, Finland and Sweden joined. At the same time, the break-up of Yugoslavia after 1990 led to a lengthy civil war and much violence in the region.

▼ Member countries of the European Union in 1999.

Explorers

There have always been people who wanted to explore. In prehistoric times people looked for new lands when food became scarce, the climate changed, or other groups of people threatened them. Over time, people reached almost all areas of the world.

The great age of European exploration began in the 15th century. The Europeans thought of themselves as discoverers of new lands, although usually these lands were already home to other peoples. Even so, the Europeans often claimed them for themselves.

Earlier explorations

Many explorers of the ancient world travelled by sea. Three thousand years ago, Greek and Phoenician traders explored the Mediterranean Sea and settled the lands around it. The Chinese sailed to the lands and islands of South-east Asia, also in search of trade. From about the 9th century AD the great explorers were the Arabs. They sailed down the coasts of Africa, and all round the Indian Ocean. The Vikings were also great seafarers. In the 9th and 10th centuries, they settled in Iceland, Greenland and North America.

But the explorers who set out on the longest voyages were the Polynesians, who settled the thousands of tiny islands in the Pacific. They probably originally came from Indonesia, and began to travel across the Pacific around 2000 BC. They finally reached New Zealand in about AD 950.

Portuguese and Spaniards

By the 15th century, Europeans had developed bigger and faster sailing ships. They had also succeeded in finding ways to navigate at sea. Prince Henry of Portugal (Henry the Navigator) launched a series of expeditions that explored the west coast of Africa, rounded the Cape of Good Hope, and reached India and the East in 1498.

The Spanish soon followed. They sailed westwards, hoping to reach Asia by that route. In 1492 Columbus landed in the West Indies. He thought he had reached Asia, but in fact he had discovered a previously unknown continent. The Spanish and Portuguese went on to conquer Central and South America. Some of the conquerors wished to take the Christian faith to new peoples, but most were after the gold and silver of the new lands.

◄ Marco Polo was an Italian merchant who in the 13th century travelled overland to China, where he stayed for 20 years. He wrote a book describing all the wonders he had seen.

• Ships from Carthage, a Phoenician colony in North Africa, probably explored the west coast of Africa in around 500 BC. In the 4th century BC the Greek sailor Pytheas sailed up the east coast of Britain and may have reached Iceland.

• The last great Chinese explorer was Zheng. In the early 15th century he sailed to India, Arabia and the east coast of Africa. After this the Chinese emperors forbade any more voyages of discovery.

• In 1804 Meriwether Lewis and William Clark explored the American West and found a route over the Rocky Mountains to the Pacific Ocean.

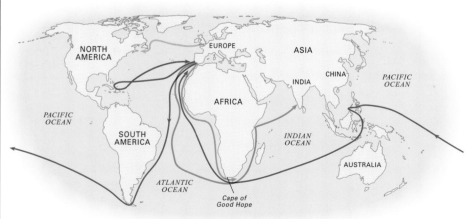

→ From 1497 to 1499 Vasco da Gama sailed all the way to India.

→ In 1519 Ferdinand Magellan set off to find a western route to Asia. He was killed in the Philippines, but one of his ships returned to Spain – the first to sail right round the world.

→ In 1488 Bartolomeu Dias sailed round the southern tip of Africa.

→ In 1492 Christopher Columbus sailed to the West Indies.

→ In 1497 John Cabot reached North America.

◄ The main European voyages of discovery in the late 15th and early 16th centuries.

▲ In 1577 Francis Drake set sail on a three-year voyage of exploration and looting. When he returned he became the first Englishman to sail around the world.

Once some European nations had found wealth overseas, others did not want to lose out. During the 16th and 17th centuries the French, Dutch and English joined the search for new lands. Some of the most dangerous voyages were made trying to find a new route to China (the Northwest passage), through the frozen seas off northern Canada and Russia.

Later explorations

Not all explorers wanted to find treasure. From the 18th century onwards many were interested in the geography, plants and animals of the world. One of the greatest of these scientific explorers was James Cook, who sailed round New Zealand and up the eastern coast of Australia.

Exploration by sea was followed by exploration of the vast inland areas of the new lands. In the 19th century expeditions explored North America, Australia and Africa. By the end of the century most of the world was mapped. In the 20th century explorers set out to conquer the last great challenges: the North and South Poles, the highest mountains, the depths of the oceans, and, last of all, the great expanse of outer space.

• In 1860 Robert Burke and William Wills led an expedition to cross Australia from south to north. They nearly reached the north coast, but died of exhaustion on the return journey.

• Robert Peary and his American expedition reached the North Pole in 1909. In 1911 a Norwegian expedition, led by Roald Amundsen, beat Robert Falcon Scott's British team to the South Pole.

find out more
Africa
Australia
Columbus, Christopher
Cook, James
North America
South America

Fascists

Fascism is a political theory that first appeared in Italy and Germany after World War I. Many Italians were unhappy that they did not gain more territory after the war, and many Germans were unhappy that they had lost so much. In addition, the economy in both countries was in a bad way.

Fascists wanted to make their own country strong, and believed that 'might was right'. They hated communists, and often disliked foreigners and people of different races. They believed that a country should be led by a dictator, a single leader with complete power. They did not believe in elections, and brutally put down any opposition.

The Italian fascists took power in 1922. The German fascists (Nazis) came to power under Hitler in 1933. Fascism also appeared in other European countries during the 1930s, such as Spain and Portugal.

The rise of fascism in Europe led directly to the outbreak of World War II. Hitler believed that Germany should reclaim the land it had lost in World War I. In pursuit of this aim Germany invaded Czechoslovakia and Poland. Britain, France and their allies went to war with Germany to stop the spread of fascism.

Fascism mostly disappeared after the defeat of Germany and Italy in World War II. However, political parties that hold some fascist ideas have since reappeared in some parts of the world.

▼ Benito Mussolini set up the Italian fascist party in 1919 and three years later took power as leader of the government. He ruled as dictator until 1943.

• Fascism takes its name from the *fasces*, the bundle of rods carried by the magistrates (government officials) of ancient Rome as a symbol of their authority.

• Both fascism and communism are forms of totalitarianism. Totalitarianism is the total control of every aspect of people's lives by the government. The government punishes anybody who does not obey or who does not agree with it.

find out more
Communists
Germany
Government
Hitler, Adolf
Holocaust
Italy
Spain
World War II

France

Before Roman times the land we now call France was lived in by Celtic peoples. It was divided into many small kingdoms and tribes. The Romans, who knew the region as Gaul, conquered it in the 1st century BC and held it for 500 years.

The name 'France' comes from the tribe of Franks who invaded Gaul in the 5th century AD. The Frankish king Clovis (465–511) defeated the last Roman governor of Gaul, accepted Christianity and established Paris as his capital.

The mightiest early French king was Charlemagne ('Charles the Great') (747–814). His huge empire included all modern France (except Brittany), much of central Europe, and northern Italy. In 800 the Pope crowned him Roman emperor. Although the empire broke up after his death, France was now an important European kingdom.

War and peace

Over the following centuries the French kings spent much of their time fighting rivals, notably the dukes of Normandy and Burgundy and the kings of England. The Hundred Years' War fought between the English and French lasted from 1337 to 1453. Inspired by Joan of Arc, the French won.

By 1483 the Burgundians had also been defeated and France's borders were much as they are today. The huge country was one of the richest in Europe. It boasted wonderful cathedrals, such as Chartres, Reims and Notre Dame in Paris, thriving cities and wealthy merchants. Most of the peasants, however, remained desperately poor.

Master of Europe

During the 16th century, France was torn by civil wars between Protestants (Huguenots) and Catholics. The conflict was ended by Henry IV, and during the 17th century France thrived. By the mid-1680s, Louis XIV, who was known as the 'Sun King', was master of Europe. Louis' palace at Versailles was the political and cultural capital of the continent.

France's strength worried its neighbours, particularly Britain. Four long wars, between 1702 and 1783, left France bankrupt and without many of its overseas territories. The French people were fed up with the unfair way they were governed.

▲ The cathedral of Bourges in France dates from the 12th–13th centuries. During the Middle Ages the French built some of the finest cathedrals and castles in Europe.

Revolution and war

In 1789 France exploded into revolution. In the name of 'liberty, equality and fraternity', the people swept away the old government and set up a parliament (the National Assembly). In 1793 they executed Louis XVI and his wife, Marie Antoinette. During a bloodthirsty Reign of Terror, 17,000 nobles and other 'enemies of the people' were executed.

In an effort to stop the Revolution spreading, other European states invaded France. The French drove them back and under Emperor Napoleon I (Napoleon Bonaparte) conquered most of western

● In the early 8th century AD Muslim Moors from Spain invaded France. They were defeated in 732 by Charles Martel, ruler of the Franks, near Poitiers.

● Louis IX was the only king of France to be made into a saint after his death. He was a just ruler, a protector of the poor, a friend of the Church, and he led two crusades against the Muslims. He was captured in Egypt on the first of these crusades, and died during the second in Tunisia in 1270.

◀ On St Bartholomew's Day 1572 the Catholic queen mother, Catherine de Medici, ordered the massacre of thousands of French Huguenots (Protestants).

Europe. The success of the French people spread the ideas of fair government and human rights across the continent.

Industry and empire

After Napoleon was defeated in 1815 France was again ruled by kings. There were revolutions against these kings in 1830 and 1848. In 1851 Napoleon's nephew seized power and the following year made himself emperor as Napoleon III. In 1870–1871 France was invaded by German armies. The French lost much of eastern France (Alsace and Lorraine) to Germany. Napoleon III resigned, and once more France became a republic. A revolution in Paris (the Paris Commune) was put down with great brutality.

Despite the political turmoil, France prospered. In the regions industrial towns expanded, and business people grew richer. Overseas the French conquered a new empire. By 1900 the French flag flew over Indo-China (modern Vietnam, Cambodia and Laos), much of north and west Africa, and many Pacific islands. Colonial trade added to France's wealth. But France's position was threatened by the new and powerful German empire. Again, in 1914, the two countries went to war.

▶ A painting depicting the storming of the Bastille on 14 July 1789, the huge prison in Paris. The act of capturing it symbolized the destruction of the once-powerful monarchy. France's national day is celebrated on 14 July each year.

The 20th century

Although the French won back Alsace and Lorraine, World War I killed nearly 2 million Frenchmen. The Great Depression of the 1930s hit France heavily. Poverty and unemployment rose and governments struggled to keep control.

In World War II German armies again invaded France. The French were defeated in 1940. Some French people co-operated with the German occupiers, but others joined the resistance movement to fight the Germans. In 1944 British and US forces liberated France.

The French seemed a broken people. But with US economic help, France's new leaders brought about an 'economic miracle'. Workers' incomes doubled in 20 years and the country grew strong and rich again. It set aside its past by working closely with Germany to found the European Union.

France also gave independence to most of its colonies. Although this usually happened peacefully, there was bitter fighting in some places, such as Vietnam. In the 1950s Algerian nationalists began to fight the French. Because so many French people had settled in the north African colony, France did not want to give Algeria its independence. It eventually did so in 1962.

France became more stable after this, but not everyone was happy with France's conservative society and government. Students and workers rioted in 1968 and the French Communist Party was prominent in opposition. After 1968 France became a more liberal society and by the 1990s it was once again a wealthy, powerful and respected nation.

• General Charles de Gaulle (1890–1970) fought in World War I, and from his base in England led the Free French (part of the French resistance) during World War II. In 1958 he was seen as the only man capable of uniting the nation and was elected president. Until 1969 he played a major part in the creation of modern France.

◀ Students demonstrate against the government in 1968. Many French felt that President de Gaulle had lost touch with the young and underprivileged.

Gandhi, Mahatma

Mahatma Gandhi led the Indian people in their struggle for independence from British rule. Many Indians think of him as the father of modern India.

Born 1869 in
Porbandar, India
Died 1948 aged 78

• Although his real name was Mohandas Gandhi, he was known as Mahatma Gandhi. 'Mahatma' means 'great soul'.

• Gandhi believed that peoples and nations should be self-sufficient. He set an example by devoting part of each day to spinning home-made cloth.

find out more
India
Pakistan
South Africa

Mohandas Karamchand Gandhi was 24 years old and working as a lawyer when he went to South Africa to work on a court case. He ended up staying for 18 years as he tried to help his fellow countrymen in South Africa in their struggle against the racial discrimination they suffered.

Gandhi returned to India in 1914 and before long he emerged as the leader of the Indian National Congress Party. The party's aim was to make India independent from Britain. Even though all the protests Gandhi led were peaceful, he was still imprisoned many times by the British.

During the long campaign for independence, Gandhi struggled in vain to overcome the growing gap between the Hindu and Muslim populations of India. Eventually these differences led to the creation of the separate Muslim state of Pakistan in 1947. India and Pakistan both became independent from Britain in that year but there continued to be explosions of violence between Hindus and the Muslims who were left in India. Gandhi appealed for peace, hoping that the two sides could work out a way of living together. His dream was cut short when he was killed by a Hindu extremist in January 1948.

▼ In 1930 Gandhi walked 400 kilometres to the seashore, where he picked up some natural salt of his own as a protest against the British ruling that Indian people had to pay tax on the salt they used.

Georgian Britain

1714 **George I**
1715 Jacobite rebellion
1721 Robert Walpole in power
1727 **George II**
1745–1746 Jacobite rebellion
1759 Wolfe captured Québec, Canada
1760 **George III**
1776 American colonies declared independence
1777 Watt built steam engine
1789 French Revolution
1793 War against France
1801 Act of Union with Ireland
1805 Battle of Trafalgar
1807 Slave trade abolished
1810 Prince George regent
1815 Battle of Waterloo
1820 **George IV**
1830 **William IV**

For over a hundred years, from 1714 to 1830, Britain was ruled by four kings called George. This time is often known as the Georgian period.

For much of this period, Britain was at war with its long-standing enemy France, until the struggle ended in 1815 with the Duke of Wellington's victory over Napoleon at the battle of Waterloo. They also clashed in the rich trading areas of India and North America, where both wanted to build an empire. Britain won control of much of India and Canada, but lost the rest of North America when the 13 American colonies won their independence in 1783. However, the first settlement in Australia in 1788 enlarged what was by then the 'British empire'.

The four Georges

George I was the Elector (ruler) of Hanover, a German state; he was a great-grandson of the English King James I. George I became king because he was the nearest Protestant heir to the throne and the Protestant ruling classes in Parliament did not want the Catholic Stuarts back in power. He left small groups of ministers, led by Robert Walpole, to make government decisions.

George II, a fiery character, also left Walpole in control of the country, until 1742. William Pitt (the Elder) became chief minister from 1756.

George III took his position as king very seriously. In 1766 he

▲ A portrait of George III. During his reign Britain lost one part of its empire, the 13 American colonies.

▲ The wealth of a country squire came from his huge estates, and his favourite sports were usually hunting and shooting.

made William Pitt (the Elder) prime minister, and after Pitt died, he gave the job to Pitt's son, William Pitt (the Younger). But George III went mad, and his son, later George IV, ruled for him for nine years as Prince Regent. George IV won little respect because of his extravagance and his wild social life. His brother William IV ruled from 1830 until 1837, when Victoria became queen.

Country life

Most of the people of Britain still lived in the countryside. Most landowners sat in Parliament as MPs, or in the House of Lords. At home, they ran local affairs. In the local lawcourts punishments were harsh. People caught sheep-stealing or poaching were hanged, or transported to the colonies.

From about 1750 many landowners created more 'enclosures', by fencing off part of their own and common land, to take advantage of new farming methods. In many places villagers were forced to work as labourers on very low wages, or they drifted to the growing towns in search of work.

Trade, industry and transport

British ships, protected by the powerful navy, brought trading wealth to merchants and bankers. At the end of the 18th century the 'Industrial Revolution' brought rapid changes in the economy, in the way people worked and lived, and in transport too. By the 1780s industrial towns like Birmingham, Manchester and Glasgow were growing fast. From the 1780s canals were built so that barges could transport heavy goods, and in 1825 the first railway opened.

Poverty

The great gap between rich and poor remained. In the country, villagers often lived in leaking, ramshackle cottages, existing on a diet of bread, cheese, peas and turnips. Many of the children in a poor family might die before the age of 5. Some villages had schools, but for the very poor, a child's wages were needed to keep the family going.

In the growing industrial towns, families were crowded into dark, stinking courtyards with one water pump which up to 50 people might share. Only a few employers, such as the social reformer Robert Owen, provided decent conditions for their workers and schools for the workers' children.

▼ William Hogarth's engraving *The Enraged Musician* (1741) shows some aspects of the lives of the poor in Georgian Britain.

find out more

Agricultural Revolution
American Revolution
France
Industrial Revolution
Ireland
Napoleon
Scotland
Slaves
Stuart Britain
United States of America
Victorian Britain

Two Jacobite rebellions

Jacobites were people who wanted the descendants of the Stuart James II (James VII of Scotland) to win back the throne. The name comes from Jacobus, which is Latin for James.

In 1715 James, son of James II, landed briefly in Scotland. Because he claimed the throne, he was called the Old Pretender ('pretend' in those days meant 'claim').

In 1745 Charles Edward, James's son, called Bonnie Prince Charlie, occupied Edinburgh for a time, and invaded England. He was defeated at Culloden in 1746.

Germany

At the time of the Roman empire, many Germanic tribes lived in the area of modern Germany. For some time the Romans tried to conquer this area. But after a terrible defeat in AD 9 the Romans gave up, and made the Rhine and Danube rivers their frontier with Germany.

In the 4th century AD the Huns, a warlike people from Asia, invaded Germany. Many of the Germanic tribes began to cross over the Roman frontiers, and in the 5th century the Roman empire in western Europe collapsed.

One of these Germanic tribes, the Franks, invaded Gaul. Charlemagne, their greatest king, created an empire that covered much of western Europe. He was crowned as emperor in Rome in AD 800. After he died, his empire was divided into West Francia (modern France) and East Francia, or Franconia.

First German empire

King Otto I of Franconia (reigned 936–973) spread his power over all the German-speaking people of Europe, down the River Rhône and into Italy. He was crowned by the Pope in AD 962, and the Holy Roman Empire was born. Some of his descendants were strong emperors, especially Frederick II, who, during his reign (1212–1250), joined southern Italy and Sicily to the empire. Others were weak and lost power to the dukes and princes of Germany.

From 1452 this empire was ruled by the Habsburgs, who also ruled Austria. Their greatest emperor was Charles V (reigned 1519–1556), but after his death the emperors gradually lost power. The Holy Roman Empire eventually collapsed in 1806, and Germany was left as a jigsaw of small states ruled by 400 princes, dukes and bishops.

One of the largest and most powerful of these

▶ When Otto von Bismarck was Prussian prime minister, his armies defeated the Danish, the Austrians and the French, and captured neighbouring lands. These victories persuaded other German states to join a German *Reich* (empire) with Prussia.

◀ Frederick II ('the Great') of Prussia. As well as being a great military leader, Frederick was also a gifted writer and musician.

German states was Prussia. In the 18th century Prussia built up one of the strongest armies in Europe, and conquered much territory in a series of wars with its neighbours. Prussia also helped to defeat the French at the end of the Napoleonic Wars.

Second German empire

By the 19th century many German-speaking people wanted to be united again in one country. In 1871 the German princes invited the king of Prussia to become emperor of Germany. The first chancellor (prime minister) was Otto von Bismarck. He tried to make life better for people by starting old-age pensions and payments for sickness and accident. People worked hard, building railways, new factories and a navy to make Germany strong.

World War I and the Weimar Republic

Rivalry between Germany and other nations led to World War I (1914–1918). Six million German people were killed or wounded, and by the end of the war many were starving. Some Germans blamed the

• The Reformation began in Germany in 1517. Several German rulers, wanting to be free of the power of the Pope and the emperor, set up their own Protestant Churches. Many wars between Catholics and Protestants followed. The worst of these was the Thirty Years War (1618–1648), in which nearly half of the population of Germany died, mostly from famine and disease.

◀ Hitler and his Nazi party set out to destroy all opposition. Young people were enrolled into the 'Hitler Youth', where they were taught that National Socialism was the only right form of government. Nazis burned any books (left) that praised democracy, denounced war or were written by Jews in their attempts to impose total control over people.

emperor (Kaiser) for this, and he was overthrown. A republic was proclaimed in the city of Weimar. This republican government soon ran into trouble. By 1923 money had lost its value and people's savings had become worthless. Unemployment was rising and by 1932 there were 6 million people without work.

Third German empire: the Third Reich

In 1933 Adolf Hitler, leader of the Nazis, became chancellor. He promised to unite all the German-speaking people into a new German empire (the Third Reich). Germans who opposed Hitler were silenced and many died in concentration camps. Jews were persecuted, and those who could migrated abroad. Hitler's armies took over Austria in 1938 and Czechoslovakia in the spring of 1939. When they invaded Poland later in 1939, World War II began.

Defeat, division and reunification

When Allied troops defeated Germany in 1945, they discovered that 6 million Jews had been exterminated in what became known as the 'Holocaust'. Most German cities had been reduced to ruins. Money was valueless.

At the end of the war, Austria became a separate country again. Czechoslovakia and Poland were restored (with changed boundaries) and expelled at least 12 million Germans. Germany was divided into four zones of occupation, and Berlin into four sectors. In 1949 the Soviet zone became the German Democratic Republic (East Germany), with the Soviet sector of Berlin as its capital. It was closely controlled by a dictatorial government.

The zones of the USA, Britain and France were combined to form the Federal Republic of Germany (West Germany), a democracy with a capitalist economy. Bonn was its capital. The three western sectors of Berlin formed an 'island' within East German territory.

By 1961 the East German economy had been greatly weakened by the loss of approximately 2.5 million people migrating to West Germany. In response to this, the communist government erected the Berlin Wall, a system of fortifications encircling West Berlin to prevent escape. The wall came down in October 1989, when massive demonstrations led to the fall of the communist government of East Germany. Free elections were held in March 1990, and Germany was reunited on 3 October that year with Berlin as the country's capital.

▼ The Berlin Wall was a powerful symbol of the East–West divide in Germany. When the communist government fell in 1989, the Berlin Wall was brought down by thousands of jubilant demonstrators.

Government

The government of a country is the organization that is responsible for running that country. Governments are headed by a monarch, a dictator or an elected prime minister or president.

The earliest form of government in most countries was monarchy, in which a king or queen rules the country. In the past the monarch in many countries was all-powerful.

When one family rules for many years, it is called a dynasty. The dynasties of ancient Egypt and China often lasted for hundreds of years. Many monarchs claimed to be descended from gods, or that God had given them the right to rule.

• When one person or political party controls a country, it is called a **dictatorship**. There is no freedom to disagree with the government and there are no free elections. In the 20th century fascist or communist parties set up dictatorships in several countries. There have also been dictatorships in countries where the armed forces have seized power.

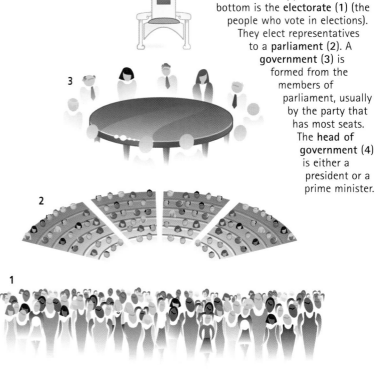

The structure of a democratic state can be seen as a pyramid. At the bottom is the **electorate** (1) (the people who vote in elections). They elect representatives to a **parliament** (2). A **government** (3) is formed from the members of parliament, usually by the party that has most seats. The **head of government** (4) is either a president or a prime minister.

Administration and law

When the first cities were built, from around 4000 BC, the rulers had many more people to control, and employed administrators to help them. As the cities developed into larger kingdoms and empires, more and more officials were needed. As societies became bigger and more complicated, many more laws were also needed. Although most monarchs had great power over their people, the laws often limited what the monarch could do.

Democracy

Democracy means 'rule by the people'. The earliest democracy was in the Greek city of Athens, about 2500 years ago. It involved a meeting of the free men of the city, who voted on what the city should do.

In ancient Rome there was also a kind of democracy. The leading citizens elected representatives to the Senate, the ruling council.

The Senate then made decisions on the people's behalf. Most democracies today work in the same way, with the people electing representatives to a parliament or congress.

Democracy was slow to appear in other countries. The English parliament developed in the 13th century, and other countries also began to have parliaments. Between the 17th and 19th centuries, parliaments began to take away more and more power from the monarch. In some places there were revolutions against the monarchy, which was replaced by a republic, led by a president. Today most countries in the world are republics.

It took a long time for most countries to become completely democratic. In Britain, for example, not all men could vote in elections until 1918, and it was not until 1928 that all women could vote.

▶ One of the oldest systems of law that we know of was put together nearly 4000 years ago by Hammurabi, king of Babylon. He had 282 laws carved on this block of black stone.

Greeks, ancient

The ancient Greeks have had an enormous influence on the modern world. Their art and architecture are copied, their literature is widely read, their plays are still performed. A system of government first used by the Greeks – democracy – is now used in most countries of the world.

▼ The Acropolis ('high city') of Athens as it may have looked in the 5th century BC.
1 Sanctuary of Zeus
2 Parthenon (the temple of Athens's goddess Athene)
3 Theatre of Dionysus
4 Erechtheum, the temple of Athene and Poseidon
5 Statue of Athene
6 Sanctuary of Artemis
7 The gateway or Propylaea

Greek civilization began about 1600 BC in a number of small but rich kingdoms on mainland Greece and on the island of Crete. Around 1200–1000 BC they were destroyed by invaders, fire and earthquakes. Some of the best-known remains are the city of Mycenae (south of Athens) and the buildings of the Minoans at Knossos on Crete.

▲ The myth of the Cretan Minotaur – the bull-headed, flesh-eating monster that lived in a maze – comes from the early period of Greek civilization. On this Athenian pot from the 6th century BC the beast is shown being killed by the young Greek hero Theseus.

City states

By the 9th century BC, after long years of war and turmoil, Greece was settling down again. The region was divided into hundreds of city states, each consisting of a city or village and its surrounding land. The city states governed themselves and made their own laws. Hard labour was done by slaves, and women had little say in what went on.

Because Greece was both rich and divided, neighbouring powers were tempted to invade. The most dangerous threat came from the Persian emperor Darius I. The wars between the Greeks and the Persians lasted from 499 to 479 BC. Although Darius's successor Xerxes burned Athens in 480 BC, in the end the Greeks drove off the invaders.

The 'golden age'

After the defeat of the Persians, Greece enjoyed a brief 'golden age' during the 5th century BC. Athens, the most successful city state, built up a trading empire in the eastern Mediterranean under the leadership of Pericles. Athens was also a centre of art, literature and philosophy (the 'love of wisdom'). Athenian craft workers produced beautiful pottery, decorated with scenes from daily life and the adventures of gods and heroes. The ruins of its grand buildings, such as those on the Acropolis, survive to this day. Open-air theatres, holding as many as 10,000 spectators, put on plays by remarkable

◀ The theatre at Epidaurus. The Greeks built their open-air theatres on hillsides so the audience had a good view and could hear every word spoken. Many modern theatres follow this basic design.

dramatists, including Euripides, Sophocles and Aristophanes.

Exercise was an important part of Greek life. Athletes from all over the Greek world met to compete in athletics games. The most famous was the Olympic Games, held at Olympia in honour of the god Zeus.

Rise and fall

Athens's great rival was the military state of Sparta, which controlled much of the southern part of the Greek mainland (the Peloponnese). Athens was wealthier and had a more powerful navy. It was also democratic ('ruled by the people'): all of its male citizens had a say in the government of the state. Spartans valued military skills above art and philosophy, and all Spartan men had to be in the army.

The two city states first went to war in 459 BC, when Sparta won. A second war broke out in 431 BC and lasted for over 25 years. Athens again lost and the city was captured. After this,

Greek power declined until the time of Alexander the Great, the Macedonian king from 336 to 323 BC, who conquered a huge empire and spread Greek ideas across Asia to northern India. His empire broke up after his death, and by the 2nd century BC Greece was under Roman rule.

Greek beliefs

The Greeks believed in gods and goddesses with semi-human personalities. These were worshipped with statues, temples, feasts, processions, sacrifices, games and plays. Because a god or goddess controlled almost every activity, from hunting to lighting a fire, the Greeks dared not forget them for an instant. Before starting something important, Greeks consulted oracles, holy places where a priest or priestess could foretell the future. The most popular oracle was at the temple of Apollo at Delphi.

Greek gods and goddesses
The chief god was Zeus, ruler of all lesser gods and mortals. He lived on top of Mount Olympus with his wife Hera, the goddess of marriage. Zeus had two brothers: Poseidon and Hades. Poseidon, married to Amphrite, ruled the kingdom of water — rivers, lakes and the sea. He dug new waterways with an enormous three-pronged spear, or trident. Hades ruled the Underworld with his wife Persephone, whom he stole from the corn goddess Demeter. Persephone was allowed back to the world for six months each year to allow crops to grow. The Underworld, where the spirits of the dead went, was a horrible maze of dark tunnels inhabited by ghosts and monsters.

Other important gods and goddesses included Aphrodite, the goddess of love and beauty; Apollo, the god of prophesy, music and medicine; Ares, the god of war; Artemis, the goddess of the Moon and hunting; Athene, goddess of wisdom; Dionysus, the god of wine and the theatre; and Hermes, the messenger god.

▲ Poseidon, ruler of the water kingdom, with his trident.

• Historians and archaeologists have long been fascinated by two 'missing' Greek cities, Atlantis and Troy. Atlantis, which was supposed to have disappeared beneath the sea, has never been found. But in 1871 the site of Troy was found in Turkey. The real city was not as grand as that of the legendary Trojan War. This is based on a real siege of about 1210 BC, when Greek armies are supposed to have captured the city by hiding men inside a wooden horse.

• Sport was so important to the ancient Greeks that during the time of the Olympic Games (held every four years between 776 BC and 394 AD) war was banned.

Ancient Greece
BC

about 2000	Minoan civilization begins in Crete
about 1600	Mycenaean civilization begins
about 1450	Mycenaeans invade Crete
about 1210	Greeks capture Troy
1100—800	'Dark Age' of Greek civilization
about 900	City of Sparta founded
about 750	Greeks setting up colonies overseas
776	First recorded Olympic Games
about 590	Tyrants driven out of Athens
508	Democratic reforms in Athens
490	Greeks defeat Persians at battle of Marathon
461	Pericles becomes leader of Athens
about 447	Parthenon built at Athens
431—404	Athens and Sparta at war
336—323	Reign of Alexander the Great
146	Greece under Roman rule

Gulf wars

There have been two recent wars around the Persian Gulf in the Middle East. The first, lasting from 1980 to 1988, was between Iraq and Iran. The second, in 1991, was between Iraq and a large United Nations force.

◄ US soldiers in action in the second Gulf war. Although the United Nations force in the war was dominated by the USA, armed forces from over 30 other countries also took part.

In 1979 there was a revolution in Iran, and the country came under the control of Muslim religious leaders, who opposed the West. President Saddam Hussein of Iraq demanded that the border between Iran and Iraq be redrawn. In 1980 a full-scale war broke out. Saddam received support from the Soviet Union, the USA and France, but still could not win. At least 1 million people died. Eventually in 1988 the United Nations arranged a ceasefire.

During the war Saddam had turned himself into a ruthless dictator in Iraq. After the war the Iraqis were poor and dissatisfied. Saddam wanted to do something to take their minds off his failings. In July 1990 Iraq accused its tiny neighbour, Kuwait, of stealing Iraqi oil. Then the Iraqi army invaded Kuwait.

The United Nations (UN) demanded that Iraq withdraw from Kuwait. Saddam refused, and the UN sent a huge force to Saudi Arabia. In January 1991 the UN attacked, and in a few days Kuwait was liberated. The UN's mission was achieved, and the UN forces stopped advancing into Iraq.

After the war the UN would not allow other countries to trade with Iraq, but Saddam continued to hold power, while his people continued to suffer.

find out more
Middle East
Muslims
United Nations

Henry VIII

Born 1491 in London, England
Died 1547 aged 55

• As an old man, Henry was a terrifying figure. He could often be unpredictable and impatient and suffered from fits of depression. He had a painful ulcer on his leg, and was so overweight that a machine had to haul him upstairs.

find out more
Elizabeth I
Monasteries
Reformation
Tudor England

Henry VIII is one of England's most famous kings. He was a powerful figure who dealt ruthlessly with anyone who opposed him, and few people close to him escaped some trouble.

After Henry VIII came to the throne in 1509, he seemed to have everything. He was handsome, religious, well educated and musical. He had a new wife, Catherine of Aragon, and a loyal minister, Thomas Wolsey, who was his Lord Chancellor.

However, Henry wanted a son to succeed him as king. Catherine had given birth to a daughter, Mary, and Henry wanted to marry Anne Boleyn, a lady of the court, instead. Wolsey failed to persuade the Pope to give Henry a divorce, and he was dismissed. To get his own way, Henry broke with the Pope and the Catholic Church. He married Anne Boleyn in 1533 (and divorced Catherine afterwards), became Supreme Head of the English Church, and destroyed the monasteries because he wanted their wealth.

Anne Boleyn produced a daughter (who became Elizabeth I), and in 1536 Anne was beheaded for alleged treason. Henry's next wife, Jane Seymour, died in 1537 giving birth to Henry's long-awaited son, Edward (who became Edward VI). Henry also married and later divorced Anne of Cleves, and Catherine Howard, who was beheaded in 1542 for being unfaithful. He finally found some peace with his sixth wife Katherine Parr.

▲ Henry VIII, king of England from 1509 to 1547, painted by Hans Holbein the Younger.

Gunpowder plot *see* Stuart Britain • **Habsburgs** *see* Austrian empire

Hindus

Hinduism is a religion that began over 4000 years ago in the Indian subcontinent. Hindus themselves call it *Sanatana Dharma*, 'eternal truth' or 'teaching'.

Hindus have many different beliefs and practices, and worship many different forms of God. Hinduism is a way of life as much as a religion, and affects what Hindus eat and who they marry as well as how they worship.

Hinduism developed in India after the arrival of Aryan peoples from central Asia around 1500 BC. But its roots lie in the earlier Indus Valley civilization. Hindu kingdoms spread all over India, and also appeared in South-east Asia and Indonesia.

In these kingdoms, each person was born into an occupation and a set place in society. At the top was the king, who was sacred. Beneath him were the priests, warriors and nobles. Then there were farmers and craftspeople, and at the bottom were the labourers. This was the origin of the 'caste' system, which was still strong in India at the end of the 20th century.

A new religion, Buddhism, spread through India and beyond from the 5th century BC. However, in India itself it had mostly disappeared by the 13th century AD. Another religion, Islam, arrived in northern India between the 8th and 14th centuries. Conflict between Hindus and Muslims led to the division of the Indian subcontinent into two independent countries in

1947: the Muslim state of Pakistan, and the mostly Hindu state of India.

◀ Ganesh is an elephant-headed form of God. His title is 'remover of obstacles', and Hindus worship him as the god of good luck.

• Over 80% of the population of India are Hindus. Other Hindus live in North America, Africa, Indonesia, Nepal, Sri Lanka, the Caribbean and Britain.

• Hindus believe that the god Vishnu had 10 avatars or incarnations (new forms) whom he could send down to Earth to help people. These include Krishna, Buddha and Rama, the hero of the epic poem, the *Ramayana*.

find out more
Buddhists
India
Muslims
Pakistan
Sikhs

History

History is the study of the past. Historians try to discover the truth about what happened in the past, and also to explain why things happened.

Different historians are interested in different aspects of the past. For example, some study what kings, queens, politicians and military leaders did. Others are interested in how people made money, or how societies have changed over time. Many historians today study the lives of ordinary people. Others look especially at the lives of women.

To be a historian you must first study the evidence. There are many different kinds of historical evidence. Oral history is what living people can

remember. Objects that have survived from the past – such as buildings, pictures, clothes, pots – can tell us a lot. Written evidence, for instance in books, letters and government papers, is especially important because it tells us what people thought.

Explaining what people did, and why they did it, means imagining what the past was like. There are often different points of view about historical events. For example, there are at least two points of view about every war. History has often been written from the point of view of a particular country, group of people, or political theory. Today historians usually try to avoid this, but they realize that it is never possible to tell the whole truth about the past.

• The earliest histories were mostly myths and legends. True history began in the 5th century BC with the ancient Greek writer Herodotus. He wrote a history of the Persian Wars, and travelled around Greece to check his facts and to talk to people who had taken part. He became known as 'the father of history'.

▲ Evidence from the past is not always reliable. These photographs of the Soviet leader Lenin look almost the same. But the one on the right was carefully altered to cut out the image of Trotsky (seen leaning against the podium in the photo above) when Trotsky was no longer in favour.

find out more
Archaeology

Hitler, Adolf

Adolf Hitler was the dictator of Nazi Germany. His determination to rule over much of Europe resulted in the outbreak of World War II.

In 1921 Hitler became the leader of the National Socialist German Workers' Party, or Nazis for short. In 1923 the Nazis tried to overthrow the government, but the attempt failed and Hitler went to prison for nine months.

While in prison he wrote *Mein Kampf* ('my struggle'), stating that all Germany's problems were caused by Jews and communists, and that Germany needed a strong Führer (leader) in order to be great again. He believed that he should be that leader. His first taste of power came in 1933 when he was made chancellor (chief minister) by President Hindenburg.

When Hindenburg died in 1934, Hitler became president, chancellor and supreme commander of the armed forces. All opposition to his rule was crushed. Millions were sent to concentration camps, and Jews gradually lost all their rights.

In 1938 Hitler's forces invaded Austria and in 1939 they occupied Czechoslovakia. They invaded Poland the same year, and this triggered the beginning of World War II. Many more Jews and others died in extermination camps, and millions of soldiers and civilians were also killed. When, in 1945, it became clear that the Nazis had been beaten, Hitler shot himself in his underground shelter in Berlin.

Born 1889 in Braunau-am-Inn, Austria **Died** 1945 aged 56

find out more
Fascists
Germany
Holocaust
World War I
World War II

◄ Adolf Hitler, centre, and other Nazi leaders at a rally. The swastika (cross with L-shaped bars) which they are all wearing was adopted by Hitler as the emblem of the Nazi Party. It was even made part of the German national flag in the years 1935–1945.

Holocaust

The word 'holocaust' originally meant 'a burnt sacrifice', but it has come to mean the horrific killing of millions of Jews by Nazis before and during World War II.

The Nazi Party rose to power in Germany between the world wars. It gained supporters by promising strong leadership at a time when there was weak government, poverty and unemployment. As soon as the Nazis were in power and Adolf Hitler became Führer (leader), Nazis were taught to believe that 'true' Germans, or 'Aryans', were superior to all other races. When Hitler declared that many of Germany's problems were caused by the Jews, a terrible persecution of all Jews began. Many were forced to live in ghettos (restricted areas), where they died of starvation and disease. Over 1 million were shot.

Concentration camps

The Nazis rounded up Jews in Germany and in the countries that they occupied during the war, and sent them to concentration camps. These were prison camps where Jews had to work hard with little food, and very many of them died. Some of the camps became 'death camps', with gas chambers in which Jews were deliberately killed. In Auschwitz, in occupied Poland, gas chambers killed and burned 12,000 people a day. In all, six million Jewish men, women and children died at the hands of the Nazis.

• As well as Jews, gypsies, mentally handicapped people, homosexuals and communists were also sent to the camps, and many died.

◄ Children standing behind a barbed wire fence at the Nazi concentration camp at Auschwitz, southern Poland, in 1945. Films and photographs of what Allied soldiers found in these camps after the war were shown all over the world, and they still cause horror when they are seen today.

find out more
Fascism
Germany
Hitler, Adolf
Jews
World War II

Holy Roman Empire

In AD 800 the pope crowned Charlemagne 'Charles Augustus, Emperor of the Romans'. Charlemagne's empire was a pale shadow of the old Roman Empire and it soon broke up. But Charlemagne's title was not forgotten.

Some 150 years later, King Otto I of Germany conquered northern Italy. In 962, as a reward for helping Pope John XII defeat his enemies, he was crowned Roman emperor. Over the next 850 years the title was given to a German prince.

From the 12th century onwards the emperors called themselves Holy Roman Emperors because they claimed to have some control over the Church. The popes, of course, did not agree and there were bitter squabbles. In 1084 Emperor Henry IV drove the pope into exile and a century later Emperor Frederick Barbarossa set up an 'anti-pope'!

▶ King Otto I ('Otto the Great').

▶ The Holy Roman Empire occupied much of central Europe from the 11th century to the 17th century.

The Habsburgs

Until the 17th century the empire stretched from northern Germany to Siena in Italy. But the emperor had only a vague control over this area and his power depended on his family possessions. In 1438 the three bishops and four princes who elected the emperor chose Duke Albert of Habsburg. Thereafter the emperor was always a Habsburg.

The most powerful emperor was Charles V, who was also king of Spain. After he resigned in 1556 the Holy Roman Empire became increasingly meaningless, so that the French philosopher Voltaire remarked that it was 'neither holy, nor Roman, nor an empire.' It was finally abolished in 1806.

1 HAMBURG
2 BILLUNG
3 NORDMARK
4 MEISSEN

KINGDOM OF DENMARK

FRIESLAND

LOTHARINGIA

SAXONY

LUSATIA

THURINGIA

FRANCONIA

BOHEMIA

MORAVIA

SWABIA

BAVARIA

AUSTRIA

CARINTHIA

KINGDOM OF BURGUNDY

KINGDOM OF ITALY

CORSICA

PATRIMONY OF ST PETER

DUCHY OF APULIA

SARDINIA

0   200 km
0   150 miles

find out more
Austrian empire
Charlemagne
Germany

Incas

The Incas were native South Americans who developed an empire in and around the Andes mountain range in the 15th and early 16th centuries. At its greatest, their territory extended for about 4000 kilometres and they ruled about 12 million people.

The Incas probably began as mountain people who moved to the valley of the Cuzco (now Peru) in about AD 1000. They gradually conquered neighbouring nations until they ruled the whole region.

Life, work and government

Almost every Inca man was a farmer, making food and clothing for himself and his family. The Incas grew maize (corn), potatoes, tomatoes, peanuts and cotton, and raised guinea pigs, ducks, llamas, alpacas and dogs.

Inca palaces, temples, irrigation systems and fortifications can still be seen throughout the Andes. The Incas also built a network of highways and minor roads over and through the mountains. They used impressive engineering techniques to construct short rock tunnels and vine-supported suspension bridges.

The ruler of the empire was thought to be a god and descended from the Sun. He was known as the Inca and he had absolute power over a highly organized system of government. Below him were the rulers, nobles, common people, and a special group of craftspeople and servants.

In 1532 Spanish invaders, led by Francisco Pizarro, arrived in Peru and captured the ruling emperor Atahualpa. The Incas resisted, but by the 1570s they had been utterly crushed by the Spaniards and their empire was at an end.

0   1000 km
0   600 miles

▲ The territory under the influence of the Inca empire at the height of its power.

◀ This young girl was buried on a volcano 500 years ago as a gift to the mountain gods, an Inca human sacrifice.

find out more
South America

India

The earliest civilization in southern Asia grew up around the city of Harappa in the Indus valley, in what is now Pakistan, and extended east into present-day India. Around 2500 BC the people of this region built huge irrigation (watering) systems, heated baths and temples, and invented their own writing.

The next stage in India's development followed the arrival of the Aryan people from central Asia in about 1500 BC. The Aryans developed the Sanskrit language and two great religious faiths, Hinduism and Buddhism.

In the third century BC, under the wise leadership of the Mauryan kings Chandragupta and Asoka, a single Indian nation began to emerge. It was based on the state of Magadha around the River Ganges, and extended west to Afghanistan and south almost to Sri Lanka.

Between AD 320 and 467 India enjoyed a golden age under the great kings of the Gupta dynasty. The many fine temples built during this period included one at Sarnath, where Buddha had first taught. Indian dance, music and poetry flourished.

Muslims and Christians

In the 8th century a third great religion was introduced into India. This was Islam, carried by Arab conquerors sweeping through the mountain passes of the north-west. Southern India was not seriously affected, and in the 9th century the Hindu Chola people set up a vast and wealthy trading empire that stretched from Sri Lanka to the Ganges.

From the 13th century onwards northern India was hit by wave after wave of Mongol invaders from central Asia. In one attack, in 1398, Tamerlane ('Timur the lame') sacked Delhi and killed most of its inhabitants. A little over a century later the Muslim warlord Babur invaded India and founded the Mughal (Persian for Mongol) empire, which lasted until 1858.

The most successful Mughal emperor was Akbar

(1556–1605). He conquered fresh lands and kept people happy by tolerating the Hindu religion. By this time, however, yet another group of people had arrived – Christians from Europe. They came as traders, but soon seized bases of their own. Then, taking advantage of squabbles between Indian princes, they gradually took over more and more of the country. ◗

◀ A figure of Buddha in the style of the ancient Greeks. Alexander the Great led an army into north-west India in 327 BC, but did not stay long. In the 2nd and 1st centuries BC other Greeks set up kingdoms in north-west India and some became followers of Buddhism.

▼ In the 3rd century BC the Indian king Asoka carved his laws on pillars. These were topped with sculptures, like these lions, which became the national emblem of India.

◀ Hinduism is one of the world's oldest religions, and is still a way of life for the majority of Indians today. Each part of the country has its own traditions. Here, thousands of people have gathered together in Puri, eastern India, for the annual Rathayatra (car festival). They haul heavy wooden images of the god Jagannatha and his brother and sister from the temple at Puri to another temple, in the country.

▲ The Taj Mahal at Agra is probably India's most famous landmark and one of the most beautiful buildings in the world. It was built between 1632 and 1649 by the Mughal emperor Shah Jahan in memory of his wife, Arjumand Banu Begam.

British rule

The British were the most successful of the new arrivals. In the 18th century they drove out their French rivals. By the 19th century they controlled most of the country. In 1876 the British queen Victoria became Empress of India.

The British ruled India less harshly than most conquerors. Efforts were made to improve agriculture and relieve famine. A fine railway system was built and Western-style education was introduced. In 1885 the Indian National Congress was set up by educated Indians to ask for more of a voice in their own government. When the British turned down their demands, a movement for full independence was born.

From 1919 the most important leader of the independence campaign was Mohandas (Mahatma) Gandhi. His successful non-violent tactics involved refusing to co-operate with the British. The British gradually gave way, and after World War II they agreed to full independence for India.

Unfortunately, the Hindu and Muslim politicians could not agree what form Indian independence should take. The British solved the problem in 1947 by dividing the country into the largely Hindu nation of India and the Muslim state of Pakistan. Millions of Hindus and Sikhs migrated to India, and millions of Muslims moved to Pakistan. There was terrible violence, and hundreds of thousands of people were killed.

An independent nation

Under prime minister Jawaharlal Nehru (1947–1964) India began to build up its industry. He also made India into the leader of the Third World countries. These countries were neutral in the Cold War struggle between the USA and the Soviet Union. India's relations with Pakistan were poor, however, and the two countries went to war in 1948, 1965 and 1971. A major cause of this fighting was Kashmir, a territory in the north-west claimed by both countries. Relations with Pakistan have continued to be bad, and both countries tested their own nuclear weapons in 1998.

Within India, religious and language differences have resulted in violence from time to time. In 1984 there was serious fighting between the Indian army and Sikhs who wanted to have their own independent state. This led to the assassination of the prime minister, Indira Gandhi (Nehru's daughter), by her Sikh bodyguards. Violence between Sikhs and Hindus continued. There have also been clashes between Muslims and Hindus.

Despite these difficulties, India has managed to remain a united country, and has also remained the world's largest democracy. India's economy has boomed, and at the end of the 20th century some people thought that India would soon become one of the world's richest countries.

• The Amritsar massacre (1919) shocked people all over India. A crowd had gathered in a small park to listen to nationalist leaders. As large meetings were forbidden, the British General Dyer told the people to leave. He then ordered his troops to open fire. 379 people were killed and about 1200 wounded in the gunfire.

• In 1984 there was a leak of dangerous gas from a US chemicals factory in Bhopal, in Madhya Pradesh. Over 3000 people died and as many as 250,000 were injured in the world's worst ever industrial disaster.

find out more
Ancient world
Buddhists
Gandhi, Mahatma
Hindus
Mongol empire
Muslims
Pakistan
Sikhs

◄ The Indian Mutiny (1857–1858). The Indian Mutiny was a rebellion by Indian soldiers and other Indians against British customs and British rule. It was brutally put down, and thousands of rebels were executed.

Industrial Revolution

From the beginning of the 18th century, machines were increasingly used to do work formerly done by hand. Later, canals and railways were built to carry raw materials and finished goods. Such developments represented a revolution in the way people lived and worked, and together make up what we now call the Industrial Revolution.

Steam engines were at the heart of the Industrial Revolution. The first was invented in 1698 by Dr Thomas Savery to pump water out of Cornish tin mines. Improvements made later by Thomas Newcomen and James Watt meant that steam engines could be used for all kinds of manufacturing work and thereby made cheap mass production in factories possible.

Textiles

Until the Industrial Revolution, linen and wool had been spun

and woven in people's homes. The introduction of machines, such as John Kay's flying shuttle, invented in 1733, speeded up the weaving process. James Hargreaves's spinning jenny (1764) enabled one person to spin as much thread as 16 had done before. By the beginning of the 19th century people no longer worked at home but in new mills and factories, which were built to house great new machines that had to be powered by water wheel or steam engine.

Iron

In 1713 Abraham Darby began using coke instead of charcoal to smelt (make) iron. This meant ironworks were not so reliant on woodland and made cast iron cheaper. By 1784 Henry Cort had developed a method of removing some of the impurities of cast iron

◀ The spinning frame, a machine for spinning cotton, which Richard Arkwright invented in 1768. Thanks to machines like this, cotton became more popular than wool and played a vital part in Britain's economy right up until the 20th century.

to make wrought iron. Ironmaking became one of Britain's most important industries and iron was used to build the tools, bridges, machines and later railways of the Industrial Revolution.

Coal and canals

Steam engines as well as the iron industry required coal for fuel, and the growing population needed coal for heat and cooking. Canals were constructed to take coal where it was needed. Between 1759 and 1840 about 6840 kilometres of canals were dug in Britain. This formed the most important transport network before the railways were built.

The continuing revolution

Later stages of industrialization included the development of steel and shipbuilding, and the chemical, electrical and motor industries. The new industrial methods spread first to Europe, then to the USA, Canada, Japan and Russia, and then to all the major countries of the world. Industrialization continues to develop and spread, particularly in electronics.

▲ Thomas Savery's first steam engine proved unsafe, and it was Thomas Newcomen who developed a much safer engine in 1712. His steam-powered water pump was rather slow, but it solved the problem of flooding in the coalmines. There is a steam-powered water pump in use in the centre of this 19th-century English painting of the pit-head of a coalmine.

find out more
Agricultural Revolution
Cities
Communications
Georgian Britain
Transport
Victorian Britain

Ireland

Around 300 BC Celtic people came to settle in Ireland, which was divided into about 100 kingdoms. Early Ireland became an important centre of Christianity. In the 9th century the Vikings founded Dublin and other ports, but were finally defeated by the Irish in 1014.

In 1171 the English king, Henry II, invaded Ireland, but only conquered a small area. In the 16th century the English fought to conquer all of Ireland. In 1601 an English army defeated the last Irish forces. James I gave land in Ulster, in the north, to English and Scottish Protestants.

In 1641 the Irish revolted against English rule. In 1649 Oliver Cromwell's army crushed the rebels and gave over more Ulster land to Protestants. Catholics briefly regained their position when Catholic James II became king, but he was defeated in 1690. For the next 100 years the parliament in Dublin was run by Protestant landowners.

Revolution and the Act of Union

Catholics resented this, and so did some Protestants. In 1798 a group of Protestants led a revolution in which many Catholics also took part. The British decided that Ireland could only be governed if it was united with England.

This happened with the Act of Union of 1801. The Dublin parliament was closed and only Protestants could be elected to Parliament in London. In 1829 Catholics were granted freedom from the laws which barred them from parliament, public office and some professions.

The fight for independence

In the first half of the 19th century a potato blight (disease) caused terrible famine and millions died or left the country. Many Irish

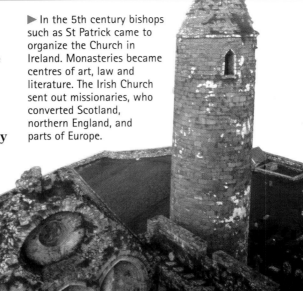

▶ In the 5th century bishops such as St Patrick came to organize the Church in Ireland. Monasteries became centres of art, law and literature. The Irish Church sent out missionaries, who converted Scotland, northern England, and parts of Europe.

blamed Britain for the famine. Many politicians began to fight for Home Rule and an Irish government run by the country's own citizens. However, this was opposed by Unionists, mainly Protestants, who feared Catholic rule.

Just before World War I, Britain promised Home Rule. After the war, the nationalist party, Sinn Féin, won the elections. Instead of going to London, they set up a parliament in Dublin. At the same time, the Irish Republican Army (IRA) began a war with Britain which lasted until 1921.

In 1921, a treaty was agreed in which six of Ulster's nine counties remained part of the United Kingdom, while the other 26 counties became the Irish Free State. In 1949 this became the Republic of Ireland.

Peace in our time?

The peace settlement of 1921 was designed to ensure continued Protestant control in Northern Ireland. This was bitterly resented by Republicans and a position of stalemate lasted until 1968, when Northern Irish Catholics began campaigning for equal civil rights. This began a period of 'troubles' – riots, shootings and bombings carried out by armed groups on both sides. In 1998 a peace plan was finally agreed. This plan gave the Republic a voice in Northern Irish affairs, in return for which it agreed to drop its claim to the province.

◀ At Easter 1916 some nationalists tried to win full independence from Britain by force. After the Easter Rising street fighting continued for about a week, until the leaders were executed.

find out more
Celts
Christians
Cromwell, Oliver
Dark Ages
Europe
Prehistoric people
Tudor England
Vikings

• Irish lawyer Daniel O'Connell (1775–1847) was a famous campaigner for Catholic Irish people's rights. O'Connell and his supporters made the British parliament pass the Catholic Emancipation Act of 1829. This allowed Catholic men to serve in the British parliament and to hold other public offices. He is most remembered for his efforts to unite all classes of Irish people, without ever using violence.

• Ireland was linked to Britain and Europe until the end of the last ice age, when the sea level rose and so formed the Irish Sea. The first human settlers were probably Middle Stone Age hunters who crossed from Britain around 6000 BC, followed by Neolithic (New Stone Age) people in about 4000 BC.

Italy

Rome, Italy's present capital, was founded more than 2500 years ago. It became the centre of the Roman empire, which included all the lands around the Mediterranean Sea.

Barbarian tribes from the north destroyed the Roman empire in western Europe in the 5th century AD. By this time most people in Italy had become Christian.

The Middle Ages

Throughout the Middle Ages, Italy was divided into many small city states. The pope was the ruler of Rome and the lands around (the Papal States). Venice was one of the most powerful states. It grew rich from its merchants, who traded all around the Mediterranean. Other wealthy and powerful states included Genoa, Florence and Milan. By the 15th century Italy had become the centre of a rebirth, or '*renaissance*', of interest in the art and ideas of the ancient Greeks and Romans, and once again Italy inspired European thinkers and artists.

Unification

Life in Italy was not peaceful. There were often wars between cities and conflicts within cities. Many different peoples invaded, and several parts of Italy came under foreign rule. In the 19th century many Italians wanted to make Italy into a united country. This movement was led by a soldier, Guiseppe Garibaldi, and a politician, Camillo Cavour, prime minister of the Italian state of Sardinia and Piedmont.

The Piedmontese, helped by the French, freed part of northern Italy from Austrian rule in

1859. In 1860 Garibaldi, with his thousand red-shirted volunteers, defeated the foreign king of Sicily and Naples, and Cavour's armies seized the Papal States. In 1861 Victor Emmanuel II of Sardinia and Piedmont was accepted as king of a united Italy. Italy took the area round Venice from Austria in 1866, and seized Rome in 1870. The pope was left as ruler of the tiny Vatican City in Rome, but refused to accept what had happened until 1929.

Italy in the 20th century

Italy sided with the Allies (French, British, Russians and Americans) in World War I (1914–1918), and gained the South Tyrol from Austria. Afterwards Italy fell under the control of the fascist dictator Benito Mussolini. Mussolini occupied Ethiopia in 1936 and Albania in 1939.

In World War II Mussolini sided with Nazi Germany, but lost power when the Allies invaded in 1943. He was executed in 1945. Italy joined the Allies, but the north of the country remained occupied by the Germans until 1945. After the war the Italians voted to become a republic. To stop the country falling into the hands of a dictator again, the new system of elections made it impossible for one party to gain power. During the 1990s Italy's government was shaken by a series of scandals.

▲ Venice was once a great trading centre, and controlled an empire in the eastern Mediterranean. In the 16th century it lost its empire to the Ottoman Turks and its trade to the Portuguese, who had opened up the sea route to Asia round the southern tip of Africa.

Invasions of Italy

5th century AD
Visigoths, Vandals, Ostrogoths

6th century
Byzantines, Lombards

8th century Franks

9th century Muslim Arabs

10th century
Magyars, Germans

11th century Normans

15th century French

16th century Spanish

18th century
Austrians, French

find out more
Columbus, Christopher
Europe
Fascists
Middle Ages
Renaissance
Romans
Twentieth-century history
World War I
World War II

◀ Garibaldi (right) meets Victor Emmanuel II in 1860, the year before the latter became king of a united Italy.

Japan

Stone Age people first settled in Japan more than 10,000 years ago. According to legend, the first emperor of Japan was Jimmu, who reigned in 660 BC, but little is known about the early Japanese empire. Emperors were seen as gods, but from about AD 800 the real rulers were the noble Fujiwara family.

In 1160 power passed to a succession of warriors, who took the title of shogun (general). European traders arrived in the 16th century, but in 1637 the shoguns banned almost all foreign trade. Japan remained cut off from the rest of the world until 1854, when a US fleet forced the Japanese to open their ports once more.

The shoguns became very bad rulers, so in 1868 the emperor Mutsuhito (Meiji) took away their powers and ruled the country himself. Japan quickly built up its industry and armed forces. In a succession of wars with China and Russia between 1894 and 1937, Japan gained control of Korea, Taiwan and large areas of China.

In 1939 World War II broke out in Europe. Japan began to attack European colonies in Asia,

◀ The *samurai* were warriors who valued honour above all, and were prepared to commit suicide if they failed to keep to their rules of behaviour. For hundreds of years they were very powerful but they lost their power in 1868.

and within five months it had conquered most of South-east Asia. The Japanese also bombed the US naval base at Pearl Harbor in Hawaii, which brought the USA into the war. Japan eventually surrendered after the USA dropped atomic bombs on two Japanese cities, Hiroshima and Nagasaki.

American and Allied forces occupied Japan until 1952. Since then Japan has adopted a democratic government, and has agreed not to develop its army and navy. Japan is now one of the world's most important industrial nations, although it suffered a severe economic crisis in the late 1990s.

• Every Japanese emperor uses a 'reign name' instead of his real name. The reforming emperor Mutsuhito took the name of Meiji, and his reign is known as the Meiji Period.

find out more
World War II

Jefferson, Thomas

Born 1743 in Virginia, USA
Died 1826 aged 83

find out more
American Revolution
United States of America

▶ Thomas Jefferson (wearing the red waistcoat) signing the Declaration of Independence. In this important document he wrote the now famous words: 'all men are created equal and independent', and therefore they have rights which no one can take away. These rights include 'the preservation of life and liberty, and the pursuit of happiness'.

Thomas Jefferson was president of the USA from 1801 to 1809, but he is most famous for his part in writing the American Declaration of Independence. This historic document formed the basis of the US constitution and renounced all connections with Britain.

When Thomas Jefferson was born, Virginia was still a colony ruled by Britain. His father died when he was 14 and he inherited an enormous plantation, together with some slaves. After going to college, he became a lawyer, and in 1769 he was elected to the House of Burgesses, a local parliament. Many Virginians felt that Britain should allow the colonists to rule themselves. Jefferson agreed. He wrote that London had no right to make laws for people who had left England. Many people read and discussed his ideas and he was chosen to draft what became the Declaration of Independence. This formed the basis of the US constitution, the theory of government on which the USA was founded. This declaration led to the American Revolution (1775–1783), which secured US independence from England.

Jefferson did not fight in the war, choosing instead to return to Virginia. He was elected governor of Virginia (1779–1781) and then rose up the political ladder, as well as serving on diplomatic missions to Europe. In 1801 he became the third president of the USA. During his presidency, the size of the USA doubled. Jefferson dedicated the last years of his life to what was one of his proudest achievements, the University of Virginia.

Jews

Jews are the followers of Judaism, the Jewish religion of the ancient Hebrews. Some Jews may feel part of the Jewish people and their culture but not the religion.

▲ The Western or Wailing Wall is the only part of the Temple which survived in Jerusalem after the Romans destroyed it in AD 70. These Jewish pilgrims have come to the Wall to pray.

find out more
Holocaust
Middle East

Religious Jews believe that God has a relationship or covenant (contract) with everyone who leads a good life. The covenant of the Jewish people with God began with Abraham in about 1800 BC and continued with Moses. Abraham is important to Jews because God led him to the promised land of Israel (in Palestine), which they have called their own ever since. Later, so it is claimed in the Scriptures, when the Israelites were slaves in Egypt, God used Moses to lead them out of Egypt back to Israel (the Exodus). The Hebrews wandered in the wilderness for 40 years until, on Mount Sinai, they made a covenant with God, who gave them the gift of the Torah (law or teaching), which includes the Ten Commandments.

David and Solomon, who lived in the 10th century BC, were two of Israel's most famous kings. David united the tribes of Judah and Israel into one nation and brought the Ark with the Ten Commandments to Jerusalem. His son Solomon's most important work was the building of the Temple, in which the Ark was placed. Later, Palestine was ruled by various empires including the Babylonian, Persian, Greek, Roman, Ottoman and British; the people were exiled and their temple in Jerusalem destroyed.

These exiles began the diaspora (dispersal) of Jews to many parts of the world. In AD 135 the Romans exiled all Jews from Jerusalem, and for the next 18 centuries most Jews lived all over the world. Wherever they went, they tried to maintain a distinctive way of life and worship. Persecutions (called 'pogroms') began because Christians saw them as outsiders. This prejudice against Jews is called anti-Semitism.

The last terrible persecution was the Holocaust (*Shoah*) in Nazi Germany in the 1930s and 1940s when over 6 million Jews were killed. After this it was agreed by the United Nations in 1947 that there should be a Jewish state in Palestine. This was to be called Israel.

Joan of Arc

Born 1412 in Domrémy, France
Burnt at the stake 1431 aged 18

Joan of Arc was a young peasant girl who, inspired by God, led French troops in a battle against the English during the Hundred Years' War. She was later captured by the English, who claimed she was a witch and burnt her at the stake.

• Twenty-five years after her death, the French king proclaimed Joan of Arc innocent, and nearly 500 years after her death the pope declared her a saint.

find out more
France

When Joan was 13 years old, she heard some voices which she believed had come from God. They spoke about the sufferings of France at the hands of the English, who had invaded under Henry V. The true heir to the French throne, Charles the Dauphin, was a refugee. The voices told Joan to lead the fight against the English.

Joan persuaded Charles of her mission. He sent her with troops to Orléans, the last city in northern France still resisting the English. Within a week of her arrival in May 1429, the siege of Orléans was over. Within two months, the English had been defeated in battle and Charles had been crowned King of France.

However, after a year she was captured by the English and King Charles made no attempt to rescue her. Joan was put on trial as a witch and a heretic (a person who disagrees with the teaching of the Church). Her accusers insisted that it was the Devil who had inspired her to wear men's clothes and to claim such power for herself. Joan was found guilty and was burnt at the stake in Rouen in May 1431.

▼ This painting of Joan of Arc in battledress at the coronation of Charles VII was made by Jean-Auguste Dominique Ingres in 1854.

Kennedy, J. F.

John Fitzgerald Kennedy was one of America's most popular and inspiring presidents. Tragically, he was in office for only two years before being shot and killed by an assassin.

John Kennedy ('Jack' to his family) was one of nine children. He did well at college, but he hurt his back while playing football and never fully recovered from the injury. During World War II, he commanded a small ship. It was sunk by the Japanese, but Kennedy, although badly injured, managed to lead his men to safety. For this he was awarded a medal for heroism.

Kennedy's father was a strong-minded man who was determined that one of his sons would become a politician. The whole family helped Jack by contributing campaign funds and canvassing voters. He became a Democrat member of the House of Representatives in 1946, and a senator in 1952.

In 1960 he was elected president of the USA. Although he was energetic and intelligent, Kennedy soon faced problems. He gave American help to Cuban refugees trying to invade communist Cuba. They failed, making the USA look foolish. Nevertheless, Kennedy did stop the USSR from building nuclear missile bases on Cuba in 1962. He also sent military advisers and troops to Vietnam, which led, after his death, to American involvement in the Vietnam War. At home, he proposed laws to give black Americans equal rights, but Congress did not pass these laws until after he was killed in 1963.

Born 1917 in Brookline, Massachusetts, USA **Assassinated** 1963 aged 46

find out more
Cold War
United States of America
Vietnam War

▼ In November 1963 Kennedy travelled to Dallas, Texas, to gather support in the American South. He was shot and killed by a gunman while travelling in this open car.

King, Martin Luther

Born 1929 in Atlanta, Georgia, USA **Assassinated** 1968 aged 39

find out more
Slaves
United States of America

▶ Martin Luther King at the Washington demonstration of 1963. His speech inspired millions of people to campaign for civil rights: 'I have a dream, that my four little children will one day live in a nation where they will not be judged by the colour of their skin but by the content of their character.'

Martin Luther King was the leader of the black civil rights movement in the USA in the 1950s and 1960s. He was an inspiring and committed leader, who finally gave his life in the struggle to win equal rights for black people.

Martin Luther King believed that the best way for black people to win equal rights was by non-violent protest against unfair laws. In 1955, he became a minister in Montgomery, Alabama. The buses there had separate seats for blacks and whites. King led a campaign to get rid of this separate seating.

King and his supporters were attacked and imprisoned for their non-violent protests, but their following continued to grow. Over 200,000 people marched to Washington in 1963, in support of equal rights for black people.

In 1964, King was awarded the Nobel Peace Prize. That same year, a new law made it an offence to discriminate against black people in public places, and the following year the US government gave all black adults the vote.

By 1966 other black leaders began to oppose his non-violent methods. He also became unpopular with some people, especially the government, because he opposed the Vietnam War. In April 1968 King went to Memphis, Tennessee, to support a strike by black refuse collectors. He was shot and killed by a sniper, while standing on the balcony of his motel room. Today, the anniversary of his assassination is a national holiday in the USA.

Knights

Knights were highly trained soldiers on horseback. In the early Middle Ages any talented warrior could become a knight. But gradually the knights formed a group which became a ruling class throughout Europe, with their own rules of behaviour known as the 'code of chivalry'.

Early knights formed the finest armies of medieval Europe. They played a vital part in the feudal system of the Middle Ages. In return for estates to live on, they had to serve their lords for about 40 days each year – in warfare, on expeditions or on castle guard. The code of chivalry they followed was meant to help to tame knights who terrorized the people of Europe in peacetime.

▼ These knights are jousting with long lances at a medieval tournament. The earliest tournaments were practice battles between two picked sides. They were rather like miniature wars, and men were often badly hurt. Jousting was more like a mock duel between individual champions.

Chivalry

Later, Christian knights formed a fixed group of warrior-governors or aristocrats. All knights were expected to serve God and the Church as well as their rulers. True knights should be brave, strong and skilful fighters. The code was used to tame unruly knights. It was an agreement between knights that they should be generous, kind and polite and always protect the weak.

Historians call the years from about 1100 to 1400 the Age of Chivalry, even though not all knights of this time behaved as well as the code suggested they should. By the end of that period most knights had stopped taking the code seriously. Instead of serving God and protecting the weak, they busied themselves with tournaments or with fighting duels of honour.

• Today in Britain men are still made knights, and given the title 'Sir', as a reward for serving the country in whatever jobs they do. Women who are given a similar reward are referred to as 'Dame' instead of 'Sir'.

find out more
Armour
Celts
Crusades
Medieval England
Middle Ages

Changing roles

By the 15th century new weapons and new kinds of warfare had come in, making the knights less important to Europe's armies. The weight of their armour greatly limited both their speed and their movement. Many stopped fighting for their rulers, and paid them instead to employ mercenaries, men who just fought for a living. The better-off knights then concentrated on running their estates.

Heraldry
Medieval knights had patterns on their shields called heraldic devices. Heraldry was the name for the study of these devices. Devices were also worn on helmets, on the drapery of horses and on special outer garments called 'surcoats'. The devices, or 'coats of arms' as they became known, were passed on from one generation to the next and so symbolized whole families, not just individuals.

Devices were often very beautiful, but they were more than just decorations. In tournaments of the Middle Ages devices were the only way of telling one knight from another. And in the heat of real battles these 'coats of arms' helped knights to tell their friends from their enemies.

Charges

Bend

Fess

Saltire

Chevron

Divisions

▶ The background colour of a shield is its *field* or *ground*. A *charge* is a picture or shape placed on the field. A few simple charges are shown here, but there are hundreds, including animals, birds and weapons. The basic field can be divided up in various ways, called *divisions* or *partitions*, two of which are shown here.

Quarterly

Paly

Lenin

Lenin was the leader of the communist revolution in Russia in 1917. Under his leadership, the old Russian empire was transformed into the Union of Soviet Socialist Republics (the USSR).

Born 1870 in Simbirsk, Russia
Died 1924 aged 53

• On the 100th anniversary of Lenin's birth, a third of the people of the world were living in countries run by communist governments. By 1991, however, the USSR had broken up and several other countries had abandoned communism.

find out more
Communists
Russia
Stalin, Joseph

As a young man, Vladimir Ilich Ulyanov (as Lenin was then called) became increasingly aware of what he saw to be the problems of his country: a weak tsar (emperor), a corrupt Church and nobility, and millions of poor and angry peasants and factory workers. Like many people, he saw revolution and the communist ideas of Karl Marx as the solution.

As a student, Ulyanov was often in trouble because of his political beliefs. Eventually he was sent to prison and then into exile in Siberia. While he was in Siberia he took the name 'Lenin', from the River Lena.

In 1898 the Russian Social-Democratic Workers' Party was formed. In an effort to gain power, Lenin helped to split the party in 1903, leading the Bolsheviks ('Majority') against the Mensheviks ('Minority'). The Bolsheviks later became the Russian Communist Party.

Lenin lived in exile for 12 years, but returned to Russia in 1917 when the tsar was overthrown and a new government came to power. That same year, he led the Bolsheviks to victory in a revolution against this government and thus became the ruler of Russia. The Bolshevik (or Soviet) government became a virtual dictatorship and defeated their opponents in the Russian Civil War (1918–1921). Lenin led his country – now the Union of Soviet Socialist Republics (USSR) – until his death from a stroke in 1924.

▼ After the 1917 revolution, posters and statues of Lenin were put up all over Russia.

Lincoln, Abraham

Abraham Lincoln was president of the USA from 1861 to 1865. His presidency was dominated by the American Civil War.

Abraham Lincoln's family was very poor and he had less than a year of proper schooling. When he was 22, Lincoln went to Illinois, where he qualified as a lawyer. It was there that he became involved in politics, eventually serving a term in the US Congress.

He first became famous as one of the leaders of the anti-slavery movement. His popularity in the Northern states resulted in him being elected president of the USA in 1861. However, on his election many Southern states (which wanted to keep slavery) reorganized themselves as an independent nation, called the Southern Confederacy. This division in the country was the beginning of the American Civil War, which lasted until 1865, when the Northern armies defeated the Southern armies.

In 1863 Lincoln made a speech at a soldiers' cemetery after the terrible battle of Gettysburg, which the armies of the Northern states had won. Few people realized it at the time, but the speech summed up the spirit of democracy. He said the soldiers had died so 'that government of the people, by the people, for the people, shall not perish from the Earth'.

After the war, Lincoln had plans for healing the division in his country, but he was killed before he could carry them out.

He was shot dead while at the theatre by John Wilkes Booth, a fanatical supporter of the Southern states.

Born 1809 in Kentucky, USA
Died 1865 aged 56

▶ Abraham Lincoln in 1864, the year after he announced his Emancipation Proclamation. He decreed that all slaves in America should be set free. People living in the Southern Confederacy refused to do this. However, after they lost the war, they were forced to comply.

find out more
American Civil War
Slaves
United States of America

Louis XIV

Born 1638 at Saint-Germain-en-Laye, France
Died 1715 aged 76

• Louis XIV's palace at Versailles was enormous. About 5000 courtiers and attendants lived inside.

Louis XIV was the king of France from 1643 to 1715. During his long reign, literature and the other arts flourished, but he had much less success in his attempts to gain new territories in Europe.

Louis became the king of France at the age of 4, on the death of his father, Louis XIII. His mother, Anne of Austria, at first ruled for him, helped by her powerful chief adviser, Cardinal Mazarin. After Mazarin died in 1661, however, Louis was determined to be the only ruler. As he said himself, 'L'état, c'est moi' ('I am the state').

Louis had many good ideas for improving the towns and countryside of France. Art, music and literature also flourished as he encouraged brilliant writers, artists and musicians to come to his court. However, there was a darker side to his reign as well. He fought expensive wars in the Netherlands and against Spain to gain new territories, but he was defeated when other countries joined together against him. At home, he was cruel to the Huguenots (Protestants) who, after a century of freedom, were told in 1685 that they had to become Roman Catholics. Two hundred thousand of them refused and left the country.

A magnificent palace at Versailles, just outside Paris, was built on Louis's orders and he moved his court there in 1682. However, the life of luxury he lived angered his subjects, many of whom were struggling to survive. When he died, he was a lonely figure, and his body was buried to the jeers of the watching crowd.

▼ Louis XIV portrayed in his coronation robes. He became known as the Sun King because he chose the Sun as his royal badge.

find out more
France

Mandela, Nelson

Born 1918 at Umtata in the Transkei, South Africa

• In 1993, together with F. W. de Klerk, the white president who released Mandela and legalized the ANC party, Mandela was awarded the Nobel Peace Prize for helping to abolish apartheid.

In 1964 Nelson Mandela was imprisoned for life for protesting against apartheid, South Africa's system of racial discrimination. During the 26 years he was detained he became an important symbol for the anti-apartheid movement, which campaigned for his release all over the world.

Although Nelson Mandela is related to the Xhosa royal family, he spent much of his early childhood herding cattle. After university, he qualified as a lawyer.

Mandela helped form the Youth League of the African National Congress (ANC) in 1943. The Youth League stressed the need for the ANC to identify with the hardships and struggles of ordinary black people against racial discrimination.

The ANC led peaceful mass protests against apartheid ('separate development'), the policy introduced by the National Party in 1948 to justify and strengthen white domination. Many protesters were imprisoned or killed. In 1960 the ANC was outlawed. In reply, Mandela and others established 'Umkhonto we Sizwe' (Spear of the Nation), a guerrilla army, in 1961.

In 1964, after months in hiding, Mandela was arrested and imprisoned for life. As a result of years of internal and international pressure, Mandela was eventually released in 1990 by President F. W. de Klerk. Mandela led the ANC in negotiations, resulting in the first democratic elections to be held in South Africa. The ANC won easily, and Mandela became president. In his new role, Mandela promoted reconciliation amongst all South Africans.

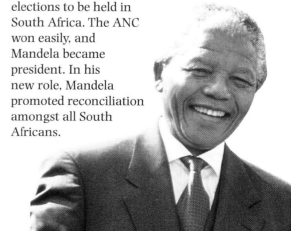

find out more
South Africa

▶ Nelson Mandela celebrates his historic inauguration as president of South Africa in Pretoria, 10 May 1994.

Magellan, Ferdinand *see* Explorers • **Magna Carta** *see* Medieval England

Mao Zedong

Born 1893 in Hunan, China
Died 1976 aged 82

• In 1937, when the Japanese invaded China, the nationalists retreated to the mountains, but Mao sent in the 'People's Liberation Army' to help people in occupied villages. This is one of the reasons why, when the Japanese were defeated at the end of World War II, the people supported Mao.

find out more
China
Communists

Mao Zedong was one of the founders of the People's Republic of China in 1949. As Chairman Mao he led China with his own brand of communism, as set out in the little red books given to all his people.

As a boy, Mao loved the stories of rebel leaders who stood up for the peasants, and he was one of the first to join the new Chinese Communist Party in 1921. At first the communists worked with the Guomindang (Nationalist Party) led by Jiang Jieshi (Chiang Kai-shek) until Jiang had many of them killed in 1927. Mao's communists and Jiang's nationalists continued to fight each other until after the end of World War II, when the people supported Mao in a civil war against the nationalists.

In 1949 Mao's forces captured the capital, Beijing, and set up the People's Republic of China. Mao encouraged the peasants to overthrow the landlords and work together on collective farms. In 1957 he ordered the peasants to join their farms into large 'communes', and to build new dams or open factories. These were part of Mao's plan for a 'Great Leap Forward' in industry. However, many of the schemes failed, and in 1959 Mao retired. Then, in 1966, he re-emerged to start the 'Cultural Revolution'. This movement was intended to keep Chinese communism free from outside influence and at the forefront of life in China. This, and many of his other plans and ideas, were lost when Mao died in 1976.

▼ The children surrounding Mao's painting are all dressed in traditional 'Mao' jackets, wearing red badges and holding copies of Mao's little red book.

Mary, Queen of Scots

Born 1542 in Linlithgow, Scotland
Died 1587 aged 42

find out more
Elizabeth I
Reformation
Scotland
Stuart Britain
Tudor England

Mary was the daughter of King James V of Scotland. He died six days after her birth, so she became queen when she was only a tiny baby.

Mary was born at a time of conflict between Scotland and England, and she was brought up in the French court for safety. In 1558 the English throne passed to Elizabeth I, a Protestant. But many Catholics viewed Elizabeth as illegitimate and thought Mary had a better claim to the throne.

Mary had been married to the French king Francis II, but when he died in 1561 she returned to Scotland. At first she managed to rule as a Catholic queen without offending the powerful Protestants in Scotland.

In 1565 Mary married her cousin Lord Darnley, but she soon came to hate him. When she drew closer to her adviser David Rizzio, her Protestant enemies involved the jealous Darnley in a plot to kill Rizzio. The murder increased her loathing of Darnley, and she in turn supported a plot in which he was blown up. Barely three months later she married the Earl of Bothwell, who was a prime suspect in Darnley's murder.

People thought this was an outrage, and in 1567 she was forced to abdicate (give up the throne) in favour of her son James VI of Scotland (later James I of England). She sought safety in England, but Elizabeth I feared her and kept her in captivity for 19 years. Eventually Mary was found guilty of involvement in a Catholic plot to kill Elizabeth, and was beheaded.

◄ Mary's beauty, the drama of her life, and the bravery with which she faced death have ensured a lasting fascination with her. This 19th-century painting shows her being led to her execution.

Maya

The ancient Mayan people of Mexico and Central America developed the highest civilization in the New World before the arrival of the Europeans.

▼ Ancient Maya occupied an area of some 495,000 sq km, including parts of what are now southern Mexico, Guatemala, Belize, Honduras and western El Salvador.

Between about 1200 BC and AD 300, the Maya were simply one of several cultures developing around the Gulf of Mexico. The Maya were a farming people, growing maize (corn), cotton, beans, chilli and cacao (source of chocolate).

Rise and fall

Mayan civilization reached its peak between AD 300 and 900.

The chief gods of the Maya were the Sun, the Moon, the Earth and four rain gods. Mayans studied astronomy and made an accurate calendar because the stars and planets were thought to influence all life on Earth.

This Mayan civilization built magnificent pyramid temples, and used stone tools and jade for decoration. They made fine woodwork, basketwork and pottery, and colourful cottons. Farmers traded in cacao beans, jaguar pelts, bird feathers and salt.

The early Mayan cities were already in decline when they were conquered by the Spanish in the 16th century. Modern Mayans live in southern Mexico, Guatemala, Belize and west Honduras.

find out more
Ancient world
Aztecs
North America

▼ This beautifully carved stone pillar from Honduras was made by a Mayan sculptor in the 8th century AD.

Medieval England

We call the years between about AD 410 and 1485 in England the 'Middle Ages' or 'medieval times'. It is not a very exact period. It did not suddenly begin when the last Roman armies sailed away in 410, or end when Henry VII came to the throne.

For much of the Middle Ages English kings had possessions in France as well as England. Henry I ruled Normandy, Brittany and Maine, while Henry II governed an empire that stretched from the Scottish border to the Pyrenees.

The medieval kingdom

King John lost some of these possessions to France, and the

kings who succeeded him fought the Hundred Years' War (really a series of small wars) to try to win them back. Edward III and Henry V had spectacular short-term successes, but

eventually the French were too powerful.

Meanwhile, English kings attempted to win control of the whole of the British Isles. Henry II conquered parts of Ireland,

◀ John, king of England from 1199 to 1216, used every means he could to raise the money to pay for wars to win back French land. When he began to act illegally, his subjects made him sign a great list of their rights called Magna Carta ('great charter').

• Because the medieval period is so long, this article covers only the years after about 1100. The time before that is dealt with in Anglo-Saxons and Normans. The period after 1485 is dealt with under Tudor England.

◄ After destroying the French army at Agincourt in 1415 (left) Henry V, king of England from 1413 to 1422, continued his assault on France until the French king let Henry marry his daughter, and so become his heir. In the nine years he ruled, Henry became the most powerful man in Europe.

but his successors were unable to retain his conquests. Wales fell to the armies of Edward I, who made his son Prince of Wales. The Scots successfully resisted English conquest.

King, law and parliament

Although medieval kings wielded immense power, an unpopular monarch rarely lasted long. The hated Edward II was murdered by his enemies, and Queen Matilda's reign was ravaged by civil war. Furthermore, ambitious barons were always ready to fight for the crown. The best known of these contests was the Wars of the Roses, fought between the families of York and Lancaster, both heirs of Edward III.

Despite war and rebellion, England was one of the best-governed states in Europe. Successful kings kept in touch with their barons and, later, with representatives from the counties. The assemblies of barons became the House of Lords and the assemblies of non-noble representatives became the House of Commons. The two Houses made up a Parliament.

God's will

The Christian Church in England was a branch of the hugely rich and powerful Roman Catholic Church, headed by the pope. It was the largest landowner and it controlled the schools and universities. The Church even had its own system of law, allowing churchmen to be tried in their own courts. This led to bitter squabbles between the king and the Church.

'Field full of folk'

In the early Middle Ages most people were agricultural peasants. They lived in small villages, where their freedom was restricted by the *feudal system*. In the feudal system society was structured rather like a pyramid. Great numbers of ordinary people formed its broad base, and their hard work on the land provided for everyone above them – the knights, lords, barons and king.

Outbreaks of the Black Death (the plague) killed more than a third of the population, causing a labour shortage. This and the peasants' own complaints made the feudal system increasingly unworkable.

Changing times

The Middle Ages were full of changes. Royal power was limited by Parliament. Towns expanded and a prosperous merchant class grew up. The broad open fields of the early Middle Ages, in which peasants farmed their own strips of land, started to be replaced by enclosed fields. By the 15th century the Church, with its wealth and services in Latin, was increasingly out of touch with people's needs.

The invention of printing meant that books were more widely available, and the Renaissance introduced exciting new art and ideas from southern Europe.

NORMANS
1100 Henry I
1135 Stephen and Matilda

PLANTAGANETS
1154 Henry II
1170 Murder of Archbishop Thomas Becket
1189 Richard I
1199 John
1215 Magna Carta
1216 Henry III
1272 Edward I
1295 English Model Parliament set up
1307 Edward II
1327 Edward III
1337–1453 Hundred Years' War
1348 First outbreak of Black Death
1377 Richard II
1381 Peasants' Revolt

LANCASTER
1399 Henry IV
1413 Henry V
1415 Henry V defeats the French at Agincourt
1422 Henry VI
1455–1485 Wars of the Roses

YORK
1461 Edward IV
1476 William Caxton sets up his printing press
1483 Edward V
1483 Richard III

◄ When Archbishop Thomas Becket refused to change the system allowing churchmen to be tried in their own courts, he was murdered in Canterbury Cathedral. This stained-glass window of Becket, later declared a saint, shows him tending a sick person.

find out more
Anglo-Saxons
Black Death
Crusades
Dark Ages
Joan of Arc
Knights
Middle Ages
Normans

Middle Ages

The Middle Ages (or the 'medieval period') covers the years between about AD 410 and 1500, the first few centuries of which are sometimes called the 'Dark Ages'. We call the period before the Middle Ages 'ancient times' (the time of the Egyptians, Greeks and Romans). After the Middle Ages come 'modern times'.

Medieval Europe was divided into dozens of small states. Countries such as Scotland and Portugal were roughly the same as they are today. Other areas, like Germany and Italy, consisted of many smaller states. Some states consisted of just a single city. At this time people's religious beliefs were more important to them than the countries they happened to live in.

One Church for all

The people of Europe described themselves as living in 'Christendom', the area where Christians lived, roughly the same as Europe. There were two branches of the Christian Church. Western Europe was Roman Catholic, under the leadership of the pope. The people of eastern Europe belonged to the Orthodox Church, which had its headquarters in Constantinople (now Istanbul). Other forms of Christianity were not allowed. Catholic services were much the same all over western Europe, and the services were even given in the same language – Latin.

For people living in the Middle Ages death was never very far away; doctors had far less knowledge and skill, and diseases like the Black Death killed many. Medieval people believed hell was real and full of torments and that going to church was the main way of pleasing God and reserving a place in heaven.

The first estate

There were three groups, or 'estates', of people in Christendom. Church men and women belonged to the first and most important estate. There were thousands of Church officials. Some were rich and mighty, like the pope, archbishops, bishops and abbots, who ran large

▲ This map shows the main countries in Europe in about the year 1200.

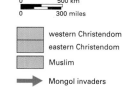

0	500 km
0	300 miles

western Christendom
eastern Christendom
Muslim
Mongol invaders

monasteries. Most, however, were poor and humble, like the parish priests, monks and nuns.

The Church's main tasks were to pray, to teach, and to help ordinary people live religious lives. Later, some said the Church was too rich, too powerful and too concerned with worldly matters. Even so, in 1500 the Church was still a mighty organization. It owned almost a quarter of all the land in Christendom and great wealth in buildings, jewels and precious metals. ◆

• Throughout the Middle Ages in Europe there were many revolts by peasants against their poor conditions. In 1358, for example, there was a massive peasants' revolt in northern France. All such revolts were crushed without mercy.

◄ The Gothic cathedral in Milan, built in the 14th and 15th centuries, still looms over the city today. In medieval Europe religion was an important part of everyone's life. On Sundays and other 'holy days', everyone had to attend religious services. Huge and splendid cathedrals like this were built by the wealthy and powerful Church all over Europe during the Middle Ages.

▶ The English king, Edward III (right, dressed in red) receives an ambassador from Robert Bruce (king of Scotland) in 1327. The 15-year-old English king is surrounded by the nobles of his court. While the Church looked after people's souls, the rulers and soldiers of the second estate were supposed to look after their bodies. Ordinary people had no say in government.

• The most important wars during the Middle Ages were the Crusades, 'holy wars' between European Christians and Muslims in the Holy Land of Palestine.

The second estate

Kings, queens and nobles made up the second estate of medieval Europe. In many parts of Europe, lay people (those not in the Church) were part of a feudal system. This placed everyone in a sort of pyramid of importance. The king was at the top and the common people at the bottom. Nobles were chief soldiers, under whom served the knights, who all swore to serve their superiors. In return, they were given lands to live on. In wartime the knights served by fighting. In peacetime, based in their castles, they served by helping their lords to rule.

The third estate

We know very little about the lives of the ordinary folk (peasants), the third and by far the largest of the three estates. Hundreds of books about the first and second estates survive, but very little was written about the peasants.

Apart from religion, the most important thing for these people was work. The nobles and the Church relied on them for food, clothing and taxes. The peasants also had to fight for their lords. Some ordinary people lived on lonely hill farms. Others lived in the growing towns and cities. But by 1500, eight or nine people out of

▶ This painting was made in the 15th century, near the end of the Middle Ages. It shows medieval country workers on an estate. Workers are shown sheep-shearing, wood-chopping, hay-cutting, apple-picking and ploughing. The lady of the house is seen carrying freshly picked flowers.

The village of Montaillou

In the 1970s some fascinating documents telling us about 14th-century village life in Montaillou, France, were discovered. Each year there were 90 religious festivals or 'holy days'. The main food was bread made from wheat or millet. A popular soup included bacon, bread, cabbages and turnips. Sweet foods were rare.

Only four or five of the villagers could read or write. Hardly any of the children went to school, and at 12 boys were expected to do grown-up jobs. People did not shave or wash very often and women spent hours picking fleas off their relatives and friends. Families normally decided who their children would marry and most villagers married someone else from Montaillou.

ten still lived in villages and worked the fields. For them, things had not changed much for hundreds of years. Virtually no ordinary medieval homes are standing today: most were rough cottages of mud, sticks and straw, which burned down or fell to ruin centuries ago.

The end of the Middle Ages

Most medieval people knew little of the outside world. They could not read about it in books and travel was difficult, dangerous and expensive. By 1500 all this was beginning to change. European explorers had sailed to India and across the Atlantic to the 'New World', later known as the Americas. Cheap printed books were helping many more people to read and write. Artists and thinkers were saying that life was more than just a preparation for heaven, and criticism of the Church and the pope was growing. People were starting to think of themselves not chiefly as part of Christendom, but as members of a nation, such as France, Castile (central Spain), or Sweden. The Middle Ages were coming to an end.

Middle East

Three continents – Europe, Asia and Africa – join in the Middle East. For thousands of years, the Middle East has been a crossroads for travellers and traders. It has also been an area of great conflict.

The Middle East has played an enormously important part in history. It was the birthplace of farming and towns. Writing was developed there, as well as the three great religions of Judaism, Christianity and Islam.

Early civilizations and empires

The earliest civilization began about 4000 BC in Sumer, part of Mesopotamia (modern-day Iraq) around the Tigris and Euphrates rivers. By 3000 BC, along the banks of the Nile, the remarkable Egyptian civilization was also flowering.

For the next 3000 years a succession of civilizations and empires rose and fell in the Middle East. These included the Babylonians, Assyrians, Hittites, Phoenicians, Persians and the Greeks who followed Alexander the Great. Later, the Romans conquered the western parts of the Middle East. After the 5th century AD, the Roman empire in the east became the Byzantine empire.

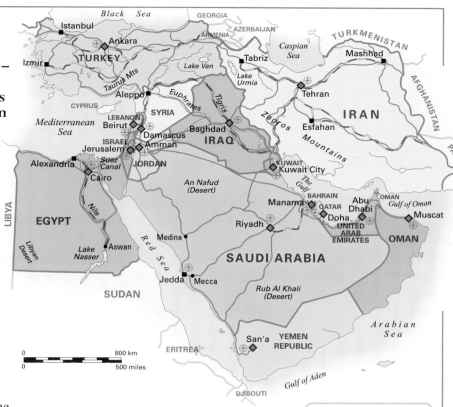

Jews, Christians and Muslims

The Jewish (or Hebrew) people, who lived at the eastern end of the Mediterranean, believed in one God. About 2000 years ago a Jew named Jesus claimed to be the son of God. His followers, the Christians, spread his teaching far and wide. Eventually Christianity became the official religion of the Romans, and then of the Byzantine empire.

In the 7th century AD an Arab named Muhammad began another new religion – Islam. The followers of this new religion, known as Muslims, swept out of Arabia and across the Middle East and beyond. By AD 750 the Muslim Arabs had conquered a huge area, including much of the Byzantine empire, and spread Arab civilization from Persia (Iran) and Afghanistan in the east to Spain in the west. From the 11th century Christian armies tried to conquer parts of the Middle East in the Crusades, but were unsuccessful.

Turks and Mongols

From the 11th century AD waves of nomadic (wandering) peoples from central Asia began to

◀ The Prophet's Mosque at Medina, Saudi Arabia, is one of the two most sacred sites in the world for Muslims. The prophet Mohammed is buried there.

Map legend:

——————	country boundary
⩘⩘⩘⩘⩘	disputed boundary
◆	capital city
■	other major cities
——————	main roads
═══════	main railways
⊕	main airports

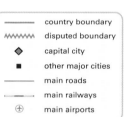

find out more
Alexander the Great
Ancient world
Byzantine empire
Christians
Cities
Crusades
Egyptians, ancient
Gulf wars
Jews
Mongol empire
Muslims
Ottoman empire
Prehistoric people
Romans

◀ An oil refinery in Saudi Arabia. In 1973–1974 the Arabs caused worldwide chaos by raising the price of their oil and refusing to supply countries that supported Israel in the Arab–Israeli conflict.

• Palestine is an area of the Middle East made up of parts of Israel and Jordan. In 1948 the state of Israel was created and Palestine was divided between Jews and Arabs. Some of the land allocated to the Palestinian Arabs was later occupied by Israel. The PLO (Palestine Liberation Organization) represents the Arab people who lived in Palestine before the creation of the state of Israel.

invade the Middle East. In 1071 one of these peoples, the Seljuk Turks, defeated the Byzantine empire and conquered much of the area now called Turkey. In the 13th and again in the 14th century Mongol armies swept through the Middle East, destroying everything in their path. But the Mongol empires did not last long.

In the 14th century another Turkish people, the Ottomans, started to expand their territory in Turkey. The Ottomans were Muslims, and by the 16th century their empire included much of the Middle East, north Africa and south-east Europe. In the 19th century the Ottoman empire began to break up. When the Turks took the side of Germany in World War I they were defeated. After the war some areas where Arabs lived, such as Arabia, became independent countries. Others, including Syria, Lebanon, Palestine, Jordan and Iraq, were governed by Britain and France until after World War II.

Modern conflicts

In Roman times the Jews had been driven from their native land and scattered all over the Middle East and Europe. In the 20th century, encouraged by the promises of European politicians, many Jews began to return to the region where their ancestors had lived. Some fled there to escape persecution in Nazi Germany.

In 1948 the United Nations allowed the Jews to set up a country of their own – Israel. But Arabs were already living there in a land they called Palestine. Fighting broke out and other Arab countries, particularly Egypt, Syria and Jordan, joined in on the Palestinian side. When the war ended in 1949 Israel had gained more territory.

In 1956 the Egyptians took over the Suez Canal, which had been owned by Britain and France. The British and French made a secret agreement with Israel to invade Egypt. People round the world were outraged, and the invaders withdrew. There were two more wars between Israel and its Arab neighbours, in 1967 and 1973. The Israelis defeated the Arabs and conquered more Arab land.

The Palestinian Arabs had no country. They lived as refugees, often in poverty and hardship. From bases in Lebanon and Syria, their young men fought the Israelis with terrorism. Only in the 1990s did the Palestinians, led by Yasser Arafat, get some say in the government of the areas where they live.

The discovery of oil made some Arab states, such as Saudi Arabia, extremely rich and powerful. The Iraqi dictator Saddam Hussein used his oil money to buy weapons to wage war against Iran (1980–1988) and Kuwait (1990–1991) – the two Gulf wars. In Arab countries without oil wealth, such as Egypt, Jordan and Lebanon, governments have struggled with poverty and Muslim extremists.

▼ Palestinian policemen trying to maintain order on the border between the Gaza Strip and Israel. The Gaza Strip was for many years an area of conflict between Israel and the Palestinian people. In 1993 an agreement with the Israelis gave the Palestinians some degree of self-rule.

Monasteries

• The Carthusians are named after their first monastery in the Grande Chartreuse, a group of mountains in the French Alps. The Cistercians are likewise named after their monastery at Cîteaux in eastern France. Both orders have strict rules about prayer, work, fasting and silence. Trappists is a later name for Cistercians.

find out more
Buddhists
Christians
Dark Ages
Hindus
Middle Ages
Reformation

▼ Buddhist monks accepting offerings. In many places monks and nuns rely on gifts of food from ordinary people.

A monastery is a religious community of monks or nuns. The places where nuns live are sometimes called convents. Monks and nuns are men and women who give over their lives completely to God. They give up all their possessions and their family, and they do not marry or have children.

As well as spending much time in formal prayer and meditation, monks and nuns may also do other things, such as teaching or caring for the sick. Monks and nuns are found in many religions, including Hinduism, Buddhism and Christianity.

Hindu and Buddhist monks

In India there have always been people who have left family life for a life of meditation. Hindus who renounce the world and live alone in this way are called *sanyasins*. There are also Hindu religious communities or monasteries. Although some Buddhist monks and nuns lead wandering lives, others are based in monasteries. The land for the monasteries and the material for building them are a gift from ordinary Buddhists and are never owned by the monks and nuns themselves. Buddhist monks ruled Tibet for centuries, until the Chinese took over the country in 1950.

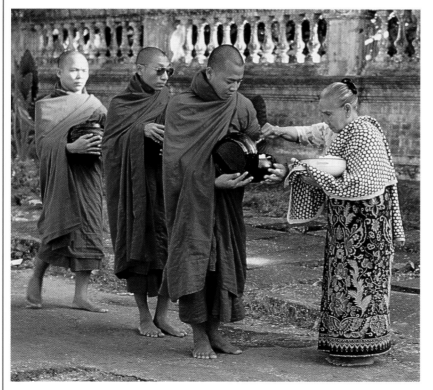

▲ Before the development of printing in the 15th century, Bibles, prayer books and collections of psalms were copied and often decorated by hand. In the early Middle Ages these manuscripts were made by monks.

Christian monastic orders

In the 3rd century AD some Egyptian and Syrian Christians gave up their possessions and went to live in the desert to be closer to God. These first monks lived alone, but they later formed communities. Their life of prayer was balanced with work, such as making reed baskets. People from the towns came to visit them to ask their advice, and they had a reputation for being wise.

In the 6th century St Benedict, a monk living in Italy, set out some rules for his community of monks. Those who followed his rules were called Benedictines, and they set up monasteries all over Europe. Many monasteries also served as farms, as hospitals and as centres of learning.

Many monasteries became very wealthy and owned a lot of land. Some men who wanted to live as monks decided that the Benedictine monasteries were too comfortable and too close to the everyday world. They joined new monastic orders, such as the Carthusians or Cistercians, and followed a harder, stricter rule. Some monks felt they should take the message of God beyond the monasteries, and became friars – penniless wandering preachers. They followed the teachings and ideas of St Francis of Assisi (Franciscans) or of St Dominic (Dominicans).

In England the monasteries were closed down in the reign of Henry VIII at the time of the Reformation (in the 16th century). But in many parts of Europe the old monasteries continued and new religious orders were founded, including the Roman Catholic order, the Society of Jesus. Jesuits, as they were called, became famous as teachers, preachers and missionaries.

Mongol empire

The Mongol empire became the largest in the history of the world. It was created by the brutal leader Genghis Khan and his followers.

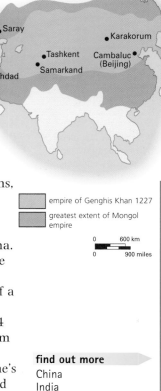

▼ Genghis Khan was one of the most terrifying soldiers in history. Here, he is entering battle behind his general, Gebe.

Genghis Khan, the son of a Mongol chief, was named Temujin when he was born. He was only 9 when his father died. When he grew up he begged 20,000 soldiers from a friendly chief, and set about making himself leader of all the Mongol tribes.

By 1206 Temujin had united eastern and western Mongolia. He won his empire through brutal leadership and unimaginable cruelty. He took the title 'Genghis Khan', which means 'universal ruler'. He and his sons and grandsons, including Kublai Khan, went on to conquer an area that stretched from Russia in eastern Europe across to China.

In the late 14th century the empire was in decline. Tamerlane, great-grandson of a minister of Genghis Khan, planned to rebuild it. By 1404 he had conquered regions from the Black Sea to the Indus. A hundred years after Tamerlane's death in 1405, the empire had completely disintegrated.

empire of Genghis Khan 1227

greatest extent of Mongol empire

0   600 km
0   900 miles

find out more
China
India
Middle East

Muslims

Muslims are the followers of the religion of Islam. Islam means submitting to the will of God. Muslims believe that obeying God (Allah), and living in the way God expects brings peace.

▲ A page from the Qur'an (Koran). Muslims believe that the Qur'an contains the messages Muhammad received from God. For Muslims this is the record of how God wants them to live.

find out more
Africa
Balkans
Crusades
India
Middle East
Ottoman empire
Pakistan

Muslims respect all the prophets who taught people to worship one God and to do good deeds. These include Abraham, Moses and Jesus. For Muslims, Muhammad is the last and greatest of these prophets.

Muhammad was born in about AD 570 in Mecca, in what is now Saudi Arabia. He and his followers were attacked for their beliefs, and Muhammad organized armed resistance to the enemies of the new faith. By the time of his death in AD 620 Muhammad ruled the whole of Arabia. His successors conquered the Middle East, North Africa and Spain. There was a great flowering of arts and learning in the Arab empire, and the Muslim rulers were generally tolerant of other religions.

Arab traders spread Islam to other peoples, in Africa south of the Sahara and as far as Indonesia. Islam became the religion of the Ottoman Turks, who later took over much of the Arab empire, and also of the Safavid empire in Persia (Iran) and the Mughal empire in India. In 1979 Muslim fundamentalists, who observe strict traditional Muslim laws, came to power in Iran. Fundamentalism has also increased in power and influence in other Muslim countries.

▼ The Arab empire in the 8th and 9th centuries.

EUROPE

SPAIN

AFRICA

Black Sea

Mediterranean Sea

SYRIA

Caspian Sea

IRAN

EGYPT

ARABIA

INDIA

Arab empire

Byzantine empire

0   1200 km
0   900 miles

Napoleon Bonaparte

Napoleon Bonaparte was a great military leader who became ruler of France. He was the emperor from 1804 to 1814 and again in 1815.

Born 1769 in Ajaccio, Corsica
Died 1821 aged 51

• Although Napoleon is perhaps best known for his military campaigns, he also made many important reforms as a statesman. He reorganized the French legal system in what became known as the Code Napoléon (Napoleonic Code). It was adopted throughout the Napoleonic empire and influenced legal systems around the world. It remains the basis of French law today.

find out more
France
Nelson, Horatio

Napoleon Bonaparte was a brilliant general who, by 1799, had led his troops to several victories in Europe. France at this time was going through a difficult phase. With his help, the old government was overthrown and Napoleon became France's new leader.

Over the next five years, he made many changes to improve the lives of ordinary people. His armies were successful abroad, although his navy was defeated by Nelson at the battle of Trafalgar in 1805. In 1804 he became emperor, and by 1807 he ruled a vast empire.

However, things began to go wrong and the French people became weary of Napoleon's rule. In 1814 he was banished to Elba, in the Mediterranean, but he escaped and regained power. This time, however, Britain, Prussia, Russia and Austria combined to defeat him at the battle of Waterloo in 1815. He died in exile in St Helena in the south Atlantic.

◄ Troops sent to stop Napoleon on his return from exile on the island of Elba in 1815 welcome him instead as their emperor. His victory was short-lived.

Native Americans

The original people of North America were called Indians by European explorers, who thought they had arrived in the East Indies. At this time Native Americans spoke many different languages and had many different customs. No one owned the land. Their religions taught respect for nature.

Different Native American peoples found different ways of living in harmony with their environment. Some were settled farmers, others fishers, and many moved from place to place gathering wild fruits and nuts and hunting animals.

As more and more Europeans arrived in North America they began to spread westwards, and take land from the Native Americans. There was fighting in some places, but by the end of the 19th century most Native Americans had been moved to reservations. The land on the reservations was often poor and unsuitable for the traditional Native American way of life.

Today some Native Americans are using the law to negotiate better deals with the US and Canadian governments. Others are using direct action such as roadblocks to enforce their claims to the lands they have lost.

▼ The Native American farmers of the south-west lived in large villages, called pueblos. The houses were made of adobe – blocks of sun-dried clay.

• The Native American peoples of Mexico, the Caribbean, Central America and South America are described in other articles in this encyclopedia.

find out more
Ancient world
Aztecs
Canada
Caribbean
Incas
Maya
North America
Prehistoric people
South America
United States of
America

Nelson, Horatio

Born 1758 in Norfolk, England
Died 1805 aged 47

find out more
Georgian Britain
Napoleon Bonaparte

Horatio Nelson was Britain's greatest admiral. He defeated Napoleon's navy at the battle of Trafalgar in 1805, and this ensured that Britain was saved from being invaded by the French.

Horatio Nelson joined the navy when he was 15, and just six years later he was given command of his own ship. In spite of frequent illnesses, he soon made a name for himself as a skilled commander who was also very popular with his men.

His first opportunity to prove himself came when Britain declared war on the French in 1793. He was blinded in his right eye during a

◀ In this painting, Nelson is shown dying on the deck of his ship, the *Victory*. Having been assured of his fleet's success, his last words were said to be, 'Thank God I have done my duty.'

battle in 1794, and more injuries followed – eventually his right arm had to be cut off at the elbow. However, this did not hold him back. He destroyed the French navy in the battle of the Nile in 1798, and in 1801 he defeated the Danes at the battle of Copenhagen. He was rewarded with the rank of vice-admiral that same year.

Nelson's greatest success was to be his last. In 1805 his fleet of 27 ships encountered 33 French and Spanish vessels at Cape Trafalgar, off the coast of Spain. Nelson signalled to his own fleet: 'England expects that every man will do his duty.' His forces won a famous victory, but during the fighting he was shot and he died on the deck of his ship, the *Victory*. England was now safe from invasion from Napoleon's forces but had lost one of its greatest heroes.

New Zealand

The first people to arrive in New Zealand were the Maori. Around 1000 years ago they sailed there from the tropical islands of eastern Polynesia, in the Pacific Ocean.

About 500 years ago improved farming methods led to an increase in population. Competition for land became intense. Tribes banded together, building large fortified villages. High-born chiefs ruled over commoners, and slaves were taken in warfare.

Maori culture had become very complex by the time that Captain Cook reached New Zealand in 1769. Soon afterwards traders, missionaries and settlers from Britain began to arrive. There were disputes

over land between the new arrivals and the Maori, which led to a series of bitter land wars. By 1870 the Maori had been defeated. As a result, the traditional Maori way of life was almost destroyed.

New Zealand began to govern its own affairs in 1856, and became completely independent of Britain in 1931. New Zealand troops fought alongside

the British in World War I and World War II. The invention of refrigeration in 1869 encouraged sheep and dairy farming, as lamb and butter could now be sold abroad. Until the UK joined the European Union in 1973, much New Zealand produce was sold there. Today, however, New Zealand has stronger trading links with Australia and South-east Asia.

▲ Maori warriors perform a war dance. The Maori fought fiercely to defend their land. It took the British settlers many years to defeat them.

● The Maori name for New Zealand is Aotearoa. It means Land of the Long White Cloud.

find out more
Cook, James

Normans

The first Normans were 'Northmen' – tall, fair-haired Vikings from Scandinavia. They came to the fertile lands of northern France to steal goods and land. In 911 the king of the Franks made a deal with Rolf, the Viking leader. The king granted him land. In return, Rolf became a Christian, and probably promised to be loyal to the king. That was the beginning of Normandy.

The dukes of Normandy, from Rolf onwards, were strong rulers and powerful fighters. They controlled their tough followers by giving them land, and they expected loyalty and obedience in return. Most of Normandy was very fertile. The coast had good harbours. The Seine joined Normandy to Paris and the heart of France, so the Normans could trade and travel easily. They became rich and independent.

The Normans learned to speak French. They had come to a Christian land and soon became Christian themselves. The Church in Normandy grew strong and well organized, run by good and well-educated bishops.

Warriors

The Normans were effective fighters, especially when fighting on horseback. They bred special warhorses, and saddles and stirrups gave them firm control of their mounts. Norman knights learned to use long, heavy lances, so when they charged, their enemies faced an array of deadly spikes bearing down on them. Norman armies

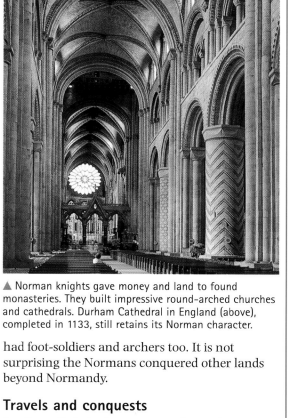

▲ Norman knights gave money and land to found monasteries. They built impressive round-arched churches and cathedrals. Durham Cathedral in England (above), completed in 1133, still retains its Norman character.

had foot-soldiers and archers too. It is not surprising the Normans conquered other lands beyond Normandy.

Travels and conquests

Southern Italy had no strong ruler, and was on the route which pilgrims took to the Holy Land. To the south lay Sicily, controlled by Saracens (Muslims). Norman adventurers turned up there from AD 1000 to make their fortunes. One such adventurer was Robert Guiscard. He and his brother, Roger, managed to win most of southern Italy and Sicily. Normans ruled there as kings of Sicily until 1194.

In 1066 Duke William of Normandy claimed the English throne when the old king, his cousin Edward the Confessor, died. But he had to defeat the English Harold of Wessex, who had already taken the crown. So 'William the Conqueror' invaded England. The battle of Hastings was long and hard, but finally Harold was killed, and the English fled. After that, the Normans ruled England.

Soon after, in 1095, two groups of Normans (from Normandy and southern Italy) joined the first crusade to win back Jerusalem from the Muslims. They helped to capture Jerusalem, and set up a Norman kingdom round Antioch, in modern Turkey. ◗

▼ Map showing Norman lands in about 1090.

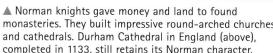

Norman states
× battle
→ Robert and Roger Guiscard, Norman adventurers to the Mediterranean 1042

SCOTLAND
IRELAND
WALES
ENGLAND
Durham
Hastings
Canterbury
NORMANDY
Rouen
Paris
BRITTANY
FRANCE
Atlantic Ocean
North Sea
Scandinavia
NORWAY
SWEDEN
DENMARK
Estonians
Lithuanians
Prussians
POLAND
THE GERMAN EMPIRE
HUNGARY
Kiev
KIEV RUS
Black Sea
LEON & CASTILE
Portugal
CALIPHATE OF CORDOVA
ALMORAVID EMPIRE
Rome
Naples
SICILY
Palermo
Mediterranean Sea
BYZANTINE EMPIRE
Constantinople
Seljuks of Rum
Antioch (Norman)
Levant
Holy Land
Jerusalem

0   500 km
0   300 miles

The Bayeux Tapestry tells the story of the Norman invasion of England. The 'Tapestry' is a long strip of linen over 70 m long with pictures embroidered on it, and a running commentary in Latin. It is over 900 years old. This section shows William in conversation before the battle of Hastings in 1066.

The Bayeux Tapestry tells the story of the Norman invasion of England. The 'Tapestry' is a long strip of linen over 70 m long with pictures embroidered on it, and a running commentary in Latin. It is over 900 years old. This section shows William in conversation before the battle of Hastings in 1066.

English rebellions

On Christmas Day, 1066, Duke William of Normandy was crowned William, King of England (William I). He faced risings against the Normans every year until 1070. In the marshy fens of East Anglia, the rebel Hereward the Wake held out until he was betrayed. Later, Vikings from Norway attacked in Yorkshire and stirred up trouble amongst those who hated the Normans. William stormed north. His soldiers killed rebels and burned villages and crops.

Normans and English

Before 1066 England had been in close touch with Normandy because Edward the Confessor was half Norman. After 1066 English customs and laws did not disappear; William's taxes were collected by the local sheriff, just as they had been in Anglo-Saxon times.

All the same, there were great changes for ordinary English people. Almost everywhere their local lord was no longer English but a Norman baron. Many churls (free men) in the village lost their land. Serfs (slaves) almost disappeared. Most of the poorest villagers became villeins, who had to work for their lord at set times. He controlled their lives in all kinds of ways, so they were really no better off.

Ordinary people still spoke English, but if you were educated and wanted to get on, you had to speak Norman French and Latin. It was about 300 years before poetry and stories were written down in English again, as they had been in Saxon times. Norman place names made from Latin or French words appeared: Pontefract, meaning 'broken bridge' in Latin; or Beaulieu, French for 'beautiful place'. Many French words have become part of modern English, including government, parliament, music and poem.

The Christian Church was already strong during Anglo-Saxon times. The Normans built churches all over England. Some were great cathedrals, as at Durham, and many were ordinary village churches.

Norman England was now closely linked to Normandy, and to the rest of western Europe. Because the Norman Conquest brought great changes, it is often called the beginning of the Middle Ages in England.

• In 1085 William decided he needed to know who owned English land, how much it was worth, who lived there, and what taxes he could expect. He divided the country into seven districts, and by the end of 1086 barons in each district had collected the information. This huge survey, called the Domesday Book, still exists today.

find out more
Anglo-Saxons
Castles
Crusades
France
Medieval England
Middle Ages
Vikings

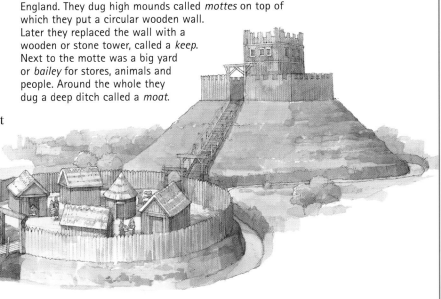

▼ The Norman invaders built castles very quickly in England. They dug high mounds called *mottes* on top of which they put a circular wooden wall. Later they replaced the wall with a wooden or stone tower, called a *keep*. Next to the motte was a big yard or *bailey* for stores, animals and people. Around the whole they dug a deep ditch called a *moat*.

North America

The first Americans came in distinct waves from Asia beginning over 25,000 years ago. They adapted their ways of life to the continent's many landscapes. There were hunters, fishers and farmers, while in Mexico, people such as the Maya and Aztecs founded great cities and civilizations.

Native Americans were called Indians by the first European explorers, who thought they had arrived in the East Indies (eastern Asia). The Italian explorer John Cabot discovered mainland North America in 1497. Shortly afterwards Spanish conquerors, called conquistadores, overthrew the Aztec empire. They used Native American people to work their new farms and mines. In the lands to the north, the Native Americans led the Europeans on explorations and provided them with food in return for iron pots and knives. But over time Native Americans were forced off their land.

Colonies

During the 16th century Spaniards had settled in Mexico and southern parts of what is now the United States, and the French were settling in Canada and along the Mississippi.

The first permanent English settlement was at Jamestown, Virginia, in 1607. These settlers grew tobacco for sale to Britain. The second colony, Plymouth Colony (later part of Massachusetts) was formed by a group of Puritans. They were called the Pilgrim Fathers because they were seeking a place where they could follow their religion without persecution. By 1733 Britain ruled 13 colonies, which ran along the Atlantic coast of North America.

Life for the first settlers in the Atlantic colonies was hard. Most people farmed, although some turned to fishing and trade. Many were Quakers, Puritans and other Protestants who led sober, hard-working lives. By 1760 the British colonies were growing prosperous. Immigrants had flocked in, lured by the prospect of owning land and making a new life. Most were from the British Isles, but others came from Germany, the Netherlands and France. Towns and cities grew up, with postal services, newspapers, and schools and colleges. The northern Atlantic colonies, called New England, had their own governors and law-makers. Each town and colony valued its independence. In the southern colonies slaves worked on huge plantations.

Wars of independence

In 1759 the British armies defeated French forces and the whole of Canada came under British rule. In the Atlantic colonies people had grown tired of paying high taxes to Britain. They fought for their independence during the American Revolution (1775–1783) and finally gained their freedom as the United States of America on 15 April 1783. In 1821, the Mexicans successfully rebelled against their Spanish rulers. Canada became an independent country in 1867.

▲ Relations between Native Americans and colonists were often hostile, but a few individuals were moved to help the 'enemy'. According to legend, Pocahontas, the daughter of a Native American leader, flung herself down and successfully saved the life of a captured English captain after she begged her father to spare him.

find out more
American Revolution
Aztecs
Canada
Caribbean
Maya
Native Americans
Slaves
South America
United States of America
Washington, George

◄ The Pilgrim Fathers coming ashore in North America in 1620. Their colony flourished when Native American farmers taught them how to grow corn (maize).

Ottoman empire

A Turkish leader, Uthman, founded the Ottoman kingdom in north-east Turkey in the 14th century. The Ottoman empire was at the height of its power in the 16th and 17th centuries. Altogether the Ottoman family ruled for more than 600 years.

The Ottoman Turks and their empire took their name from Uthman (1258–1326). The capital of their empire, Constantinople, was captured from the Byzantine emperor in 1453. To win the city, Mehmed II, the Turkish sultan, had his ships dragged overland to the harbour to bypass Constantinople's sea defences.

The sultan was the religious head over all Muslims within the empire. All his ministers and servants were originally military slaves, and so were his personal troops, the Janissaries. They were taken as boys from the Balkan lands, spent all their lives in barracks and were not allowed to marry.

In 1683 the Ottoman army threatened to capture Vienna but Austrian and Polish troops turned them back. From about 1800 the empire began to break up. The Greeks fought and won their independence in 1829.

In World War I, the Turks fought on the side of Germany and Austria and were defeated in 1918. The lands of the old empire became independent countries and the new Republic of Turkey was created in Asia Minor.

▶ The greatest of the sultans was Suleiman the Magnificent, who ruled from 1520 to 1566. He filled his court with painters, poets and craftsmen, and employed architects to build aqueducts, bridges, public baths and mosques.

• Constantinople actually became Istanbul after the Turks took over in the 15th century, but the name was not officially changed until the Turkish Post Office changed it in 1926.

find out more
Balkans
Byzantine empire
Holy Roman Empire
Middle East
Muslims

Pakistan

The Indus valley was the site of the great civilization of Harappa and Mohenjodaro (about 2500–1600 BC). The invasion of Alexander the Great in the 4th century BC was the first of a series of invasions into the rich lands of the Indus valley and the Punjab (the land of the five rivers). Muslim rulers controlled the region from the 13th century until the 1750s, when the British East India Company began to take control.

From 1858, for almost a hundred years, Pakistan was part of British India. From the 1920s Indian nationalists campaigned for independence from Britain. But the Muslim minority in India demanded the creation of a separate country for Muslims. When in 1947 India gained independence, it was divided into two nations: India, which was mainly Hindu, and Muslim Pakistan. Pakistan was in two parts, West and East, separated by Indian territory. India and Pakistan both claimed the territory of Kashmir, and went to war over it in 1948 and 1965.

There were also difficulties between West and East Pakistan. The people in the East campaigned for independence, but in 1971 West Pakistani forces invaded. Millions of refugees fled to India. This led to another war between India and Pakistan, in which the West Pakistani forces were defeated. In 1972 East Pakistan became independent as Bangladesh.

Since the creation of Pakistan, democratic government has alternated with times when the army has had control. Pakistan's constitution is based on Islamic (Muslim) law.

▶ Part of the remains of Mohenjodaro. Four thousand years ago Mohenjodaro was an important trading city on the River Indus.

find out more
Ancient world
India
Muslims

• The name Pakistan comes from two words in the Urdu language. *Pak* means 'pure', and *stan* means 'land'.

Peace movement

At the time of World War I, faced with the slaughter of millions of young men, many people became pacifists (opposed to all war). Today, there are more than 1400 peace groups in the world, with a membership of millions.

Peace campaigns often focus on nuclear weapons, but the numerous peace organizations do differ in their aims, some wanting an end to all weapons manufacture, others simply opposed to any increase in arms. The anti-nuclear peace movement began almost as soon as the first atomic bomb was dropped on Hiroshima, Japan, in 1945. The first mass rallies began in the 1950s.

In the 1960s the peace movement switched its attention from nuclear weapons to war. In the USA and Europe huge demonstrations forced the US government to withdraw from the Vietnam War. Later, many Europeans protested against the US nuclear missile bases in Europe. With the end of the Cold War between the communist countries and the West, the movement felt one of its main aims had been achieved.

▼ Crowds of anti-nuclear protesters at a rally in Germany.

• There are a number of environmental groups such as Friends of the Earth and Greenpeace (both founded in 1969), which have many of the same aims as the peace movement itself. Together, these environmental groups are called the green movement, and in some countries there are green political parties and members of parliament.

• The main peace organization in Britain is the Campaign for Nuclear Disarmament (CND).

find out more
Cold War
Vietnam War
Weapons

Pirates

• When Elizabeth I was queen of England, the English and the Spanish were enemies. Elizabeth allowed her most famous sea captain, Francis Drake (1543–1596), to steal from Spanish ships, as long as he was doing it 'unofficially'. Drake was behaving little better than a pirate, but he was popular in England for his daring deeds.

• Anne Bonny and Mary Read wore men's clothing and made a living by piracy until captured in 1720. Their accomplices were hanged, but Anne and Mary were spared execution because they were pregnant.

Pirates are robbers who steal from ships at sea. They appeared as soon as people had learned how to make sea-going ships, at least 7000 years ago.

By the time of the ancient Greeks and Romans, piracy was a constant danger to Mediterranean sea travellers. The 16th and 17th centuries saw the 'golden age' of piracy. After this, with powerful navies patrolling the world's oceans, piracy declined. However, pirates still roam the islands and channels of the Caribbean and South-east Asia.

Pirates around the world
Spanish ships passing through the Caribbean with treasure plundered from the Americas were easy targets for pirates famous for their cruelty. Edward Teach, known as Blackbeard, scared his victims by hanging lighted fuses about his head, and seized their rings by cutting off their fingers.

For centuries the pirates most feared by Europeans were the Muslim corsairs of North Africa, who sailed massive galleys with up to 300 oarsmen. The great Corsairs Dragut Reis and the Barbarossa (Red Beard) brothers captured slaves for sale or ransom.

European pirates arrived in the 17th century, using Madagascar as a base. The most successful pirate of this era was Henry Avery, an ex-naval captain who disappeared with a shipload of diamonds.

Piracy in the Far East was on a grand scale. The 17th-century Chinese pirate Ching Chihlung commanded over 1000 boats.

◄ The corsair Dragut Reis fires a gun from the bow of his ship.

Persia, Phoenicians *see* Ancient world • **PLO** *see* Middle East • **Polo,** Marco *see* Explorers

Prehistoric people

• When 19th-century European archaeologists began to find prehistoric stone and metal tools they divided prehistory into three periods: the Stone Age, the Bronze Age and the Iron Age.

Prehistory is the name archaeologists give to the enormous period of the past before written records began. It includes the evolution of modern humans from the ancestors that we share with today's great apes. Archaeologists have to work out how people developed and lived in that time from what little physical evidence survives.

▲ Evidence of how prehistoric peoples lived is also found in the cave paintings they made. The most famous are in the woods of Lascaux in the Dordogne area of France. The cave walls are covered in a range of animals, dating from between 15,000 and 14,000 BC.

Homo sapiens made carvings, delicate stone tools, clay models and wonderful cave paintings.

modern humans

Neanderthal people wore clothes and used flint knives. They also buried their dead.

Homo erectus ('upright man') had a bigger brain than *Homo habilis*, was able to make better tools, and to make fires.

Homo habilis ('handy man') was less ape-like than *Australopithecus*, stood about 1.6 m tall, had a larger brain and probably used tools.

other australopithecines (types of 'southern ape')

One of the best examples of *Australopithecus afarensis* is known as Lucy. She was 1.5 m tall and had a small brain. She could walk upright, although she would have spent time climbing trees.

Australopithecus ramidus (*Australopithecus* means 'southern ape')

▲ How modern humans evolved over the last 5 million years. Many human-like species, such as *Homo habilis* and Neanderthals, are not the direct ancestors of modern humans. Some of these species overlapped with each other in time.

Our ancestors separated from the ancestors of modern gorillas nearly 7 million years ago, and from the ancestors of modern chimpanzees over 5 million years ago.

Millions of years ago

The further back you go in time, the more chance there is that things people used will have rotted away. It is usually only bones, and the stone tools or metal parts of things that survive.

The evolution of people

The animals that eventually evolved into humans separated from the ancestors of the great apes over 5 million years ago. Some human-like species which evolved later are not direct ancestors of modern humans.

The earliest kinds of fossil that are believed to be from ancestors of humans have been found in Africa and are over 4 million years old. Scientists think that the modern kind of human beings evolved from *Homo erectus* ('upright man'), although the fossil record does not tell us where and when *Homo sapiens* ('thinking man'), which is what we are, first arose.

Neanderthals were *Homo sapiens* and their fossils have been found in Europe and western Asia. Genetic evidence suggests that a newer type of human, *Homo sapiens sapiens*, developed in Africa about 100,000 years ago and spread to other continents, gradually replacing the Neanderthals. The fossil record is not good enough to make us sure of all the details, but by 10,000 years ago modern people lived almost everywhere.

Hunters and gatherers

Through most of prehistory, people everywhere obtained their food from wild plants and animals. They hunted, fished and gathered fruits, roots and other plant foods. They moved seasonally

Presidents *see* Government *and page 125* (US presidents)

Prehistoric people

▶ This timeline shows the development of prehistoric peoples around the world, from the time when the first human-like 'hominids' evolved, about 5 million years ago, until 700 BC.

5,000,000–2,000,000 BC	2,000,000–250,000 BC	250,000–120,000 BC	80,000–30,000 BC	50,000–25,000 BC	25,000–10,000 BC	10,000–8000 BC
Early tree-dwelling 'hominids' evolve in Africa.	Upright humans *Homo erectus* evolve, spreading to Asia and Europe.	Modern humans *Homo sapiens* evolve in Africa and spread north.	*Neanderthals*, a now extinct type of *Homo sapiens*, live in Europe and western Asia.	Modern humans, like those of today (*Homo sapiens sapiens*), spread through Europe and Asia into Australia and the Americas. A wide variety of tools (knifes, axes, adzes, scrapers, awls, harpoons, needles) made in a variety of materials (wood, bone, stone, antler, reed, leather, flint).	Early round houses, cave-painting and carving in Europe and western Asia.	Climate changes as ice age ends.

▼ This drawing shows what archaeologists think a hunters' camp looked like in a place called Pincevent, on the banks of the River Seine in France, about 12,000 to 10,000 years ago. The people hunted reindeer for food and skins, gathered plant foods and cooked their meals in the open.

from camp to camp and became expert observers of plant and animal life in the landscapes they occupied. They were the world's first 'ecologists'. They made tools, mostly of stone and wood, and lived in small family groups, occasionally joining other groups at tribal gatherings. They did not need to spend all their time getting and processing food, and had leisure to express themselves artistically in rock and cave paintings and by carving models of animals and people.

Farmers

From about 10,000 years ago, at the end of the last ice age, some hunter-gatherers began to cultivate plants and keep animals in small herds. This change took place earliest in the Middle East, where some people were already living all year in small settlements. Their populations grew and they became more dependent on the cultivation of cereals, such as barley and wheat, and other grain crops, such as peas and lentils, the seeds of which were nutritious, easily stored, and could be sown for future harvesting.

They raised goats, sheep, and later pigs and cattle, which provided regular supplies of meat and other useful products. As agriculture developed, settlements became larger and people began to specialize in different crafts such as pottery, weaving and metal-working.

In a few other parts of the world people also began to cultivate plants they had previously gathered, such as rice in China, maize in Mexico and sorghum in tropical Africa. Agriculture gradually spread from these early centres and, as it did so, more plants and animals were 'domesticated': for example, asses, horses and camels in western Asia, and llamas and alpacas in South America. By 3000 BC farming had largely replaced gathering and hunting as the dominant way of life in Europe. And in the Middle East the first civilizations had become established. ▶

8000–7000 BC	7000–6000 BC	5000–4000 BC	4000–3000 BC	3000–2000 BC	2000–1000 BC	1000–700 BC
Beginning of farming in western Asia. Wild cereals (wheat and barley) and legumes (peas, lentils) cultivated. Village settlements in the eastern Mediterranean, Syria and Jordan.	Goats, sheep, pigs and cattle domesticated in western Asia. Linen, textiles and pottery first made. Copper used in Anatolia, Turkey. Rice cultivated in China.	Copper and lead used in Anatolia. Domestication of asses, horses and camels in western Asia.	Sumerian civilization. First writing. Metalwork in copper, tin, bronze, lead, silver, gold. Irrigation. Sails. Maize cultivated in Mexico. Cotton grown in Peru. Llama domesticated in Peru. Agriculture established across Europe. Stone temples and tombs in Europe.	First pharaohs in Egypt; hieroglyphic writing system. Chariot invented in Mesopotamia. Indus civilization with cotton textiles. 'Beaker culture' spreads copper and textile technology through western Europe.	Bronze technology throughout Europe. Stonehenge completed.	Olmec culture in Mexico. Celts spread into central Europe and Britain. Iron technology in Europe by 700 BC.

▲ Stone circles were built in Europe from about 3000 BC to about 1200 BC as ceremonial or religious monuments. Archaeologists think that Stonehenge (pictured) in England was also used to observe the Sun and Moon.

Prehistoric technology

In many parts of the world prehistoric people used flint and other types of stone, such as obsidian, to make their tools and weapons. As they became more skillful, they developed specialized tools, such as stone axes for butchering large animals, flint blades for skinning them, and differently shaped stone and bone barbs for spears and arrows with which to kill birds, fish, reptiles and small mammals. They also made baskets for collecting plant foods, but these are seldom found by archaeologists because they decay easily. The first farmers needed additional tools, especially stone axes for felling trees to make room for fields, and grindstones for processing grains. Most prehistoric peoples also learned how to make pottery and to spin and weave wool, hair and other fibres.

Discovering metals

The discovery of how to use metal was made at different times and in different parts of the world.

Copper was the first metal to be used, before 6000 BC in western Asia. Later it was found that mixing copper and tin produced a harder and more useful metal, bronze. Later still, people discovered that they could make iron by 'smelting': melting iron ore and charcoal together. While hot, the iron was beaten into shapes with stones to make knives and other tools and weapons.

The first people to use iron lived in Anatolia (part of Turkey today) in about 2000 BC. In Britain people began using iron in about 700 BC. Some of it was made into bars and used for currency. In China iron was being smelted by the 6th century BC, and in West Africa iron was being worked before 500 BC.

Prehistory to history

The period of prehistory varies from place to place depending on the time when writing began in an area. In China prehistory ends with the invention of writing in the Shang period (from about 1600 BC). In most of America prehistory lasted until the Europeans arrived in the 16th century. In Britain the prehistoric period ended with the Roman invasion in AD 43, as it did for other countries too, as they were conquered by the Romans, who kept written records.

find out more
Africa
Ancient world
Archaeology
Aztecs
Celts
China
Evolution
Human beings
Hunter-gatherers
Incas
Maya
Prehistoric life

▼ On 19 September 1991 two hikers in the Alps found the remains of a man whose body had been preserved in the ice for 5300 years. He still had clothes and boots, a quiver and two arrows, a copper axe, a stone-pointed 'fire striker', a small flint dagger, a simple haversack, a sewing kit and lots of trapping equipment. He had apparently died while hunting in the mountains.

Reformation

In 1500 all Christians in western Europe belonged to the Catholic Church, with the pope in Rome at its head. Fifty years later, European Christians were bitterly divided into separate Churches. We call this change the Reformation.

Some people had been critical of the Catholic Church long before the Reformation. Popes often behaved more like powerful kings than religious leaders. Bishops and abbots of great monasteries were often wealthy landowners and also royal advisers at court. But ordinary priests were often so poor and ignorant that they could hardly do their job properly. For many ordinary people, visiting church must have been rather strange and mysterious. Churches were full of detailed pictures and statues, the altars were elaborately decorated with a cross and candles, and services were read in Latin, a language few understood.

Protest in the Church

The Church was further undermined by the row over indulgences (pardons for sins) which people could buy. In 1517 a German monk, Martin Luther, wrote a long list of reasons why he disagreed with indulgences, and pinned it on the church door in his home town of Wittenberg in Saxony. Perhaps this would have been just a local row if printing had not been invented. But Luther's list, and other churchmen's arguments against it, were printed throughout Germany. Luther's ideas spread.

The ruler of Saxony, and other German princes who wanted to be free of any interference by the pope, backed Luther. They drew up a 'Protest' in 1529. Soon the 'Protestants' set up a separate Church. The nickname stuck.

Protestants

Luther taught that people must work out their own faith in God from the Bible, so they did not need the pope or priests. People could only read the Bible for themselves when it was translated from Latin into ordinary languages, and when plenty of copies were printed. Protestant churches were plain and simple, and services were held in local languages by ministers in simple black gowns. Long sermons were preached to teach the Bible. In John Calvin's church in Switzerland church members chose their own ministers and lived simple, strict lives.

In time the Reformed and Non-conformist Churches developed from these movements. They include the Lutherans, especially in Germany, Calvinists in Switzerland and Scotland, and Anglicans (Church of England) and the Anglican Communion Overseas, which includes the Episcopal Church in the USA.

Counter-Reformation

The Catholic Church began to reform itself and tried hard to win back Protestants (the Counter-Reformation). Both sides believed that they were right, and that those who disagreed with them would go to hell. Rulers did not want different Christian Churches in their kingdoms because of possible conflicts. So, in the 16th and 17th centuries, there were terrible religious wars and persecutions in Europe. It was a long time before Protestants and Catholics began to respect and tolerate each other.

▲ Martin Luther, the monk who started the Protestant Reformation in Germany. In Luther's Church bishops and priests were less powerful than in the Catholic Church. There were no monks, nuns, friars or pope.

• There were Christians who criticized the Catholic Church long before the Reformation. In England in the 14th century, John Wycliffe gained a following for his attacks on the wealth and power of the Catholic Church. He organized the first translation of the Bible from Latin into English so people could read it for themselves.

find out more

Christians
Tudor England

▼ The trunk and branches of this 'tree' represent the divisions in the Christian Church.

Protestant branches

Calvinist Presbyterians in Scotland

Puritans in England

Calvinists in the Netherlands

Huguenots in France

Church of England 1559

Roman Catholic Church

Calvin from 1541

Lutherans in Germany and Scandinavia

Luther from 1517

Eastern Orthodox Church in Greece, Balkans and Russia

The Catholic Church and the Eastern Orthodox Church split in 1054

Catholic Church in western Europe

Renaissance

Renaissance means 'rebirth'. It is the name used for the great flowering in the arts, learning and science that reached its peak in 15th- and 16th-century Italy. The influence of the Renaissance quickly spread throughout Europe.

For centuries the Catholic Church had been at the centre of learning and art in western Europe. But by 1400 educated people were beginning to find out more about the ancient civilizations of Greece and Rome. Scholars and artists began to be less concerned with God in their writing and art, and more interested in human beings.

Learning

The scholars of the Renaissance studied the writings of the ancient Greeks and Romans. They translated many documents in Greek, which few people understood, into Latin, which many educated people did understand. This opened up the great discoveries and literature of the Greeks to many more people. The invention of printing in the middle of the 15th century helped to spread this new learning.

The scholars of the Middle Ages had mostly thought and wrote about God and the Church. The scholars of the Renaissance are called *humanists* because they were interested in human achievements. Most were still Christians, but some called for the Church to reform itself. Their ideas played a part in the Reformation, in which the new Protestant Churches broke away from the Catholic Church.

Art and architecture

The artists of the Renaissance found that people no longer just wanted paintings and sculptures of stories from the Bible. Stories from the myths of ancient Greece became very popular, and so did portraits of living people. Renaissance artists also developed the technique of *perspective*, a way of making some things in the picture look further away than others, just as they do in the real world.

Architects too learnt much from the ancient Romans, particularly in Italy, where there are many impressive

▲ Michelangelo's sculpture *David* shows the beauty of the naked human body. Paintings and sculptures of the nude in the style of the ancient Greeks became popular during the Renaissance.

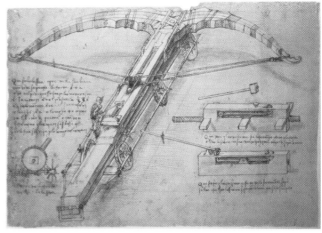

▲ A design for a giant catapult by Leonardo da Vinci (1452–1519), one of the greatest figures of the Renaissance. As well as being a famous artist, Leonardo was also a poet, scientist, architect and engineer.

remains of Roman buildings. They began to design new churches and palaces using ideas borrowed from classical Greek and Roman architecture, such as domes, rounded arches, and pillars.

Science

At the time of the Renaissance more people began to study the world around them. What they found led them to question many ideas that had been held for centuries. One of the greatest revolutions in thinking came from the Polish astronomer Nicolas Copernicus. By studying the night sky he realized that all the planets, including the Earth, move round the Sun. Before that, the Church had taught that God created the Earth at the centre of the Universe.

▶ This map showing the Sun at the centre of the Solar System was published by Copernicus in about 1530. From the time of the ancient Greeks people had believed that the Sun and the other planets moved round the Earth.

● During the Renaissance, learning and art became fashionable, as rulers and important churchmen in rich and powerful cities like Rome, Milan, Venice and Florence employed scholars and artists at their courts. Wealthy merchants also became patrons of the arts.

● Before the 16th century doctors had very mistaken ideas about human anatomy (the way the body is built). Then the Flemish anatomist Andreas Vesalius actually began to cut up and study the insides of dead human bodies, completely changing many ideas.

find out more
Communications
Europe
Italy
Reformation

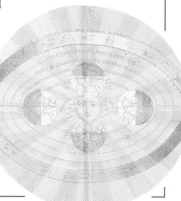

Romans

The Latini, a Latin-speaking people, took over the town called Rome from its Etruscan kings in 509 BC. As Romans they spread their way of life, their laws and their language throughout Italy and then over the Mediterranean area and much of Europe.

• The Latin language developed into many European languages spoken today, including Italian, Spanish and French. Roman law is the basis of the laws of many European countries. The English names for the months are Roman. The English alphabet is Roman and Roman numerals are often used.

• Romans liked their food with lots of spices, and the main meal of the day (eaten at about four o'clock in the afternoon) usually had three courses. Many people, especially those who lived in the flats, went out to fetch 'take-away' meals from the hot-food shops.

▼ In AD 79 the Roman town of Pompeii in Italy was buried under ash when the nearby volcano Mount Vesuvius erupted. This picture shows the forum (meeting place) with Vesuvius in the background. Many of the remains are remarkably well preserved and have told us a huge amount about Roman life.

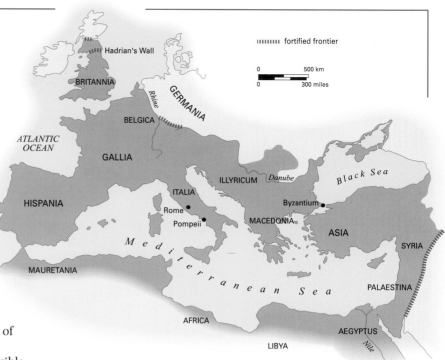

▲ This map shows the extent of the Roman empire in the 2nd century AD. The names of many modern countries come from the Latin names of the Roman provinces.

Wherever the Romans went as conquerors, they established their own way of life. Although many local customs survived, it is possible to talk about 'Roman everyday life' throughout the empire. Archaeologists often find the same sorts of evidence, either buildings or things that people used, all over the Roman world.

Town and country

Roman towns were usually well planned with straight streets dividing the town into regular blocks. A block of houses was called an *insula*, the Latin for 'island'. In the big towns and cities many people lived in blocks of flats or in apartments above shops or small factories. Those who were rich enough lived in private houses with rooms for slaves and a secluded garden. They may also have had mosaic floors and hypocausts (underfloor heating).

Roman towns usually had regular supplies of water and an efficient system of sewage disposal. Water pipes, of lead, wood or pottery, brought supplies from aqueducts to private houses, to businesses, and to fountains and public baths or basins in the streets.

The central government in Rome wanted farmers to work as much land as possible. New farmhouses and estates appeared. These villas had the same comforts as city houses.

The Roman army

Soldiers were organized into units called legions. Each legion was made up of about 5000 men and had a name and a number. The men trained and fought in groups of 80 with a centurion (the name for a commander of about 100 men) in charge of each. The legionary soldiers were well armed and fought on foot. Other army units, called the cavalry, fought on horseback. Some were trained to use artillery weapons such as catapults. Some were engineers.

The provinces

The army helped create the Roman world by conquering peoples, building forts and roads and keeping Roman-run countryside secure from attacks. Boundaries to the Roman world were established, sometimes using rivers, mountains or seas as a barrier, and in many places the Romans had to build a barrier. Inside the boundaries the Romans created provinces.

In the provinces the Romans encouraged the newly conquered peoples to live just like Romans. They introduced their religion into the provinces and built temples to gods and goddesses such as Jupiter, Minerva and Juno. Quite often, though, people in the provinces worshipped their own gods too. Celtic gods and goddesses were still worshipped in Roman Britain and in Gaul.

From republic to empire

At first Rome was a republic. Some people (men who owned property) were allowed to vote for the politicians who formed the government. At the head were two men, called consuls. Each year one was elected to lead the government and one the army. They were the chief judges as well. A sort of parliament, called the senate, discussed the way the state was governed and made new laws.

In the 2nd century BC politicians began to fight each other for power and in the next

▼ Augustus put a great deal of time and money into making Rome a great city. He is said to have claimed that he found Rome a city of brick and left it a city of marble. This is the Forum Romanum (Roman forum) at the time of Augustus.

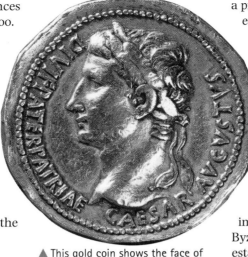

▲ This gold coin shows the face of Augustus, the first Roman emperor. It was made in the 1st century AD, when he was about 70 years old.

century civil war broke out. Julius Caesar beat a rival politician, Pompey, and made himself dictator of Rome. The next dictator was Octavian, who in 27 BC made himself an emperor and called himself Augustus. This was the beginning of the period in Roman history called the empire.

Although men could still vote for their leaders it was not a proper democracy. The emperor decided who should rule and handed out jobs to people he could trust.

Under the rule of the emperors, Rome gradually conquered an even greater area.

The end of an empire

Eventually this vast Roman empire was divided in two with one capital city in Rome and the other in Byzantium. Byzantium was established by the emperor Constantine as his capital in AD 330, and was renamed Constantinople.

By the 5th century AD the western part of the empire had been overrun by Goths, Huns and Vandals. The eastern empire became the Byzantine empire and survived until AD 1453, when it fell to the Ottoman Turks.

The emperor Claudius soon returned to Rome. Under his commander-in-chief, Aulus Plautius, the army gradually brought more of what is now

• A Roman town might have a theatre, a stadium (for chariot racing) and even an amphitheatre. One of the spectacles at the amphitheatre was a cruel sport in which trained men, called gladiators, fought to the death in single combat. Sometimes animals were chased and killed in the arena, or even human beings. At various times, persecuted people, such as Christians, were 'thrown' to wild animals.

Roman Britain
In AD 43 the emperor Claudius invaded Britain and set about adding this new province to the Roman empire. A Roman way of life was established over the whole of England, but Wales and Scotland proved more difficult to conquer.

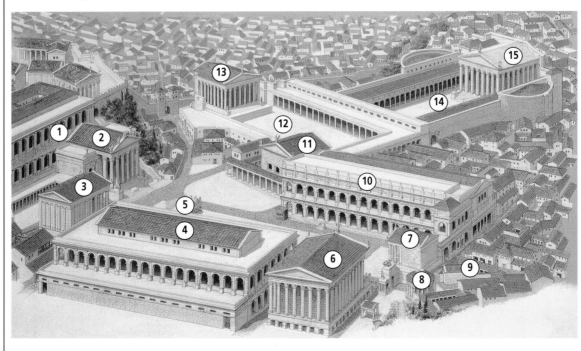

1 Tabularium (records office)
2 Temple of Concord
3 Temple of Saturn
4 Basilica Julia
5 *rostra* (the speaker's platform)
6 Temple of Castor and Pollux
7 Temple of the Deified Julius Caesar
8 Temple of Vesta
9 Regia (office of high priest)
10 Basilica Aemilia
11 Curia Julia (senate house)
12 Forum of Julius Caesar
13 Temple of Venus Genetrix
14 Forum of Augustus
15 Temple of Mars Ultor

◀ This Roman mosaic shows two fishermen surrounded by the fish they are catching. It comes from Utica, a Roman settlement in North Africa, and dates from the 4th century AD.

England under Roman control. In AD 58 a new governor of Britain, Suetonius Paulinus, led an invasion of Wales.

While this invasion was going ahead successfully, the people in East Anglia revolted against their Roman masters in AD 60. Led by Boudicca, the queen of the tribe called the Iceni, they attacked Roman towns, villages and farms, burning and killing as they went. Eventually, after many setbacks, the Roman army took control and peace was re-established.

The area of Roman Britain changed over the years. By the middle of the 2nd century AD the Roman army had moved up the east coast of Scotland. But by the 3rd century it was back at Hadrian's wall, the fortified frontier established by the emperor Hadrian across the far north of England. In the 4th century the army had to build special forts along the southern and eastern coasts against invasions.

By the beginning of the 5th century, there were attacks by barbarians in many parts of the Roman empire. The Roman army left Britain to deal with these attacks. This in turn left Britain open to invasions by Anglo-Saxons, who eventually took over all of England.

find out more

Anglo-Saxons
Byzantine empire
Caesar, Julius
Celts
Dark Ages
Greeks, ancient
Slaves

Roosevelt, Franklin Delano

Franklin Delano Roosevelt was president of the USA from 1933 to 1945. He was the only president to be elected four times.

Roosevelt was already a well-respected politician when, at the age of 40, he developed polio. He never gained full use of his legs again. However, he worked hard to get himself fit, and he returned to politics. In 1928 he was elected governor of New York State, and in 1933 he became president of the USA.

This was the time of the Great Depression. One worker in four was out of work and many families faced poverty. Roosevelt promised a 'New Deal'. This was an economic programme to put the country back on its feet. He also began radio broadcasts to the nation, known as his 'fireside chats'. The success of these and later measures ensured his re-election as president in 1936.

In 1940 Roosevelt was elected for a third term. In December 1941 the USA entered World War II after the Japanese bombed the US naval base at Pearl Harbor in Hawaii. Roosevelt worked closely with the leaders of Britain and the Soviet Union, Winston Churchill and Joseph Stalin, to try and end the war. He won a fourth election in 1944, but six months later, with victory in the war in sight, he collapsed and died.

Born 1882 in Hyde Park, New York State, USA
Died 1945 aged 63

◀ Franklin Delano and Eleanor Roosevelt in 1932. Eleanor Roosevelt was famous for her humanitarian work. She was a US delegate to the United Nations, and in 1946 she became the chairwoman of the United Nations Human Rights Commission.

find out more

Twentieth-century history
United States of America
World War II

Russia

Over 1400 years ago there were tribes of Slav people living in parts of central and eastern Europe. In the 6th century AD some began to migrate further eastwards. Although the new territory was open to attacks from Huns, Scythians and Goths, the Slavs settled down as farmers.

▲ Ivan IV (known as Ivan the Terrible) crowned himself first tsar of Russia in 1547. Although he did much to bring Russia in line with Europe, he is remembered most for his brutality. In his last years he had thousands of people executed. After killing his own son in a fit of rage, he became insane.

From the 6th to the 9th century, Vikings from the north came to trade in Kiev, Novgorod and other cities. Kiev also traded with Greeks in the south, and it was from the Greeks that the Russians took their Christian religion. In 988 Grand Prince Vladimir of Kiev was converted to Christianity.

In 1240 the Golden Horde of Mongol-Tartars from the Gobi Desert, in what is now Mongolia, overran Russia. They occupied the country for about 250 years. The princes of Moscow gradually beat them off, and in the 16th century Ivan the Terrible finally defeated the Tartars at Kazan. He became tsar (emperor) in 1547. After that the country turned more towards Europe than to Asia.

Rise of the Russian empire

After Ivan died, there were quarrels over the throne until Mikhail Romanov was made tsar. The Romanovs ruled Russia from 1613 until they were overthrown in 1917. Mikhail Romanov's grandson, Peter the Great, made Russia a world power, and introduced many political and social reforms. Before he died, in 1725, he brought Estonia and part of Latvia and Finland under Russian control.

In 1762 a young German princess took the throne. Catherine the Great ruled for 34 years. She expanded Russia southwards to the Crimea and Black Sea, eastwards into central Asia, and westwards to occupy Lithuania and much of Poland. At first she was a tolerant ruler, but she was scared by peasant revolts and the French Revolution of 1789. During the last years of her rule her government used secret police to arrest people who disagreed with its policy and exiled some to Siberia.

Russia in crisis

By the middle of the 19th century, Russia was in crisis. A costly war fought against Britain and France in the Crimea only revealed how backward its military was, and the country's serfs (poor peasants) had rebelled against the landowners. Many Russians wanted to modernize the country. In 1861 the tsar, Alexander II, freed the serfs and gave them land. However, most Russians were still very poor and there was a lot of discontent.

In 1905, factory workers marched on the Winter Palace in St Petersburg to present their demands for political reform to Tsar Nicholas II. They were met by troops, who shot and killed 130 of them. As news of this massacre travelled, a revolutionary movement swept the country. In order to keep the peace the tsar agreed to a few of

▼ The Winter Palace, St Petersburg, was taken by the Bolsheviks in 1917. The Russian Revolution brought to an end the Romanov family dynasty.

◀ Inside a gilded metro (underground) station in St Petersburg, which was built in the 1950s. The city was named after is founder, Peter the Great, but its name was changed to Leningrad after the Russian Revolution. It became St Petersburg again in 1991.

Independence

Under the leaderships of Khrushchev from 1953 and Brezhnev from 1964 communist rule remained strong. In 1985 Mikhail Gorbachev became leader and tried to reform the Soviet Union. But he failed and in 1991 the Soviet Union collapsed. Boris Yeltsin became the first president of the new Russian Federation, consisting of 21 self-governing republics, various territories, provinces, and a self-governing Jewish region. Yeltsin also organized the Commonwealth of Independent States.

Yeltsin's period as president from 1991 was a troubled one. Not all of the nationalities of the Russian Federation wanted to stay part of it. The Chechens, who live in the Caucasus Mountains region, fought the Russian army from 1994 to 1996 and won greater self-government. There have also been violent political clashes in Moscow and a steep drop in the standard of living of most Russians.

Commonwealth of Independent States

When the Soviet government voted itself out of existence, the republics became independent. Some of the republics thought it was important to keep in touch with each other. The Commonwealth of Independent States (CIS) was formed in 1991 to include 12 of the 15 republics of the former USSR both in Asia and Europe. Members meet to make agreements in areas such as trade, foreign policy, law enforcement, defence and transport.

find out more

Cold War
Communists
Crimean War
Europe
Lenin
Mongol empire
Stalin, Joseph
Twentieth-century
  history
Vikings
World War I
World War II

the political demands. However, the unrest continued.

Russia's entry into World War I increased the nation's hardship and anger. Riots by starving people in February 1917 quickly spread. The tsar was forced to give up his throne, and Russia became a republic. For eight months a temporary government ruled, but it was overthrown by the Bolshevik Party led by Lenin. The new government had the tsar and his family shot in 1918. The Bolsheviks became the Communist Party. Under their rule all farms and factories were owned by the state.

The Soviet Union

The hopes of peace were short-lived. Civil war broke out and the new republic was invaded by foreign troops, including British and American. Millions of people died. At the end of the civil war the communist government divided the territories of the old empire into

▶ President Boris Yeltsin negotiating with coalminers in 1991. Since becoming president of Russia, Yeltsin has battled to transform the country's economy and to give more choice and freedom to the Russian people.

republics; the Republic of Russia was by far the largest of these. In 1922 the new country was named the Union of Soviet Socialist Republics (USSR), or the Soviet Union.

Under the harsh rule of Stalin, from 1924 to 1953, millions of people starved because the state-owned farms on which they were forced to work did not provide enough food. Anyone who opposed Stalin was either imprisoned or killed.

During World War II Germany invaded the Soviet Union, and 27 million Soviet people were killed. In 1945 Soviet armies liberated much of eastern Europe from German occupation.

Scotland

The Highlands of northern Britain were the only part of the British mainland not to fall to the Romans. About AD 500 the area was settled by Scots from Ireland. Over the next 700 years the Scots, Picts, Britons, Anglo-Saxons and Vikings living to the north of England gradually united into a Christian kingdom – Scotland.

Scotland's early kings struggled to keep out the English. In 1286 Edward I of England began a series of wars to take Scotland. Led by heroic soldiers such as William Wallace and King Robert the Bruce, the Scots eventually defeated the English in 1314. For the next 300 years the Scots kings struggled to rule their country. Many died violent deaths. During Queen Mary's reign, conflict raged between Protestants and Catholics. The Protestants triumphed, Mary was removed, and her young son James VI placed on the throne.

In 1603 James VI became king of England as well as Scotland. In 1707 Scotland's parliament was abolished and the country was united with England. At first some Scots were uneasy about the union, and the Jacobites (supporters of the Stuarts) rebelled in 1715 and 1745–1746. But wealth was increasing, new industries sprang up and Edinburgh became a centre of culture. At the same time poor farmers in the Highlands were being driven off the land to make way for sheep farming. In the 20th century the Scots began to rediscover their old longing for independence, and in 1997 they voted to have their own parliament once again.

▲ Glencoe was the site of a massacre of the MacDonald clan by the Campbells in 1692. The MacDonalds had delayed signing an oath of allegiance to the British crown, and the Campbells were acting on behalf of the British government.

find out more
Britain since 1900
Celts
Europe
Georgian Britain
Industrial Revolution
Mary, Queen of Scots
Stuart Britain

Sikhs

The Sikh religion began in the Punjab in northern India where most Sikhs still live. The most important thing for a Sikh is learning about God, and in the Punjabi language the word *sikh* means 'learner'.

The founder of the Sikh religion was Nanak, who lived in the Punjab from 1469 to 1539. He was the first of the ten Sikh *gurus*, or teachers. The last guru died in 1708. The earlier gurus were against war. But after the Muslim rulers of northern India executed the fifth guru in 1606, the Sikhs turned themselves into 'warrior-saints'. Eventually they created their own Sikh state in the Punjab. After two wars against the British in the 1840s the Sikhs were defeated and the Punjab became part of British India.

After India became independent from Britain, some Sikhs called for an independent Sikh state in the Punjab. A few Sikhs turned to violence and fought the Indian army. In 1984 Indian troops attacked the Sikh fighters in their holiest shrine, the Golden Temple in the city of Amritsar. A few months later the Indian prime minister, Indira Gandhi, was assassinated by her Sikh bodyguards. This was followed by many attacks by Hindus on Sikhs, and more Sikhs began to demand independence.

• Sikhs share some of the ideas of both Hindus and Muslims. But they do not accept the Hindu caste system, in which everybody is born into an occupation and a set place in society.

◄ The Golden Temple at Amritsar in the Punjab, India, is built on an island in a lake. Both the lake and the temple are sacred to Sikhs.

find out more
Hindus
India

Slaves

Slaves are people who are treated as if they were somebody else's property. They are bought and sold just like any object. There have been slaves in many different parts of the world, and at many different times in history.

▼ Romans could be very cruel to their slaves, whipping and branding them for disobedience. In this picture a slave has been killed just for an experiment. He is being weighed to find out whether the departing of the soul leads to weight loss (it doesn't!).

The trade in slaves began long ago. The ancient Egyptians used people they had conquered as slaves, as did Greeks and Romans. Slavery continued in Egypt until the 19th century.

Ancient Greece and Rome

In ancient Greece, slaves often worked in rich people's houses. Women slaves cooked and cleaned, and served the lady of the house. They entertained guests at feasts as flute girls and dancers. Male slaves in Athens sometimes kept order in the streets like policemen.

The Romans too used slaves to run their homes, and to do hard and often dangerous jobs. Slaves also trained as gladiators who fought each other or wild animals, to entertain huge crowds in Roman theatres. Some well-educated slaves ran

shops and became important government servants.

The Middle Ages

When the Roman empire broke up, slaves gradually disappeared in northern Europe. Powerful barons gave the people who worked for them a little land to live on. In return, these *serfs* had to work for their lord for fixed times, and could not leave their land. They were not owned, but otherwise they were like slaves.

However, slavery did not disappear in the Mediterranean. Slaves there were often black Africans or Slavs from the Balkans and further east. The word 'slave' comes from 'Slav'.

African slaves

Arab traders sent slaves from East Africa to Arabia and Asia, probably from the 12th century. Prisoners taken in wars between different tribes were used as slaves. In North Africa, from the 15th century, Muslims used European Christians as slaves.

Between the 16th and the early 19th centuries, Europeans bought millions of West African slaves and sold them across the

Atlantic in the Caribbean, Brazil and North America. There the slaves were made to work on sugar, tobacco and cotton plantations. They also worked in the houses, cooking and cleaning. Since slaves were so useful, some owners treated them quite well. But other owners were harsh and cruel, especially when they feared trouble.

An end to slavery?

Sometimes slaves rebelled against their owners. In Haiti, an army of former slaves defeated French and British troops and set up an independent country there in 1804. In the early 19th century, many white Americans and Europeans began to realize how wrong the slave trade was. The British abolished slavery throughout their empire in 1833.

In the American Civil War (1861–1865) the Southern states of the USA fought the Northern states for their right to own slaves. The Northern states won the war, and in 1865 the Congress of the USA abolished slavery throughout the country.

• Many citizens of the United States are descended from West Africans who were taken to North and South America during the 17th, 18th and early 19th centuries to work as slaves. They used to be called negroes, but now prefer to be known as Afro-Americans, African Americans, or blacks.

▶ African slaves on plantations endured long hours cutting tough sugar canes under the blazing sun.

South Africa

The first inhabitants of South Africa were hunters and gatherers, the Bushmen (San) and Hottentots (Khoikhoi). Together these peoples are known as the Khoisan. Later the Bantu-speaking peoples, including the Xhosa and the Zulus, arrived in South Africa from the north.

Dutch settlers established a settlement at Cape Town around 1652. The Dutch brought in slaves, and they also forced the Khoisan to work for them. During the Napoleonic Wars of 1792 to 1815, Britain captured the Cape. British settlers began to arrive in the 1820s. They fought the Xhosa peoples for farmland.

The Zulu and Boer wars

In the 1830s many Boers (Dutch farmers) wanted to control their own territory and to have more land. They moved north and founded the republics of the Orange Free State and the Transvaal. In Natal, Zulu chief Shaka (1787–1828) had established a powerful empire, and the Zulus strongly resisted the invading Boers. The British eventually defeated the Zulus in 1879.

In 1877 the British tried to take over the Transvaal, but were defeated by the Boers in 1881. The discovery of diamonds and gold led to conflict between the British, led by Cecil Rhodes, and the Boers, led by Paul Kruger. This resulted in the Anglo–Boer war of 1899–1902, when the British defeated the Boers and took over their territory. South Africa became a self-governing British dominion in 1910.

Segregation of the races

In the new South Africa only whites were allowed to be members of parliament. Black South Africans (over 75 per cent of the population) could not vote, and nor could Asians and people of mixed race (coloureds). After 1948 the laws for keeping whites and non-whites apart were made much stricter. This was the system of apartheid ('apartness'). While most whites lived in luxury, non-whites generally lived in

◀ In January 1879, at the battle of Isandhwlana, the Zulu army of King Cetawayo destroyed a British force of 1700 men. But by July the British had taken the Zulu capital, and Zululand came under British control.

poverty in overcrowded townships on the edges of cities, or were moved to separate black 'homelands'.

The end of apartheid

Within South Africa opposition to apartheid was led by the African National Congress (ANC). For many years the ANC campaigned peacefully, but from the late 1950s it began to organize acts of sabotage. Its leader, Nelson Mandela, was imprisoned in 1962.

Apartheid was condemned around the world. As more and more countries refused to trade with South Africa, the white government was forced to reform. They gave seats in parliament to coloureds and Asians, but blacks were still unable to vote.

In 1989 F. W. de Klerk was elected president, and things began to change. He released Mandela from prison and abolished the apartheid laws. In 1994 South Africa held its first democratic elections. The ANC won, and Mandela became president.

Steve Biko
Steve Biko was the leader of the Black People's Convention, an organization that fought the oppression of apartheid. His activities brought him into conflict with the government and he was often arrested. In 1977, while under arrest, he was so badly beaten in the police cells that he died. He became a symbol of the anti-apartheid movement.

◀ Archbishop Desmond Tutu opposed the apartheid system for many years. When the ANC came to power, he was chosen as head of the Truth and Reconciliation Commission. The Commission encourages people who have been accused of crimes under the apartheid regime to admit to what they did.

find out more
Africa
Mandela, Nelson

South America

In South America, before the arrival of European explorers, Native Americans developed large empires. Great civilizations came and went, including the Nazcas and Chimus. Agriculture supported the city populations of these great empires.

Native South Americans had their own forms of government and boundaries between nations. Their religions often taught a respect for nature. Most people were peasant farmers who grew food for their own families, sold a small surplus at village markets, and gave the rest to government officials.

Conquering South America

The discovery of new lands in the west by Columbus in 1492 led to a race to claim and exploit them. Spain and Portugal were the main rivals for the new lands across the Atlantic Ocean. So in 1493 Pope Alexander VI drew an imaginary line on the map of the world called the Line of Demarcation. Spain was to have all the lands to the west of it, Portugal all the lands to the east. By the Treaty of Tordesillas, a year later, the

line was moved westward, which gave Portugal the right to the area that is now Brazil.

In 1498 the explorer Christopher Columbus landed in South America on his third voyage, paid for by the Spanish. A Portuguese expedition reached the Brazilian coast north of Rio de Janeiro in 1500. Spanish and Portuguese became the main languages of South America, and for the next 300 years Europe was to control South America.

Conquistadores

The conquistadores (conquerors) were inspired by a greed for gold, of which there was plenty in the Americas, and by a desire to bring Christianity to the Native American peoples.

When the conquistador Francisco Pizarro arrived in Peru in 1532, he invaded and conquered the Inca empire, and within a few years the Spanish had begun to spread their rule over much of the continent. They converted large numbers of Native Americans to Christianity, often by force.

The Spanish empire

At its height in the 16th and 17th centuries Spain's empire included half of South America, all of Central America and the Caribbean, and other parts of North America.

Many of the conquistadores married local Native American women. A class structure grew up. Those with all Spanish ancestors owned most of the wealth and had all the power. Those of mixed race often had small farms or were traders. ▶

▲ The Spanish conquistador Francisco Pizarro captured the Inca emperor Atahualpa by treachery. Atahualpa filled his cell with gold to buy his freedom, but Pizarro had him killed anyway.

• America was named after Amerigo Vespucci, an Italian navigator who explored the South American coast. The German mapmaker, Waldseemüller, first used the name because he believed Vespucci discovered America before Columbus. This is unlikely, but Vespucci was certainly one of the first to realize that the land might be a separate continent, not part of Asia as Columbus believed.

◀ Machu Picchu, an Inca city high in the Andes of Peru. The Spanish conquistadores destroyed other Inca cities, but never found Machu Picchu. It was only discovered in 1911.

◀ Simón Bolívar (left) was a brilliant general who led the struggle against the Spanish rulers of South America. In 1825 he helped to defeat the Spanish armies in upper Peru, and the people decided to form a separate republic. They named it Bolivia, in honour of their liberator.

The poorest of all were the Native Americans and African slaves, who were forced to work in the silver mines and sugar plantations, and to produce crops such as cotton and tobacco, which were exported to Europe. Many died of overwork in poor conditions, or from the diseases Europeans brought with them.

Wars of independence

The unequal wealth of the people in South American colonies led the citizens to rebel. The Wars of Independence began in 1809. At first they failed, but from 1816 onward they were successful everywhere.

Two men were outstanding among the South American leaders. José de San Martín liberated Argentina, Chile and Peru. In the north Simón Bolívar won freedom for four countries: Bolivia, Colombia, Ecuador and Venezuela. He also helped San Martín defeat the Spanish in Peru.

There was no fighting in Portugal's South American colony, Brazil. In 1825 Portugal recognized Brazil as an independent empire. In 1889 the emperor left Brazil to seek refuge in Europe, and the Brazilians formed a republic.

Many European immigrants flocked to South America, lured by the prospect of new land and a new life. Most inhabitants of South America today are descendants of European settlers who married Native Americans.

After independence

Independence did not bring peace to the people of South America. Some of the new countries began to fight each other. In 1864–1870 one-third of the population of Paraguay died in a war with Argentina, Uruguay and Brazil. In the War of the Pacific (1879–1883) Chile seized territory from Peru and Bolivia, and in the Chaco War of 1932–1935 Paraguay and Bolivia fought over land in the Chaco desert.

Many of the countries of South America remained desperately poor. Most of the wealth was in the hands of big landowners and foreign mining companies. Sometimes the people started revolutions to change things, and sometimes they elected governments to make reforms. But often when this happened

the army took power, and military dictators ruled in favour of the rich. Today, democracy is widespread in South America, but poverty is still a major problem.

The Guianas

Three small countries in the north of South America are rather different from the rest. The only English-speaking nation in South America is Guyana, which was the colony of British Guiana until 1966. Most people there are descended from African slaves or Indian labourers, brought to work on plantations. In Suriname (which used to be called Dutch Guiana) many inhabitants are descendants of people from the Dutch East Indies (now Indonesia), brought to work there when Suriname was a Dutch colony. Suriname became independent in 1975. French Guiana is an administrative district of France. This means that its people are French citizens.

• The traditional way of life of Native Americans is fast disappearing. Many Native Americans have moved to the cities, but there they often earn low wages and live in shanty towns. The Native Americans of the tropical forests are losing their homes as farmers, mining companies and ranchers clear the forests where they live.

find out more
Caribbean
Columbus, Christopher
Explorers
Incas
Slaves

▼ General Augusto Pinochet, backed by the US government, overthrew the democratically elected government of Chile in 1973. Thousands of Pinochet's opponents were killed or tortured.

Spain

By the 5th century BC, Phoenicians, Greeks and Celts had established settlements in Spain. The country was divided among many small, warlike tribes. It is a difficult country to attack because it is very mountainous. The highly efficient Roman army finally conquered the Spanish peninsula and made it part of the Roman empire.

Roman rule lasted for almost 600 years. Then a Germanic tribe, the Visigoths, swept in and took over. They set up a kingdom whose nobles warred among themselves. In AD 711 one of these nobles, Count Julian, called in Berber warriors from Morocco to help him rebel against his king, even though they were Muslims not Christians.

Under their Arab leader, Tarik, the Berbers landed at a rocky point which ever after was called Tarik's Rock – in his language Gebel Tarik (Gibraltar). In seven years the Berbers, aided by a host of fellow Muslims – Arabs, Moors and Syrians – had conquered all but the north of the country. For almost 500 years most of Spain was an Islamic country, though Muslims were generally tolerant of Christians and Jews. Spain under the Moors became famous for its universities, its medicine, and its art and architecture. The Alhambra palace at Granada is one of the most elegant and finely decorated buildings in Europe.

The years of power

The Muslim rulers quarrelled among themselves, and by the 11th century Spain was divided into over 20 small states. The Christian kingdoms of the north, led by Castile, took the opportunity and reconquered Spain bit by bit, until only the kingdom of Granada in the south remained a Muslim state. The two Christian kingdoms of Castile and Aragon united in 1479, and almost

▲ In the 16th century Spain was the most powerful country in Europe. At the battle of Lepanto in 1571 the Spanish and Venetian fleets defeated the Ottoman Turks. This stopped the Turks from spreading into the western Mediterranean.

all Spain was under one rule again. In 1492 two very important events occurred: the Muslims were driven out of Granada, and an expedition led by Christopher Columbus landed in the Caribbean. Columbus was from Genoa in Italy, but it was Queen Isabella of Spain who provided the funds, and Spain that reaped the benefit.

In the following hundred years Spanish adventurers, known as the conquistadores, conquered a vast empire in Central and South America, and untold gold and silver were looted and brought back to Europe. In the late 16th century, under King Philip II, Spain became one of the richest and most powerful countries in Europe.

Spain's 'golden age' did not last. A series of disastrous wars and feeble kings weakened the country. It declined rapidly in the 18th century, and eventually its American colonies rebelled and became independent. ◗

▼ The Alhambra is a fortified Moorish palace outside Granada in southern Spain. It was built between 1238 and 1358, and was the last stronghold of the Moors in Spain.

• A wedding led to the unification of Spain in 1479. The couple were cousins – Prince Ferdinand, heir to the throne of Castile, and Princess Isabella, heir to the throne of Aragon. When they succeeded to their thrones, the two kingdoms effectively became one. Isabella and Ferdinand were strict Roman Catholics. They introduced the Inquisition, a court which used torture and execution to force all Spain's people to join their religion. At least 2000 people were burned at the stake, and the Jews were driven out of Spain.

• Gibraltar is a tiny country linked to Spain by a narrow strip of lowland 3 km long. Gibraltar has been a British dependency since 1704.

Spanish Armada *see* Elizabeth I *and* Tudor England

◄ Troops supporting General Franco fire on rebels from behind a makeshift barricade in Toledo. Over 750,000 people were killed in the Spanish civil war.

• The Basques are a people who live in the border regions of France and Spain. In 1959 some Spanish Basques formed a group called ETA ('Basque-land and Freedom') to fight for independence. Spain created a Basque parliament in 1980, but terrorist attacks by ETA have continued.

From dictatorship to democracy

In 1931 the king, Alfonso XIII, was driven into exile and a republic was set up. Five years later a military revolt against an elected left-wing government plunged the country into civil war. Spaniards suffered terribly during the three years of fighting between the Republicans and their allies on the one side and the fascist 'Falange' on the other. In 1939 Spain fell under the rule of a fascist dictator, General Francisco Franco, who held power until his death in 1975.

Although he was friendly with the dictators of Germany and Italy, Adolf Hitler and Benito Mussolini, he kept Spain out of World War II. However, he was not a popular ruler. When Franco died, Alfonso's grandson, Juan Carlos, became king, and free elections were held.

find out more
Columbus, Christopher
Europe
Fascists
Holy Roman Empire
Muslims
South America

Stalin, Joseph

Joseph Stalin was leader of the Soviet Union from 1924 to 1953. He became a ruthless and much-feared dictator.

Joseph Vissarionovich Dzhugashvili was expelled from college at the age of 20. Two years later he joined the Russian Social-Democratic Workers' Party and became a revolutionary. His escapades led to him being imprisoned or exiled for a number of years. In 1912 he joined the Bolshevik (Communist) Party, and took the name 'Stalin' (man of steel).

In 1917 the Bolsheviks seized power and Lenin became ruler of the Russian republics (renamed the Soviet Union, or USSR, in 1922). Stalin became Secretary of the Communist Party in 1922 and took over as leader of the USSR after Lenin died in 1924.

In the years that followed, Stalin built a strong nation through a series of Five Year Plans, which were intended to industrialize and modernize the Soviet Union. His greatest achievement was to lead his country to victory over the Nazis in World War II.

However, all Stalin's reforms were made at great human cost. He had all of his rivals killed until he became dictator. Soviet people lived in fear of arrest, torture and execution by the secret police (later called the KGB). During the 1920s and 1930s, millions of people died of starvation, and millions more were sent to labour camps for opposing Stalin's wishes.

Born 1879 in Georgia, then part of the Russian empire
Died 1953 aged 73

find out more
Cold War
Communists
Lenin
Russia
Twentieth-century history
World War II

▼ The leaders of the Communist Party in Russia denounced Stalin in 1956, and in that same year his statue was pulled down in Budapest, capital of Hungary.

Stuart Britain

The Stuart royal family inherited the English throne from the Tudors in 1603. They ruled until 1714, when the last of the Stuart monarchs, Queen Anne, died.

While the Tudors had provided strong government, there were so many difficulties between the Stuart kings and Parliament that they led to civil war. Neighbours, friends and even members of the same family sometimes found themselves on opposite sides.

Troubled times

Both King James I and his son Charles I were extravagant with money and often asked Parliament to raise extra taxes. But Members of Parliament (MPs) in the House of Commons were angered when the kings refused to listen to their complaints about royal spending and often voted against them. There were also religious disagreements. Many MPs were Puritans who wanted the Church of England to have plainer services and churches. The Puritans hated and feared Catholics. Charles I had a Catholic wife and Parliament was afraid he was going to make England Catholic.

Because of all these disagreements Charles I decided, in 1629, to rule without Parliament. However, in 1640 a Scottish rebellion forced Charles to call a Parliament to raise extra taxes. MPs immediately began to work to limit the king's power.

Civil war

These problems finally led to civil war. From 1642 to 1646, Cavaliers (for the king) fought Roundheads (for Parliament). Parliament's New Model Army won the war, and peace was restored. But when Charles I joined forces with the Scots in 1648 and fighting started again, Parliament decided they no longer wanted to be ruled by a king. In 1649 Charles was put on trial and executed.

For the next 11 years, England did not have a king. It was called a 'Commonwealth'. From 1653 Oliver Cromwell, who had led the army

▼ The execution of Charles I, 30 January 1649. This is the only time an English king has been put on trial and executed. Even many Roundheads were horrified at his death.

against the king, ruled as Lord Protector. He kept England peaceful and made it strong abroad. However, he too found it difficult to get on with Parliament, and had to raise taxes to pay for an army to help him rule.

Restoration of the monarchy

Cromwell died in 1658. In 1660 Charles I's son Charles II was invited back from exile and crowned as king. This was called the Restoration. The next king, James II, was a Catholic and ignored laws made by Parliament. His reign lasted only three years. In 1688 he was forced to escape into exile in France. Parliament asked his Protestant son-in-law and daughter, William and Mary, to become joint king and queen. They agreed to share power with Parliament. This change (which was peaceful in England, but not in Scotland and Ireland) is often called the Glorious Revolution. By the time of the last Stuart, Queen Anne, rulers of England had become 'constitutional monarchs' who had to obey Parliament's rules. ◆

◀ In the civil war each side gave the other a nickname. 'Roundheads' were those who fought for Parliament. 'Cavaliers' were Royalists, who fought for the king.

1603 **James I** (James VI of Scotland)
1605 Gunpowder Plot
1625 **Charles I**
1642 1st civil war
1648 2nd civil war
1649 Charles I executed
1650 **Commonwealth**
1653 Cromwell Lord Protector
1655 Jamaica captured from the Spaniards
1660 **Charles II** Restoration of the monarchy
1665 Great Plague
1666 Fire of London
1685 **James II**
1688 **Mary II and William III**
1690 Battle of the Boyne. William III defeated James II in Ireland
1695 Mary II died
1702 **Anne**
1707 Union of England and Scotland
1714 Death of Queen Anne
The next king was George I. There is an article on Georgian Britain.

The Gunpowder Plot

In 1605, in what became known as the Gunpowder Plot, a small group of Catholics plotted to blow up the Houses of Parliament on 5 November, when King James I was to open Parliament. They wanted to make England Catholic again. They hid 35 barrels of gunpowder in a cellar under the House of Lords, guarded by one of the conspirators, Guy Fawkes. The plot was discovered just in time, and Guy Fawkes and the other conspirators were captured and executed. Since then, bonfires have been lit on 5 November each year to celebrate the failure of the plot.

▲ The Gunpowder Plot conspirators. Guy (Guido) Fawkes is third from the right.

Stuart life

As the wealthy landowners and merchants in Parliament got even more say in running the country, they became even more powerful and prosperous. Change was much slower for ordinary people. They still could not vote or sit in Parliament. Times were often hard, especially when there was a bad harvest. But by the end of the 17th century, the country was generally more prosperous. Slightly fewer people died young, so the population increased.

London was the biggest city in Britain, with a population of about half a million by the 1660s. Slums full of filthy tumbledown houses grew up to the north of the city; the rich built grander houses to the west. There were fashionable new coffee houses, bull-baiting rings, bear-baiting pits, and theatres. The smoke from coal fires polluted the air. Disease spread easily. The Great Plague of 1665 was the last of several outbreaks of bubonic plague.

Trade

Trade grew enormously. At the beginning of the Stuart reign, England had only one important industry, the woollen cloth trade. Corn often had to be imported to feed everyone. By 1700 enough corn was grown to export some, and new goods, including tobacco, tea, coffee and chocolate, were imported. Much more sugar was coming into the country, and some of it was refined in London. Cotton, silks, fine china, dyes and jewels came from the East. Huge profits were made from the trade in slaves. Trade led to wars with Dutch and French rivals and to the establishment of colonies in North America and the Caribbean. The East India Company, which brought many of the luxury goods from the East, established settlements in India too. In the next century these colonies grew into an empire.

• Ireland was governed by English rulers. Most Irish were Catholics, except in Ulster where Protestant English and Scots settled. There was a Catholic rebellion in 1641. In 1649–1650 Cromwell led a harsh campaign to bring Ireland under English control again. By 1714 Irish Catholics owned only 7% of the land of Ireland. English and Scottish landowners had taken the rest.

• Scotland had the same Stuart kings as England, but remained a separate kingdom. In 1650–1651 Cromwell defeated the Scots. Scotland was occupied. In 1707 the Act of Union united England and Scotland as part of a united kingdom. After the Glorious Revolution many Highlanders became Jacobites, who supported the exiled James II and his descendants.

• Wales was ruled in the same way as England, with similar law courts and counties.

◄ With wooden houses cramped together in narrow streets, fire was a common danger in Stuart London. This painting shows the most famous and devastating one, which raged across the city in 1666.

find out more
Cromwell, Oliver
Georgian Britain
Ireland
Scotland
Slaves
Tudor England
Wales

Transport

The invention of different forms of transport – from the wheel to the jet airliner – has had a great effect on how people have lived through the centuries.

Transport firsts

1825 George Stephenson opens the first passenger railway, which ran between Stockton and Darlington in England.

1885–1886 The Germans Gottfried Daimler and Karl Benz build the first vehicles powered by petrol engines.

1903 The American brothers, Orville and Wilbur Wright, make the first flight in a powered aeroplane.

1907 The American Henry Ford begins to manufacture motor cars in large numbers.

1930s Germany becomes the first country to build a network of motorways.

1952 The world's first jet airliner, the British De Havilland Comet, starts carrying passengers.

• One of the earliest canals is the Grand Canal in China. Work started on the canal in the 6th century BC, and continued over hundreds of years. Today, the canal is 1794 km long.

▶ A United States mail train crossing the Sierra Nevada in 1870, a year after the completion of the first railway line across the United States from the Atlantic to the Pacific. This helped to open up the interior of North America to settlement, trade and industry.

find out more
Communications
Industrial Revolution
Twentieth-century
  history

Between 5000 and 4000 BC people in the eastern Mediterranean area first domesticated horses and donkeys, for riding and for carrying goods. The wheel was probably invented around 3500 BC in Sumer (now part of Iraq), although before that people had used logs as rollers to move heavy objects.

Boats, ships and canals

Boats were another early form of transport. Dugout canoes and rafts were used in prehistoric times. It was often much easier to go by boat along a river than to struggle through marshes and forests. Even when roads began to be built they were usually very bumpy and muddy. People also began to build bigger boats – ships – so that they could travel along the coasts or across the open sea. Early boats and ships used sails or oars to move through the water.

▲ In 1783 the first people to fly in a hot-air balloon travelled 9 kilometres across France in a balloon designed by the Montgolfier brothers.

People also linked rivers by building artificial waterways, called canals. Many canals were built in Europe in the 18th century at the start of the Industrial Revolution. Until the coming of the railways in the 19th century most goods travelled by ship or by horse-drawn barges on canals.

The age of steam

Steam-powered locomotives (railway engines) were first developed in Britain in the early 19th century. By the end of the century thousands of kilometres of railway lines had been built all over the world. Trains carried more goods than horse-drawn barges or carts, and they travelled much faster. The railways also brought great changes in the way people lived. They made it possible for people to travel long distances every day to work.

Travel by sea also changed in the 19th century, as steam ships replaced sailing ships. At the same time ships became bigger, and from the 19th century millions of Europeans emigrated by ship to North America, Australia, New Zealand and South Africa.

The petrol engine

The petrol-powered engine, and the first automobiles, were invented towards the end of the 19th century. By the early 20th century cars, buses and lorries began to be produced in large numbers. By this time people had begun to build much better roads, with hard surfaces. Gradually road transport became as important as the railways, both for people and goods. Cars changed the way people lived in the 20th century as much as railways did in the century before.

The beginning of air travel

The petrol engine was also used to power aeroplanes. The first powered flight took place in 1903. For many years aeroplanes were mostly used by the armed forces, and it was not until after World War II that airliners powered by turboprop or jet engines began to carry large numbers of people. More and more people are now able to visit faraway places in a matter of hours, and the world has become a much smaller place as a result.

Tudor England

The Tudors were a royal family who ruled England from 1485 to 1603. The first Tudor monarch was Henry VII, and the Tudor family dynasty which began with him ended with the death of Elizabeth I.

The first Tudor king, Henry VII, won his crown by defeating the unpopular Richard III at the battle of Bosworth in 1485. His victory ended the 'Wars of the Roses', a struggle for the throne between the families of York (one of whose badges was a white rose) and Lancaster (often represented by a red rose). In the unsettled 30 years of war before 1485 there had been five different kings.

Tudor rule

Henry VII was descended from the Lancastrians. Henry faced plots and rebellions, and his first son and heir died young. Fortunately, by the time Henry

▶ The Spanish Armada and the English fleet doing battle in 1588. Catholic King Philip II of Spain sent his ships to crush the Protestant English. The Armada failed and there was no Spanish invasion. But Philip rebuilt his fleet, and the war dragged on until 1604.

died in 1509, a second son, Henry, was old enough to inherit the throne.

Henry VIII became intent on producing a son and heir to the Tudor line. He went through three marriages and a major quarrel with the pope before his son Edward was born, 27 years after he became king. Edward VI was only 9 when his father died in 1546, and was too young to rule by himself.

When Edward died in 1553, his only heirs were his two sisters, Mary and Elizabeth. Mary I married Philip of Spain, but she died, childless, five years later. When Elizabeth I became queen in 1558, she proved that a woman could be a successful ruler. She never married and so was the last Tudor monarch.

Ambitions beyond England

The Tudors ruled England reasonably successfully. They also tried to control more of the British Isles. Their family came from

◀ The Protestant Thomas Cranmer was Archbishop of Canterbury during Henry VIII's reign. When the Catholic Mary I became queen, she arrested him for heresy (not accepting the official Catholic teaching) and he was burnt at the stake for his beliefs.

Wales, and under their rule Welsh landowners had a better chance of doing well in England. In 1536 the Act of Union gave Wales the same local government as England, and made English the official language there, which made life difficult for ordinary Welsh-speaking people.

Henry VIII made himself King of Ireland in 1541 (until then English kings had been only 'Lords of Ireland'). Mary I and Elizabeth I tried to strengthen English control by giving Irish land to English settlers. This resulted in six serious rebellions in Ireland during Elizabeth's reign.

Scotland was an independent kingdom ruled by Stuart kings. The Scots had long defended themselves against English attempts to conquer them. Henry VII tried to make peace by marrying his daughter Margaret to the Scots king, James IV, in 1503. But this failed to bring peace, and Henry VIII tried unsuccessfully to conquer Scotland. However, when Elizabeth I died, Margaret Tudor's great-grandson James VI became James I, the first Stuart king of England.

Richard III was the last English king of the Middle Ages.
1485 **Henry VII**
1509 **Henry VIII**
1534 Henry VIII Supreme Head of the Church of England
1536–1550 Monasteries destroyed
1538 English Bible printed
1542–1550 Wars with Scotland
1547 **Edward VI**
1553 **Mary I** Catholic Church restored
1558 **Elizabeth I** Church of England established
1568 Mary, Queen of Scots, imprisoned
1577–1580 Drake's voyage round the world
1587 Mary, Queen of Scots, executed
1588 Armada defeated
1596–1603 Rebellion in Ireland
1601 Poor Law
1603 Death of Elizabeth I
The next king was James I (Stuart). There is an article on Stuart Britain.

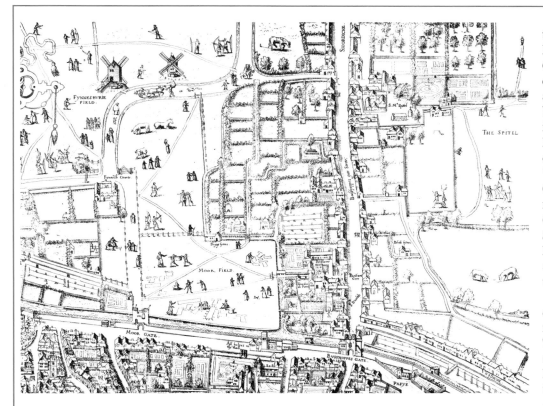

▲ Moor Field (now Finsbury Circus), London, 1553–1559. People can be seen drying washing, practising archery and setting up 'tenter' frames for stretching cloth.

Tudor life

In Tudor times most people still lived in villages and the local landowners were the most powerful people. The rich could afford to buy luxuries such as silks, spices, cotton, furs and carpets, which were brought to England from abroad. But for ordinary people life was much the same as it had been for centuries. Diseases were often killers; about one baby in five died before its first birthday. Poverty was a great problem. There were harsh punishments for beggars, and thieves were executed. Only at the end of the Tudor period, in 1601, did the new Poor Laws bring some relief to the poor.

Although some villages had schools, most poor children worked with their families in the fields. Wealthy boys often went to grammar schools in towns, but most girls just learned to read and prepared for marriage by helping their mothers at home.

A time of change

In Tudor times food prices increased because there were more people to feed. There was more unemployment because there were not enough jobs for everyone.

Printed books were becoming cheaper and more widely available, so information began to spread more quickly and there were probably more people who could read. The English Bible became a best-seller. Printed pictures began to appear too.

The Church changed as the Reformation spread through Europe. The Reformation was a movement to reform the Roman Catholic Church which led to the establishment of Protestant churches. After a dispute with the pope, Henry VIII made himself Supreme Head of the Church in England and destroyed all the monasteries and sold all their lands. Mary I brought back the old Catholic faith and persecuted Protestants. Elizabeth's Church of England aimed to be a 'middle way'. However, Mary, Queen of Scots' ambitions to retake the English throne and Catholic King Philip II of Spain's attempt to invade England resulted in harsh laws against Catholics, who became very unpopular once more.

In Tudor times sailors and explorers travelled new sea routes to discover foreign lands. They brought back new goods such as tobacco and potatoes to England. Some explorers went to make a new life in North America and this was the beginning of England's colonies abroad.

▼ Mary, Queen of Scots, who, after 19 years of imprisonment, was found guilty of being involved in a Catholic plot to kill her Protestant cousin, Queen Elizabeth I, and take her throne. On Elizabeth's orders Mary was beheaded in 1587.

Twentieth-century history

The world changed at breathtaking speed in the 20th century. We invented flying machines, conquered many diseases, travelled into space, and sent words and pictures around the Earth in seconds.

In 1900 most people lived in villages. Important cities were much smaller than they are today. Over the century people moved into the rapidly expanding towns and cities. While for some people town life was convenient and pleasant, for the poor living in city slums it could be grim and violent. By the 1990s some 30 million children lived on the streets.

Technology and religion

At the beginning of the century few houses had toilets, running water or electricity. Although millions still live like this, in the richer countries – Europe, North America, and East Asia – life has been transformed by central heating, air-conditioning and a host of household gadgets, from washing machines to personal computers.

In some societies, particularly in Europe and communist China, the number of people regularly going to a place of worship greatly declined. However, in the Americas and the Muslim world religion was as important as ever. The last quarter of the century saw an alarming increase in conflicts between different religious groups.

Women's and children's rights

In 1900 most of the world's population could not read or write. Even in the West, most children had only a few years' early education. By the end of the century, the great majority of children went to school and many went on to college. As life became more complicated, people needed education to get jobs.

In 1900 women were largely seen as second-class citizens, without education or paid work. By the end of the century most governments agreed that men and women should be treated equally and given the same opportunities.

Communications

The arrival of cheap, mass-produced cars changed the way people lived and altered the shape of cities and the countryside. Air travel, telephones,

radio, television and satellite communications also brought people closer together. Athletes met for international sporting events, such as the Olympic Games. In 1945 the United Nations was set up to help settle disagreements peacefully and tackle such problems as poverty and racism. Multinational companies began operating in dozens of different countries.

Conflict

Sadly, better communications did not bring less conflict. In two terrible world wars (1914–1918 and 1939–1945) cities were destroyed and millions were killed. World War II left the world dominated by the two 'superpowers' – the

▲ Then and now – a city street in Tokyo, Japan, in 1905 and in 1996. Modern forms of transport have speeded things up since 1905, but car exhaust fumes have filled the air with poisonous pollution.

● The 20th century was powered by the fossil fuels coal and oil. This made countries with large oil reserves, such as Saudi Arabia, rich and powerful.

• During the 20th century the world's population grew from around 1.5 billion to about 6 billion. The population explosion meant that more food had to be grown and distributed where it was most needed. It also led to serious environmental problems, such as forest clearance and pollution.

capitalist USA and the communist USSR. Their rivalry led to a period of dangerous tension known as the Cold War.

The Cold War cast a shadow over the second half of the century. Billions of pounds were spent on arms. Concrete and barbed-wire barriers divided eastern and western Europe. The struggle between capitalists and communists spread around the globe.

Nuclear weapons made another world war almost unthinkable. But there were many smaller conflicts, such as the Korean War (1950–1953), the Vietnam War (1963–1975) and the Afghan War (1979–1989). The Middle East saw a series of wars between Israel and its Arab neighbours (1948–1973) and a long, bitter war between Iran and Iraq (1980–1988).

The Cold War ended when the USSR collapsed in 1989. By this time relations between democratic nations and communist China had improved. Although a major war now seemed unlikely, bloody civil wars were fought in Yugoslavia, Somalia, Rwanda and several other places.

Empires and nations

At the beginning of the century Britain and other European countries had empires stretching across the world. Europeans ruled most of Africa, the Caribbean, Oceania and huge areas of Asia. Before 1914 much of the Middle East was part of the Ottoman empire. Gradually these empires fell apart as the power of the European states grew less, and dozens of new nations won back their independence. Over the years many more independent states were created, sometimes after periods of conflict.

▶ In 1957 Ghana was the first black African state to gain independence, under its first president Kwame Nkrumah (centre).

▲ At the beginning of the 20th century space exploration would have seemed fantastic and impossible. Today, orbiting astronauts can study the Earth below because of the huge technological advances science has made since then.

Mass killings of one group of people by another (genocide) haunted the 20th century. The Nazi destruction of some 6 million Jews was the worst example. But the massacres in Cambodia (1975–1979) and Rwanda (1994) were equally horrifying. By the end of the century most governments had laws to stop racism. The greatest anti-racist triumph was the fall of the all-white regime in South Africa in 1993–1994.

Unsolved problems

The 20th century was marked by the tragedies and triumphs of science. Huge technological advances were made, but many other difficulties remained. The gap between rich and poor was as wide as ever. Pollution threatened to poison the planet. People still turned to war to settle their differences. Learning to work together to solve these problems is the challenge of the future.

United Nations

The United Nations (UN) is an international organization whose purpose is to maintain peace and security all over the world.

• An organization similar to the UN, called the League of Nations, was founded in 1919 after World War I. It was unable to keep the peace, partly because the USA decided not to join. Also, no action was taken against Japan, Italy and Germany when they invaded other countries in the 1930s, which led to World War II.

The UN tries to help countries settle disagreements by getting them to talk to each other. It also provides a place where the representatives of countries can discuss all sorts of problems. Nearly all the countries of the world are now members of the UN. In 1997 there were 185 member countries. The only major countries which are not in the UN are Switzerland and Taiwan.

The General Assembly

Every member country of the UN has a seat in the *General Assembly*. Representatives discuss problems such as disarmament, environmental pollution and world poverty, and occasionally pass resolutions. At the heart of the UN is the *Security Council*. This is a body of selected member countries which takes decisions on behalf of all the members when there is a crisis. The *Secretary-General* of the UN

carries out decisions of the Security Council and works on the plans of the General Assembly. He also takes part in UN peace-keeping work.

Keeping the peace

Since 1945 the UN Security Council has tried to deal with many conflicts. Sometimes it sends a military force, made up of troops from different countries, to keep the peace between warring groups. UN forces have served in Korea, Cyprus, Lebanon, Cambodia and the countries of the former Yugoslavia. While the troops keep the warring groups apart, the Secretary-General and UN staff try to get the groups' representatives round a table

▲ The United Nations was founded in 1945 at the end of World War II. The idea arose among the allied nations who fought against Nazi Germany and Japan. At a conference in San Francisco, USA, they drew up a document called the Charter of the United Nations. The UN Charter has become its rule book.

to discuss solutions to their problems. Unfortunately, these peace-keeping efforts do not always succeed and the UN is often blamed when talks break down and wars continue.

Specialized agencies

Much of the work of the UN is carried out by specialized agencies. These deal with matters such as food aid, agriculture, health, education and finance. Member countries pay for the work of these agencies according to how rich they are. Some governments also give voluntary contributions to UNICEF and UNHCR for their work with children and refugees.

Some UN specialized agencies

FAO Food and Agriculture Organization
IMF International Monetary Fund
ITU International Telecommunication Union
UNESCO UN Educational, Scientific and Cultural Organization
UNHCR UN High Commission for Refugees
UNICEF UN International Children's Emergency Fund
World Bank
WHO World Health Organization

find out more
Balkans
Cold War
Twentieth-century history

◄ Bosnian Serbs welcome a Russian United Nations battalion in Pale on 20 February 1994. UN peace-keeping troops were sent to the former Yugoslavia in the early 1990s, when wars broke out between different ethnic groups and the country divided into smaller states.

United States of America

The history of the United States began on 4 July 1776, when the 13 British colonies in North America declared themselves independent of Britain and its king, George III.

After defeating the British in the war of independence known as the American Revolution (1775–1783), the colonies wrote a constitution for their new country. This divided power between the states and a central (or 'federal') government, which was run by an elected president. The successful general George Washington became the first president of the United States of America and the new capital city, Washington, was named after him.

Across the continent

The USA expanded fast. Four new states had joined by 1803. In the same year President Jefferson doubled its size by buying a huge area of central America from France (the Louisiana Purchase). The USA now stretched from the east coast to the Rocky Mountains. It expanded south in 1819 when it bought Florida from Spain.

The USA continued to grow throughout the 19th century. It absorbed Texas in 1845. Three years later, following a war with Mexico, it took over territory that became the states of California, Arizona and New Mexico. Further states were added when Britain gave up its claim to lands in the north-west, and in 1867 Russia sold Alaska to the USA for 7.2 million dollars.

Opportunity and repression

New territory brought new opportunities. Pioneer settlers moved west as farmers and cattle ranchers. In 1849 miners from all over the world flocked to California in search of gold. The population grew rapidly, boosted by thousands of European immigrants hoping for better lives in the New World. Towns and cities expanded and multiplied. The

▲ Before the first railroad was built across the USA in 1869, settlers looking for new land in the American West made long, hard journeys in covered wagons.

development of telegraphs and railroads speeded up communications across the vast country. The first railroad to cross the continent opened in 1869.

The new opportunities were not open to all. For the Native Americans, driven westwards and robbed of their ancestral lands by European settlers, it was a time of great hardship and misery. Until the Civil War (1861–1865), most African Americans were held in slavery and were often mistreated. Although slavery was abolished in 1865, African Americans were discriminated against for many years to come.

Industry and war

The USA changed dramatically in the years after the Civil War. Immigrants continued to flood into the country, including many from eastern Europe. As the population soared, so industry and business boomed. The world was flooded with new American inventions, from the sewing machine and typewriter to electric lighting and the combine harvester. The output of coal, iron and steel, machinery and, later, oil rose at a spectacular rate. Grain from the Midwest was exported around the world. The

◄ Sitting Bull, a Sioux Indian chief, is most famous for his defeat of General Custer at the battle of Little Bighorn in 1876, fought over Indian land rights.

• In the USA people vote separately for their president and for their parliament, which is called Congress. The Congress has two houses: the Senate contains two people elected from each of the 50 states; the House of Representatives has 435 members, divided among the states according to their population size. Each state also has a congress and a governor.

107

▲ The battle of Winchester (1864), fought between the pro-slavery southern states (Confederates) and the anti-slavery northern states (Unionists) during the Civil War of 1861–1865. The Unionists finally won, but only after terrible slaughter. One in 50 Americans (about half a million) died in the war.

development of canning and refrigeration greatly helped the meat industry.

By 1914 the USA had become the richest country in the world. But the industrial revolution brought problems too. Officials and politicians struggled to control child labour, slum dwellings, urban crime, pollution and corruption. Abroad, before the USA entered World War I in 1917, it used its new-found power to gain control over Puerto Rico, Hawaii, the Philippines and Cuba.

Boom and bust

After World War I the USA went its own way. It refused to join the League of Nations, the peace-keeping body set up after the war, and it cut immigration and imports from other countries. The US economy flourished for a decade. The greatest advances were made in the oil and automobile industries. New factories, which attracted many African-American workers from the south, turned out a vast range of consumer goods. The most famous, Henry Ford's Model T car, had sold 15 million by 1928.

The boom suddenly ended in 1929, throwing the USA into the worst depression in its history. Thousands went bankrupt, unemployment rocketed, factories ground to a halt, and farmland lay uncultivated. President F. D. Roosevelt's New Deal programme went some way toward helping the situation, but the USA did not really get back on its feet again until the outbreak of World War II in 1939.

Superpower and world leader

By 1950 the world was dangerously divided between communist nations, led by the Soviet Union and China, and democratic nations, led by the USA. Guided by its mistakes in the past, the USA accepted its new role. It supported the United Nations, and in order to deter communist aggression, it built up a huge arsenal of weapons.

The USA used force in Korea and Vietnam to try to halt the advance of communism. In 1962 President Kennedy brought the world to the brink of nuclear war when Soviet missiles were discovered on Cuba. The hostility between the USA and the USSR (known as the 'Cold War') lasted until the collapse of Soviet power in the late 1980s.

Modern America

The USA continued to prosper during the last half of the 20th century. Its scientists put a man on the Moon in 1969, and it dominated the new computer and software markets. American culture, from Hollywood movies to jeans and chewing gum, became the international culture.

However, city centres deteriorated and sometimes flared into riot. Crime and drug-taking rose. Women and racial minorities, particularly African Americans and Hispanics, campaigned vigorously for equal rights. As the 'American century' drew to a close, many of the nation's traditions and values were under threat. No one was quite sure what would replace them.

► The Statue of Liberty, which stands at the entrance to New York Harbour, was given by France to the American people in 1886. Her torch represents freedom and her book the law.

• Of the 42 presidents to 1997, all of whom were men, Franklin Delano Roosevelt served longest (1933–1945). Two of the most famous, Abraham Lincoln (1861–1865) and John F. Kennedy (1961–1963) were assassinated. Several had made their names as soldiers. Ronald Reagan (1981–1989) had been a film star and Jimmy Carter (1977–1981) a peanut farmer. Theodore Roosevelt (1901–1909) had the teddy bear named after him.

find out more
American Civil War
American Revolution
Cold War
Kennedy, J. F.
King, Martin Luther
Lincoln, Abraham
Native Americans
North America
Roosevelt, Franklin D.
Slaves
Twentieth-century history
Vietnam War
World War I
World War II

Victorian Britain

The Victorian period runs from 1837 to 1901, the years during which England was ruled by Queen Victoria.

• In Victorian times rich boys usually went to 'public' schools, which were not public but fee-paying. The North London Collegiate School founded in 1850 was one of the first to provide a good education for middle-class girls. The Church provided some primary schools, but not until 1870 were there 'elementary' schools for all children between the ages of 5 and 10. By 1901 these schools were free for everyone up to 12.

▶ Life for the poor in Victorian times was grim. Towns grew too fast for proper town planning. This meant overcrowding, poor water supplies and a lack of sewage and rubbish disposal. Disease thrived and cholera epidemics swept the country.

▲ On 1 May 1851 Queen Victoria, with Prince Albert by her side, opened the first Great Exhibition in the Crystal Palace in London. On show were samples of industry from countries all over the world. Over half the exhibitors were British, because in 1851 Britain had a vast empire and was the leading industrial nation of the world.

During Victoria's reign Britain's empire grew stronger than ever. The empire brought vast wealth for some and Britain ruled over millions of people. Many Victorians worked in India as soldiers, traders and government officials. Victorian explorers were beginning to go deep into Africa. Under Benjamin Disraeli, prime minister in 1868 and again from 1874 to 1880, Britain took control of the Suez Canal, the shortest route to India, and Parliament gave Victoria the title of 'Empress of India'.

Country life

Landowners continued to be the richest and most powerful people in Britain. The squire who lived in the big house in a village usually owned the villagers' homes, and most of them worked on his land. Owners of small farms were often well-off and quite independent. The poor, ordinary villagers lived in damp, cold houses with no indoor water supply.

Things began to change in about 1880. Cheap wheat and frozen meat began to be imported. Margarine was invented, and was cheaper than butter. All this competition hit British farming badly. Landowners did less well, wages fell and jobs were lost. More people left their villages to find jobs in the growing towns.

City and town life

Victorian Britain became the leading industrial nation in the world. More industry meant more cotton mills, bigger coalmines and more factories all over the country. Existing and new cities grew quickly. By 1880 the industrial town of Middlesbrough with 50,000 people had grown up on the River Tees. In 1830 there had been one farmhouse on the site.

This huge change in people's lives brought problems. Factories and mines were dangerous and unhealthy places to work. There were no rules about hours of work or wages. Workers' houses were built as cheaply as possible, huddled together with no taps or toilets indoors. Filthy drains were often close to

the pumps that provided drinking water.

For the better-off rail travel made it easier to get to work, and so suburbs grew up on the edge of towns, with bigger houses, trees and gardens. By 1901 big cities like Birmingham and Manchester had fine new town halls, libraries, art galleries and parks.

Struggles towards change

The 1830s were bad years for working people, with low wages and much unemployment. In 1836 a group of skilled workers in London, led by Francis Place and William Lovett, decided to draw up a Charter. This demanded several reforms by Parliament, in particular the vote for all adult males and payment for MPs so that working people could be elected to Parliament. Workers all over the country campaigned to get it accepted but the Chartists did not immediately get the reforms they wanted.

Gradually workers realized that if they joined a trade union, they could help each other, and perhaps force their employers to improve wages and working conditions. In the late 1880s, strikes by women making matchboxes (match girls) and dockers were both successful. But strikes were very

risky as employers often 'locked out' strikers, so they lost their jobs and their families starved.

Reforms

Many Victorians worked hard for reform, and most of the changes the Chartists wanted came about in the end. By 1884 most men over 21 could vote. By 1901 there were even a few working-class MPs, though MPs were not paid until 1911.

Many people began to realize that rules were needed to make

▼ The Chartists collected petitions, written requests signed by supporters of their cause, and took them to Parliament. This is the procession taking the 1842 petition. All three petitions were rejected.

▲ Victorian women had few rights. Working-class women lived hard lives and many worked as domestic servants. Most rich women found themselves dependent on their husbands. Better schools gave girls the chance to do more, and in about 1875 the first women studied at Oxford and Cambridge Universities. These women students are taking tea in their rooms at Holloway College, London, in about 1900.

towns healthy and workplaces safe. William Gladstone, prime minister four times in Victoria's reign, brought many reforms. In 1870, when he was in office, schools were provided for all children under 10 and in 1884 working men got the vote.

There were other reforms during Victoria's reign. By 1875 Parliament had passed laws enforcing clean water supplies, proper drains and dustbin collections. Cholera gradually disappeared.

The 7th Earl of Shaftesbury spent his life campaigning for laws to help people in the cities. These laws stopped children working in mines and factories and limited a factory worker's day to 10 hours. There were also rules about safety at work. Things improved, but poverty and disease did not disappear.

1837 Victoria becomes Queen
1840 Victoria and Albert marry
1851 Great Exhibition
1865 First woman doctor
1867 Workers in towns get the vote
1870 Education Act; Trade unions legal
1875 Public Health Act
1884 Workers in country get vote; Irish demand home rule
1892 Keir Hardie elected first Labour MP
1899 Britain fights Boer War in South Africa
1901 Death of Victoria

● Robert Peel was Britain's prime minister twice, but today he is best remembered for starting the police force in London. The arrival of 'Peelers', as they were called, in 1829 helped to stop a lot of petty crime.

find out more
Britain in the twentieth century
Crimean War
Georgian Britain
Industrial Revolution
Ireland
South Africa
Women's movement

Vietnam War

The Vietnam War was fought between the two halves of a divided country. From 1954 until 1975 communist North Vietnam fought against the US-backed South Vietnamese to unite the whole country.

During the 19th and early 20th centuries, Vietnam was part of France's empire in Indo-China. In 1946 communist leader Ho Chi Minh and his Vietminh forces declared war on the French. In 1954 Vietnam was divided into North Vietnam with Ho Chi Minh as president, and non-communist South Vietnam supported by the USA. Ho Chi Minh was determined to reunite the two. The North Vietnamese backed the South Vietnamese communists, the Vietcong, who were fighting their government and the Americans.

At war with America

The Americans believed in the 'domino theory' which said that if one country fell to the communists, the one next door would fall, then the one next to that, and so on. To stop this happening, the Americans decided to resist communists everywhere. In 1965 the US began to bomb North Vietnam. By the summer of 1967 there were 2 million US soldiers involved in the war.

The Americans were not trained to fight in the jungles and swamps of Vietnam, where their tanks and heavy artillery were useless. They tried massive air raids on North Vietnam and on neighbouring countries. Civilian targets were also attacked. Huge areas of the jungle were destroyed with fire bombs and chemical weapons. But nothing stopped the Vietcong advance.

By 1968 the Americans realized they could not win, and in the following year peace talks began. By 1973, when a cease-fire was agreed, all American forces had been withdrawn. The cease-fire broke down in 1974 and a year later South Vietnam fell to the communists and the country was reunited.

► This Vietnamese woman and her child were hit by a US grenade thrown into a bunker.

find out more
Cold War
Twentieth-century history
United States of America

Vikings

In the Middle Ages the word Viking meant a robber who came by sea. Today we use Viking as the name of Norse peoples who lived in the Scandinavian countries of Norway, Denmark and Sweden.

In their own countries the Vikings were farmers. In the 8th century AD they began to look for more land. They made raids across the seas and settled in other countries. They were great traders, too, reaching as far east as Constantinople (Istanbul) and westwards across the Atlantic to Newfoundland.

Everyday life

Most Vikings were farmers and they built the same sort of farmhouse wherever they settled. The most important part was the great hall. In earlier times this was where the family lived, ate and slept. Later the hall was divided into eating and sleeping rooms. Houses were often smoky inside because cooking was done over an open fire in the middle of the room.

Viking farmers grew all sorts of crops to eat, such as wheat, oats, barley and vegetables like cabbages, beans and carrots. They kept cattle, sheep, pigs and chickens, but they also hunted animals, birds and fish. Some of this food would be smoked in the roof of the hall, or dried or salted to eat during the winter.

Viking men and women liked bright clothes and decoration and jewellery. Women often wore headscarves, an ankle-length dress of wool or linen, with an overdress held on by great brooches. They might also wear necklaces, bracelets and rings. Men wore woollen trousers with a tunic on top.

Traders and raiders

The Vikings were famous for the goods they made themselves and for their trade with far-off countries. They traded as far north as Iceland and with the Lapps (for ivory and furs), as far south as Baghdad (for silk and spices) and into Russia (for slaves and furs). ◗

• Vikings settled in many lands, including Iceland, Greenland and parts of England, Scotland and Ireland. The Normans of north-west France were originally 'Northmen' (Vikings).

▼ Archaeologists have found many Viking remains in York (called Jorvik by the Vikings). This is a leather boot on a skate made of animal bone.

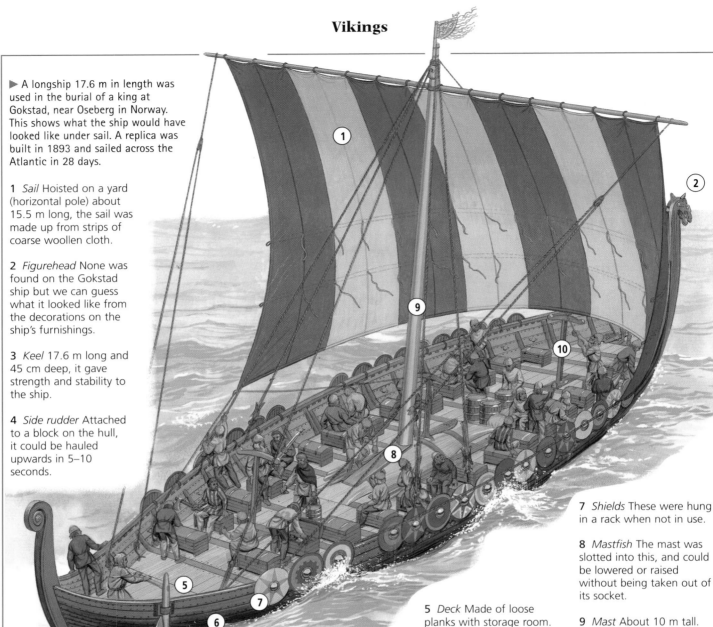

▶ A longship 17.6 m in length was used in the burial of a king at Gokstad, near Oseberg in Norway. This shows what the ship would have looked like under sail. A replica was built in 1893 and sailed across the Atlantic in 28 days.

1 *Sail* Hoisted on a yard (horizontal pole) about 15.5 m long, the sail was made up from strips of coarse woollen cloth.

2 *Figurehead* None was found on the Gokstad ship but we can guess what it looked like from the decorations on the ship's furnishings.

3 *Keel* 17.6 m long and 45 cm deep, it gave strength and stability to the ship.

4 *Side rudder* Attached to a block on the hull, it could be hauled upwards in 5–10 seconds.

5 *Deck* Made of loose planks with storage room.

6 *Hull* 16 rows of over-lapping planks reinforced with cross-beams.

7 *Shields* These were hung in a rack when not in use.

8 *Mastfish* The mast was slotted into this, and could be lowered or raised without being taken out of its socket.

9 *Mast* About 10 m tall.

10 *Crutches* These carried the yard and mast when the ship was being rowed.

In towns, craftspeople made a variety of products; for example, pots and pans for the kitchen, clothes and jewellery, tools and weapons of bronze and iron. They exchanged goods but they also minted their own coins.

However, the Vikings are probably best known as fierce raiders of other peoples' lands. They first invaded Britain in AD 793. Raiders were looking for rich plunder, but also for slaves. Slaves, called *thralls*, worked on the farms for freemen, who were called *karls*. More important than freemen were the rich landowners, who were also chieftains. They were called *jarls*. Warriors on raiding parties were heavily armed with swords, shields, spears and axes. They wore helmets and chain mail.

Viking ships

The key to the success of the Vikings in trading and raiding was the ship. The Vikings built fast, strong ships that could withstand even an Atlantic crossing. In about AD 1000 the Viking explorer Leif Ericsson went all the way to Newfoundland in North America.

The Vikings built not only 'longships' for raiding (one of which held 200 fighting men), but also wider, deeper ships called *knarrs* for trade, and little rowing boats called *faerings*. Ships had both oars and sails.

• Norse myths are stories about the gods and heroes of the Norse people. The Vikings worshipped many gods including: Bragi, the god of poetry; Frigg/Freya, one of the twin gods of love; Loki, god of fire; Odin, king of the gods; Thor, the storm-god.

find out more
Anglo-Saxons
Archaeology

Wales

Wales first appeared in recorded history when the Romans attacked it in the 1st century AD. The people living there were Celts. The Romans conquered all but the mountainous heart of the country and introduced the Christian religion. The next wave of invaders, the Anglo Saxons, also failed to master Wales. So did the Normans.

The country was finally conquered after the death of the Welsh prince Llywelyn ap Gruffudd in 1282. The new ruler, England's Edward I, built massive castles to keep the Welsh under control. Sometimes they rebelled and were penalized by harsh laws and heavy taxes.

In 1536 Wales was divided into counties and its government united with England's. The Welsh language was banned for all official business, but it did not die out.

The Welsh people eagerly accepted the Protestant religion. They did not take kindly to the Church of England, and in the 18th and 19th centuries thousands of non-conformist chapels (which refused to conform to certain

Church practices) sprang up. Meanwhile, in the south a huge coalmining industry developed.

In the early 20th century demand for coal, steel and slate dropped and times were hard. But in the late 20th century new businesses from Japan and other foreign countries moved into Wales, and in 1997 the country voted for an assembly to discuss its own affairs.

▲ Caernarfan Castle is one of the mighty fortresses built by Edward I of England.

find out more
Celts
Henry VIII
Romans

Washington, George

George Washington was the first president of the USA, a post he held from 1789 to 1797. Before becoming president, he led the Americans against the British in the American Revolution.

At the time of George Washington's birth, America was divided into colonies. Some were ruled by Britain and some by France, but both countries wanted to be in control. Washington was born in Virginia, which was a British colony, and when he was 21 he joined the British army to fight against the French. His success as a leader made him well known in Virginia, and by the

time he left the army he had become a colonel.

Washington settled down to be a farmer on his Virginia estate. However, like many others, he believed that people in the American colonies should be able to govern themselves rather than be ruled by the British. The only way for this to happen was to fight for freedom. In 1775 he was made commander-in-chief of the American colonists' army. His job was to recruit men and train them to be soldiers. The American Revolution (War of Independence) began soon after. Washington's grit and perseverance kept his forces going. The British were finally defeated in 1783 and the United States of America was formed.

After the war, Washington went back to Virginia. Although he was a national hero, he did not want public office. Nevertheless, in 1789 he was unanimously elected as the first president of the USA and he dutifully accepted the job. He was re-elected in 1792 but refused to serve for a third term.

Born 1732 in Virginia, USA
Died 1799 aged 67

• The USA's capital city was named in George Washington's honour.

◄ After he died, it was said of Washington that he was 'first in war, first in peace, and first in the hearts of his countrymen'.

find out more
American Revolution
United States of America

Weapons

Since the earliest times, people have used weapons to defend themselves and their homes from attack by their enemies. Prehistoric people used simple weapons, such as sticks, stones and axes. Following the discovery of gunpowder, more powerful cannons and smaller firearms were developed. Modern weapons are very powerful and complicated, and some can kill many people at a time. The largest rockets can carry nuclear bombs to hit targets thousands of kilometres away.

Prehistoric people learned to use sticks and stones as weapons, then pointed sticks as spears and sharpened stones as knives and axes. When metal-working developed, bronze daggers replaced flint ones. Swords were made of bronze and, later, iron.

Bows were used as much as 20,000 years ago to fire arrows further and more accurately than a man could throw a spear. By the 10th century the Turks were making bows made from wood and animal bones. The crossbow was used across much of Europe during the 1100s. Later, the longbow was developed and was an important weapon in battles fought between the English and the French during the Hundred Years' War.

▲ The longbow had a range of 180 metres.

The first firearms

Before the discovery of gunpowder, weapons could only cut or hit. Now weapons could be developed which used the explosive power of gunpowder to fire a bullet or a shell. Firearms such as guns and cannons, and later bombs, started to appear.

Guns were developed in Europe in the 14th century, but the early ones were inaccurate, took several minutes to load, and could sometimes blow up in your face. In the 16th century they greatly improved with the development of the musket, which fired bullets that could penetrate a soldier's armour. In the 19th century a new development, the rifled barrel, made bullets spin in flight, so they could travel further, and in a straighter line. These new rifles could hit targets over 1000 metres away.

Cannons work in much the same way as guns but they fire bigger missiles over much longer distances. They were first used for attacking castles and fortified towns in the early 14th

▲ Musketeers fired their muskets from a rest stuck in the ground.

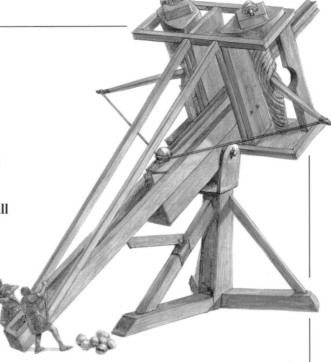

▲ A catapult used by Roman soldiers to throw huge rocks at enemy castles.

century. By the late 15th century no defences could withstand a cannon assault. During the course of 200 years they changed the face of warfare, and after their appearance most wars were decided on the battlefield. Field guns, which came after the heavy unwieldy cannons, were lighter and easier to transport. By the 18th century no army was complete without a battery of two-wheeled field guns. The basic design of the cannon remained unchanged until the 19th century, when breech-loading guns appeared. These were loaded at the rear, and fired shells that exploded on impact.

Weapons in the 20th century

Modern weapons have changed a lot from the early ones, although the guns carried by soldiers today are similar to those used in World War I. Aeroplanes, tanks and submarines were first used in World War I, and became even more important in World War II. Tanks could quickly push deep into enemy territory, supported by aeroplanes dropping bombs and firing guns. Aeroplanes could also sink the biggest battleships, and submarines fired torpedoes to sink the enemy's ships. By the end of World War II the invention of the long-range rocket and the nuclear bomb changed the face of warfare. Computers, radar and lasers are now used in many weapons to help them hit small targets with great accuracy.

Wellington, Duke of *see* Georgian Britain

Witches

Witches in stories have pointed hats and black cats, and ride broomsticks through the sky. They chant magic spells. They are wicked, frightening women, until the hero or heroine tricks them and escapes.

If you had lived 400 years ago, you would not have laughed at stories of witches. Almost everyone believed that some women were the servants of the Devil.

If a child or an animal became ill, people sometimes thought that it had been cursed. They looked around for the guilty person – a witch. It was usually poor, old women who were accused of being witches.

One way of testing a witch was to tie her up and throw her into water. People thought that water rejected evil and that only the guilty would float. So the innocent drowned, and those who floated were killed. In most of Europe witches were burnt; in England they were hanged.

During the 17th century, witch-hunting became a mania. In parts of Germany there were a hundred burnings a year. In England over 200 women were hanged in just two years.

As scientific knowledge grew, belief in witchcraft faded, and there were few trials after 1700. In Salem, in Massachusetts in the USA, 30 people were executed for witchcraft in 1692. Only five years later, the judge and jury publicly admitted their mistake.

• A female witch is called a witch or a sorceress. A male witch is called a wizard, sorcerer or warlock.

• A witch who does good, like healing sick people, is often called a white witch.

◀ This German woodcut of 1555 shows three women accused of practising as witches being burned at the stake. They are condemned to suffer burning in death and in the afterlife (shown to the right). A demon is clutching one of them as she burns.

Women's movement

For many centuries there have been people who want women to have the same rights as men. While different women's groups may campaign for different things, the movement as a whole is often called the women's movement.

From about 1850 there were campaigns in both the USA and Britain for married women to be able to own their own property, instead of everything belonging to the husband when they married. Women also campaigned for 'suffrage' or the right to vote. In Britain, many women became suffragettes to force a change in the law. By the end of the 1920s, the right to vote had been won by women in many countries.

After this, women's organizations campaigned for such things as childcare to enable them to work. In the 1960s, the women's liberation movement started in the USA. Feminists began to work for equal pay, equal education and equal opportunities.

In the 1990s women's groups are an accepted part of society. In business, sport, music, trade unions and many other areas, there are women's organizations which meet regularly and give positive advice and support to each other.

◀ Emmeline Pankhurst, suffragette leader, being arrested for an attack on Buckingham Palace, May 1914. The suffragettes, led by Emmeline and her daughter Christabel, became known for their dramatic publicity stunts. They burned empty buildings, smashed windows and chained themselves to railings.

Writing for women's equality
A Vindication of the Rights of Women, Mary Wollstonecraft (1792)
The Second Sex, Simone de Beauvoir (1949)
The Feminine Mystique, Betty Friedan (1963)
Sexual Politics Kate Millet (1969)
The Female Eunuch Germaine Greer (1970)
Women and Sex Nawal El Saadawi (1972)
The Beauty Myth Naomi Wolf (1992)

find out more
Peace movement

World War I

World War I was known at the time as the Great War. It started in August 1914 and ended in November 1918. For four years it was the biggest and most terrible conflict between nations that the world had ever seen.

▲ British troops going 'over the top' during the Battle of the Somme (1916) on the Western Front. Trenches provided some protection from enemy gunfire and were difficult to capture, but they were terrible places to live. They were often cramped, waterlogged and rat-infested. In battle soldiers ran across open ground ('no man's land') towards men firing rifles and machine-guns.

• Sea battles did not play an important part in World War I, as neither side wanted to risk serious damage to its fleet. The only major (but indecisive) sea battle was at Jutland in the North Sea in May 1916. The most effective sea warfare was the German submarine, or 'U-boat', campaign against ships used by Britain to import food and goods.

The countries of Europe had been arguing for some time, jealous of each other's power. Conflict was almost inevitable. Then, on 28 June 1914, Archduke Ferdinand of Austria was killed by a Serb in the Bosnian capital, Sarajevo. Austria threatened Serbia, and by August Europe was at war.

The Western and Eastern Fronts

The Germans marched through Belgium, hoping to take France by surprise. The plan was to knock France out quickly and then turn to deal with Russia. The British and French stopped them. Where the two sides met, a 'front' developed which stretched from the English Channel to the Swiss border. Long trench battles were fought, and millions were killed and injured.

The same thing happened in the east, where the Austrian and German armies faced the Russians. The hardships caused by the war added to Russian discontent. This anger led to the Russian Revolution in 1917, after which the Russians left the war.

A world at war

In 1916 in the southern Alps the Germans and Austrians faced the Italian army, while at the Gallipoli peninsula in north-west Turkey British troops, with others from Australia and New Zealand (Anzacs), fought the Turks (the Ottoman empire was allied with Germany and Austria). Other troops came from countries of the British and French empires to fight in France on the Western Front. In Africa, British, French and African troops occupied the German colonies.

In the Far East, Japan declared war on Germany and occupied the Qingdao peninsula, which Germany held, and German island colonies in the Pacific.

In the Middle East, Britain encouraged the Arabs to revolt against their Turkish rulers. In 1917 an Anglo-Indian army entered Baghdad, the capital of Iraq. At the same time troops from Egypt, with Arab supporters (led by T. E. Lawrence – 'Lawrence of Arabia'), advanced into Palestine and occupied Jerusalem.

The end

In April 1917 the USA declared war on Germany. American weapons and reinforcements for the Western Front arrived from the USA. This was crucial in the final victory. In 1918 an armistice (end to the fighting) was called for at 11 a.m. on 11 November. Over 7 million people had died in the war.

find out more

Austrian empire
Britain since 1900
France
Germany
Italy
Ottoman empire
Russia
Twentieth-century history
United States of America
Weapons
World War II

▶ Britain and France's allies included Russia, USA, Romania, Belgium, Italy, Serbia, Japan and Portugal. On the other side were Germany, Austria-Hungary, Bulgaria and Turkey (the Ottoman empire).

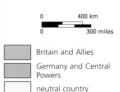

Britain and Allies

Germany and Central Powers

neutral country

World War II

When the Nazi leader Adolf Hitler came to power, he gained popularity by saying that Germany should reclaim the land it had lost in World War I, and take over nearby lands where there were German-speaking people. It was this German expansion into neighbouring countries that eventually led to war.

Allies and neutral countries

German conquests and allies

Japanese conquests and allies

—— limit of Japanese conquests

▲ ▶ The countries allied to Germany were Bulgaria, Finland, Hungary, Italy, Japan, Romania and Thailand. The Allies were Australia, Belgium, countries in the British empire, Canada, China, Czechoslovakia, Denmark, France, Greece, the Netherlands, New Zealand, Norway, Poland, South Africa, USA, USSR and also countries in South America and the Middle East.

▶ The USA entered the war in December 1941, after the Japanese attack on Pearl Harbor. They gradually took island after island back from the Japanese in the Pacific. Here they are invading the island of Okinawa, about 500 km from Japan, in 1945.

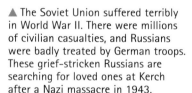

Germany began its expansion in 1936 by reoccupying the Rhineland. Then in 1938 German soldiers marched into Austria, which was made part of Germany. In 1939 Czechoslovakia fell. Britain and France allowed these things to happen without much protest

because they hoped that when Germany regained its 1918 position, it would stop threatening other countries.

War breaks out

In August 1939, the German Nazi government made an agreement with the Soviet Union so that if war came, the Germans would not have to fight Russia on their eastern front. In September 1939, German troops marched into Poland, as did others from the Soviet Union. The Germans used a tactic called 'Blitzkrieg', or 'lightning war': troops and tanks moved quickly, backed up by very effective dive-bombing. This time, Britain and France declared war.

▲ The Soviet Union suffered terribly in World War II. There were millions of civilian casualties, and Russians were badly treated by German troops. These grief-stricken Russians are searching for loved ones at Kerch after a Nazi massacre in 1943.

In spring 1940 the German army invaded Norway, Denmark, France, Belgium and the Netherlands, and the British army had to retreat in ships and small boats from the French port of Dunkirk. Germany was soon in control of most of Europe, and Britain stood alone, in danger of invasion.

USSR: the great patriotic war

In April 1941 German forces occupied Yugoslavia and Greece. Then, in June 1941, with western Europe under Nazi rule, the Germans invaded the Soviet Union, breaking the agreement made in 1939. German troops drove deep into Russia and besieged Leningrad (St Petersburg) and Stalingrad (Volgograd). The Russian losses were enormous.

The Germans had expected a quick victory, but the Russians resisted with determination. They were helped by the Russian winter, which killed

◀ Allied commandos landing on 6 June 1944 (D-Day) on a beach in Normandy, northern France. British and Canadian troops landed on the eastern beaches and Americans landed to the west.

many German soldiers. In January 1943 the Germans were defeated at Stalingrad and over 90,000 German soldiers were taken prisoner. This was the beginning of the end for the Nazis, although two years of war were still to come.

Global war

World War II was a truly global war. Japan allied itself with Germany and overran several British and French colonies in the Far East. In December 1941 a Japanese air raid destroyed US ships at Pearl Harbor Naval Base in Hawaii, in the Pacific Ocean. After this attack, the USA entered the war on the side of Britain and the USSR.

Fighting went on across the Far East, the Pacific, the Atlantic Ocean, the Middle East and North Africa. American, Soviet, British and Commonwealth forces, together with 'Free' forces from France and other countries in German hands, fought against Germany, Italy and Japan in the conflict.

Land, sea and air

The main land weapon was the tank. Commanders tried to get their armies into positions where the tanks could be given freedom to travel across the countryside against the enemy. Great tank battles were fought, especially in Russia and the deserts of North Africa. There were also heavy guns, and infantrymen marching on foot with rifles and bayonets.

By 1939 the big battleship was already becoming old-fashioned, because it was too easily attacked from the air. Aircraft-carriers and submarines became the most important fighting ships. Submarines ranged far from home, attacking cargo ships and warships. The Germans had a large and very effective fleet of submarines or 'U-boats'.

Commanders tried to get air supremacy – a situation in which their aircraft could roam the skies attacking targets at will. The 'Battle of Britain' was a battle for the skies over southern Britain in 1940. Had the British Royal Air Force lost, a German invasion would have been possible.

Victory

Once the Soviet Union and the USA were in the war, the defeat of Germany, Italy and Japan was only a matter of time. From early 1943, the Soviet Red Army rolled the Germans back towards their border and then pressed on to Berlin. In 1942 American forces began to recapture the Pacific islands taken by the Japanese. In November 1942 the British defeated the Germans and Italians at El Alamein in North Africa, and in 1943 Allied troops crossed the Mediterranean to invade Italy itself. Then in June 1944 came the long-awaited 'Second Front': the invasion of northern France by British and American troops on 'D-Day'.

Now Germany was under pressure from east, west and south. Gradually its troops were pushed back as far as Berlin, and Germany surrendered in May 1945. The Japanese surrendered in August after American planes dropped atomic bombs on the cities of Hiroshima and Nagasaki.

• As the great armies battled to and fro, millions of people were forced from their homes and took to the roads with their possessions. Many never succeeded in returning home, and many children lost contact with their families.

find out more ▶
Britain since 1900
Churchill, Winston
Cold War
Fascism
France
Germany
Hitler, Adolf
Holocaust
Italy
Japan
Roosevelt, Franklin D.
Russia
Stalin, Joseph
United States of
  America
Weapons
World War I

◀ Devastation in the city of Hiroshima in August 1945. Within one minute 80,000 people died. Around 70,000 more people were injured, of whom about 60,000 died within a year. The city was rebuilt, but there is a Peace Memorial Park on the site where the bomb exploded to remind the world of the true horror of war.

Writing

Before writing was developed, many early people kept 'oral' records of their history or beliefs. Some people would learn the record by heart (perhaps in a long poem) and recite it to others in their society.

One of the earliest forms of writing was the *pictogram*, in which pictures of objects, such as a circle for the Sun, represented the object themselves. Another early form is the *ideogram*, in which the whole idea of the word is explained in a shape rather like a picture. The Chinese and Japanese writing systems use ideograms instead of an alphabet.

The earliest true writing was developed by the Sumerians in the land of Mesopotamia (now Iraq). The oldest examples date from about 3250 BC. The Sumerians used wedge-shaped signs on clay tablets to develop a type of writing known as *cuneiform*. Cuneiform was used for about 3000 years.

Hieroglyphics

Hieroglyphics are a form of writing which uses pictures and symbols instead of words. The ancient Egyptians developed hieroglyphics around 3100 BC and invented a sort of paper called papyrus, made from crushed reeds. The Egyptians used hieroglyphics for 3500 years, but other peoples have used them as well.

The Mayan people of Central America also used hieroglyphs for writing. They are preserved on a type of document, called a codex, made of folded strips of deerskin or tree-bark. The Spanish destroyed most of the codices when they conquered the Maya in the 16th century.

Alphabets

Most languages today are written using an alphabet. The first true alphabet was probably developed in the 15th century BC by the Canaanite people of Syria. It had 32 letters.

The Phoenicians reduced the Canaanite alphabet to 22 letters and spread it through the Mediterranean. It is from this alphabet that the Greek, Roman, Arabic and Hebrew alphabets developed.

English is written in the same alphabet as Latin, the Roman language. The ancient Roman alphabet had 23 letters. After the collapse of the Roman empire the Latin language survived in changed forms in many countries in Europe. In most European countries people still use the Roman alphabet to read and write their language. It is the most widely used alphabet in the world today.

horse

to stand upright

▲ Chinese ideograms. The earliest forms were simple but recognizable drawings. Over the centuries they changed into stylized shapes that are easy to write.

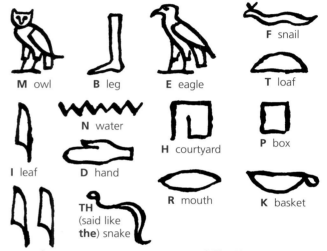

M owl **B** leg **E** eagle **F** snail

I leaf **N** water **D** hand **H** courtyard **P** box **T** loaf

Y two leaves **TH** (said like **the**) snake **R** mouth **K** basket

▲ The hieroglyphs represent particular sounds. To make a word the Egyptians used these signs and some of the other 700 pictures.

The Cyrillic alphabet has 32 letters and is used in Russia, and some countries of the former Soviet Union.

А Б В Г Д Е Ё Ж З И Й К Л М Н О П Р С Т У Ф Х Ц Ч Ш Щ Ъ Ы Ь Э Ю Я

а б в г д е ё ж з и й к л м н о п р с т у ф х ц ч ш щ ъ ы ь э ю я

The Devangari alphabet has 46 letters. It is the main alphabet of northern India.

ऋ ऋ इ ई उ ऊ ऋ ए ऐ ओ औ अं ऋः क ख ग च ङ च छ ज झ ञ

ट ठ ड ढ ण त थ द ध न प फ ब भ म य र ल व श ष स ह

The Arabic alphabet has 28 letters and is used by people all over the Arab world.

ا ب ت ث ج ح خ د ذ ر ز س ش ص

ض ط ظ ع غ ف ق ك ل م ن و هـ ي

◄ The Cyrillic, Devanagari and Arabic alphabets are three of approximately 50 different alphabets used today. The letters in each alphabet are shaped differently. Most alphabets have between 20 and 30 letters. The Arabic alphabet is written from right to left.

find out more
Ancient world
Communication
Egyptians, ancient

Timeline of world history

	Before 10,000 BC	10,000 BC	5000 BC	3000 BC	2000 BC
Asia	· Hunter-gatherers · A variety of stone tools used – knives, axes, needles, harpoons	· Rice and millet farming begins and spreads · Pottery made in Japan and China	· Horses domesticated on steppes (grasslands) · Cities in China · Decorated pottery made in Japan · Jade worked in China	· Silk weaving in China · Cities of Harappa and Mohenjo-daro in Indus valley · Cotton grown in Indus valley	· Aryans invade northern India · Beginnings of Hindu religion ▲ The Hindu god Shiva
Americas and Oceania	· Hunter-gatherers · Cave drawings in Australia from about 40,000 BC	· Hunter-gatherers · Canoes and sledges used	· Maize (corn) cultivated in Mexico · Pottery first made in South America · Llamas domesticated in Andes · Root crops cultivated in New Guinea	◀ A sailing canoe · Temples and monuments built in Peru, and cotton cultivated · Colonization of Pacific islands by canoe begins	· Metalworking and cotton weaving in Peru · Colonists reach Samoa in the central Pacific
Africa and Middle East	· First humans · From about 100,000 BC people spread through all continents · Cave drawings in south-west Africa from about 27,000 BC · Female figurines made · Bow invented	· Cereals farmed from about 9000 BC · Grain ground with hand mills · Wheel invented · Dogs, cattle, sheep and goats domesticated · Woven textiles · Copper used about 6000 BC	· Plough invented · Horses and camels domesticated · Sails used on River Nile · Bronze made · Writing invented · Wheeled vehicles made · Pottery made in East Africa	▶ The Great Pyramid at Giza, built 2600 BC · Pyramids built in Egypt · Sumerian civilization · Stone cities in Middle East · Troy founded	· New kingdom in Egypt · Hittites establish empire · Beginnings of Jewish religion
Europe	· Hunter-gatherers · Cave paintings from 30,000 BC · Female figurines made · Bow invented	· Farming in Balkans and Greece from 7000 BC · Canoes and sledges used · Animals domesticated and herded	· Standing stones and circles built · Flint mines worked · Farming spreads · Ploughs drawn by animals	· Bronze objects made · Sailing boats in Aegean · Megalithic ('large stone') tombs built	◀ Golden burial mask from Mycenae ('Mask of Agamemnon') · Minoan civilization in Crete · Mycenaean civilization in Greece

Timeline of world history

1000 BC	750 BC	500 BC	250 BC	AD 1	AD 249
· Zhou dynasty in China · Taoism founded in China · The epic poem, the *Mahabharata*, composed in India	· Iron working in China · Confucius (Kongzi) and Buddha lived ◀ Statue of Buddha	· Mauryan empire in India · Alexander the Great invades India	▶ Terracotta horse from the tomb of the Chinese 'First Emperor' · Great Wall of China built · Qin dynasty unites China · Great Silk Road across Asia opens	· Han dynasty in China · Buddhism reaches China and South-east Asia · Paper invented in China · Emperors in Japan	
· Settlements in Polynesia · Chavin culture in Peru · Pottery made in North American Arctic	· Olmec civilization in Mexico	· Olmec civilization ends	· City of Teotihuacán founded in Mexico ◀ A Mayan hieroglyph · Early Maya culture in Central America · Hieroglyphic writing develops in Mexico	· Large states in Central America · Large temples built in Peru	
· Kingdom of Kush in East Africa · Assyrian empire · Kingdom of Israel	· First coins in Lydia, Turkey · Persian empire established · Zoroastrian religion develops in Persia · Assyrians conquer Israel	· Nok culture in Nigeria · Persian empire conquered by Alexander the Great · Alexandrian Library founded	· Romans destroy Carthage, and conquer Syria, Palestine and Egypt · Birth of Jesus	· Jews expelled from Jerusalem · Beginnings of Christianity · Kingdom of Axum, Ethiopia	
· Celts move into Germany and France · Etruscans settle in northern Italy	· Greek alphabet develops · Greek city states · Roman republic founded · Hillforts in western Europe	· Great age of Athens · Alexander the Great conquers Greece · Romans conquer Etruscans, rule all Italy, and conquer Spain	· Growth of Roman empire · Julius Caesar conquers Gaul · Augustus first Roman emperor	◀ Colosseum, Rome, completed AD 80 · Roman empire reaches greatest extent · Christianity spreads	

121

Timeline of world history

	AD 250	500	750	1000	1250
Asia	• Gupta empire in India • Horse-collar harness first used	• Large Chinese empire under Tang dynasty	• Beginning of Fujiwara period in Japan • Tang dynasty in China • Chinese invent gunpowder • Printing invented in China	• Genghis Khan creates Mongol empire • Mongol Golden Horde conquers Russia • Muslim conquests in northern India • Khmer kingdom in South-east Asia	• Yuan (Mongol) and Ming dynasties in China • Conquests of Tamerlane • Russia defeats Mongols • Growth of Vietnam state • Portuguese reach India via southern Africa
Americas and Oceania	• Maya civilization in Central America growing • Nazca civilization in southern Peru	• Maya civilization at its height	• Toltec civilization in Mexico	• Vikings sail to North America • Polynesians settle Hawaii, New Zealand and Easter Island • Growth of Inca empire, Peru	◄ A Khmer temple, Angkor, Cambodia • Aztec and Inca empires at their height • Columbus reaches America
Africa and Middle East	▶ Madonna and child from a Byzantine icon • Byzantine empire succeeds Roman empire in east	▶ Islamic mosque, Persia • Muhammad founds Islam • Sassanid (Persian) empire at its height • Arab conquests in northern Africa	• Abbasid caliphate rules from Baghdad • Empire of Ghana, West Africa • Cairo founded by Fatimids • Great Zimbabwe founded, East Africa	• Christian crusaders invade Middle East • Saladin defeats crusaders • Turks conquer Palestine	• Mongols destroy Abbasid caliphate, Baghdad • Empires of Benin and Mali powerful in West Africa • Black Death ▶ Bronze cast from Benin
Europe	• Collapse of Roman empire in west • Spread of Christianity continues • Frankish kingdom founded	• Gregory the Great establishes the power of the pope • Muslims conquer Spain	▶ A Viking longboat • Viking raids and settlement • Empire of Charlemagne • England united • Beginning of Holy Roman Empire	• Break between Roman and Greek (Byzantine) Churches • Normans conquer England and Sicily	• 100 Years War between England and France • Ottoman Turks capture Constantinople • Black Death • Fall of last Muslim state in Spain • Printed books made • Beginning of Renaissance

Timeline of world history

1500	1600	1700	1800	1900 2000
· Babur founds Mughal empire · Beginning of Sikh religion in Punjab, India	· Qing (Manzhou) dynasty in China · Tokugawa shoguns (governors) in Japan · Taj Mahal built in India · European trading forts established · Russian expansion reaches the Pacific	· Qing dynasty continues · Decline of Mughal empire · British defeat French and control much of India	· Europeans dominate trade in Asia · Opium Wars in China · Taiping rebellion in China · Indians rebel against British · Japan begins to modernize	· China becomes a republic, then a communist state · Rise and fall of Japanese empire · India and other countries gain independence · Vietnam War
· Spanish conquer Aztec and Inca empires, and establish colonies in Caribbean · Fleet led by Ferdinand Magellan finds a route round the Americas and sails round the world	· Europeans found colonies in North America · Slavery grows	· British defeat French in Canada ▲ The first US flag, 1776 · USA gains independence · First European settlers in Australia	· Spanish and Portuguese colonies gain independence · USA expands through Louisiana Purchase and Mexican War · American Civil War · European settlement of Australia and New Zealand	· USA becomes leading world power · Civil rights movement grows · *Apollo 11* puts first astronauts on Moon · Technological revolution in industry, transport and communications
· Ottoman (Turkish) empire at its height under Suleiman the Magnificent · Atlantic slave trade begins	· Slave trade expands · Dutch settlers in South Africa ◄ The Globe Theatre, London, where Shakespeare's plays were performed	· Atlantic slave trade continues to grow · Ottoman power declining · Ashante kingdom in West Africa	· Africa divided into European colonies · Atlantic slave trade ended · Suez Canal opened ▼ Stephenson's 'Rocket', an early steam locomotive	▲ A communications satellite · Turkey becomes a republic · African and Arab states gain independence · State of Israel founded · South Africa adopts and later abandons apartheid
· Reformation (split between Catholics and Protestants) · Ottomans invade central Europe · Wars of Religion · Shakespeare's first plays	· Netherlands gain independence · Thirty Years War · France replaces Spain as greatest power · Civil wars in Britain · Isaac Newton explains law of gravity	· England and Scotland united · Russia dominant in northern Europe · Rise of Prussia · French Revolution · Big advances in farming · Start of Industrial Revolution	· Napoleonic wars · Industrial Revolution continues · Italy united · Germany united · Growth of railways · Rise of socialism	· Einstein's theory of relativity · World Wars I and II · Russian Revolution · Ireland gains independence · Eastern Europe under Soviet communist control · European Union founded

British royal family

▼ Elizabeth II became queen after her father's death in 1952. She is one of the longest-serving monarchs of the United Kingdom. As queen, she is the head of state and undertakes more than 400 public engagements a year, many of them abroad. In her free time she loves country life and being around dogs and horses.

▼ Charles, Prince of Wales (centre), is the heir to the throne. He works for many charities and travels widely as a representative of the crown. He is particularly interested in architecture and in the environment. In 1981 he married Lady Diana Spencer, who became Princess of Wales. The couple had two sons: William (left) and Harry (right).

▼ Diana, Princess of Wales, was born in 1961. She was the daughter of Earl Spencer. Diana worked actively for many charities, especially those connected with children, and was immensely popular. Diana and Charles separated in 1992 and later divorced. On 31 August 1997 Diana was killed in a car crash in Paris, France. She was only 36.

Victoria (1819–1901)
married Albert of Saxe-Coburg-Gotha

Edward VII (1841–1910)
married Alexandra of Denmark

3 brothers and 5 sisters

George V (1865–1936)
married Mary of Teck

2 brothers and 3 sisters

Edward VIII (1894–1972)
married Wallis Simpson

George VI (1895–1952)
married Lady Elizabeth Bowes-Lyon (*Queen Mother*)

3 brothers and 1 sister

Elizabeth II (1926–)
married Philip, *Duke of Edinburgh*

1 sister

Charles, *Prince of Wales* (1948–)
married Lady Diana Spencer

Anne, *Princess Royal* (1950–)
married (1) Mark Phillips
(2) Timothy Laurence

Andrew, *Duke of York* (1960–)
married Sarah Ferguson

Edward (1964–)

William (1982–)

Henry (Harry) (1984–)

Peter (1977–)

Zara (1981–)

Beatrice (1988–)

Eugenie (1990–)

Rulers of England and of the United Kingdom (with the dates they reigned)

Saxon kings	
Alfred	871–899
Edward the Elder	899–925
Athelstan	925–939
Edmund	939–946
Eadred	946–955
Eadwig	955–959
Edgar	959–975
Edward the Martyr	975–978
Ethelred the Unready	978–1016
Edmund Ironside	1016
Danish (Viking) kings	
Canute (Cnut)	1016–1035
Harold I (Harefoot)	1035–1040
Hardicanute (Harthacnut)	1040–1042
Saxon kings	
Edward the Confessor	1042–1066
Harold II (Godwinson)	1066
House of Normandy	
William I (the Conqueror)	1066–1087
William II	1087–1100
Henry I	1100–1135
Stephen and Matilda	1135–1154
House of Plantagenet	
Henry II	1154–1189
Richard I	1189–1199
John	1199–1216
Henry III	1216–1272
Edward I	1272–1307
Edward II	1307–1327
Edward III	1327–1377
Richard II	1377–1399
House of Lancaster	
Henry IV	1399–1413
Henry V	1413–1422
Henry VI	1422–1461
House of York	
Edward IV	1461–1483
Edward V	1483
Richard III	1483–1485
House of Tudor	
Henry VII	1485–1509
Henry VIII	1509–1547
Edward VI	1547–1553
Mary I	1553–1558
Elizabeth I	1558–1603
House of Stuart	
James I of England and VI of Scotland	1603–1625
Charles I	1625–1649
Commonwealth (declared 1649)	
Oliver Cromwell, Lord Protector	1653–1658
Richard Cromwell	1658–1659
House of Stuart	
Charles II	1660–1685
James II	1685–1688
William III and Mary II	1689–1702
(Mary died 1694)	
Anne	1702–1714
House of Hanover	
George I	1714–1727
George II	1727–1760
George III	1760–1820
George IV	1820–1830
William IV	1830–1837
Victoria	1837–1901
House of Saxe-Coburg-Gotha	
Edward VII	1901–1910
House of Windsor	
George V	1910–1936
Edward VIII	1936
George VI	1936–1952
Elizabeth II	1952–

Prime ministers and presidents

Prime ministers of Great Britain and of the United Kingdom

(1721)–1742	Sir Robert Walpole	*Whig*
1742–1743	Earl of Wilmington	*Whig*
1743–1754	Henry Pelham	*Whig*
1754–1756	Duke of Newcastle	*Whig*
1756–1757	Duke of Devonshire	*Whig*
1757–1762	Duke of Newcastle	*Whig*
1762–1763	Earl of Bute	*Tory*
1763–1765	George Grenville	*Whig*
1765–1766	Marquis of Rockingham	*Whig*
1766–1768	William Pitt (the Elder)	*Whig*
1768–1770	Duke of Grafton	*Whig*
1770–1782	Lord North	*Tory*
1782	Marquis of Rockingham	*Whig*
1782–1783	Earl of Shelburne	*Whig*
1783	Duke of Portland	*coalition*
1783–1801	William Pitt (the Younger)	*Tory*
1801–1804	Henry Addington	*Tory*
1804–1806	William Pitt (the Younger)	*Tory*
1806–1807	Lord William Grenville	*Whig*
1807–1809	Duke of Portland	*Tory*
1809–1812	Spencer Perceval	*Tory*
1812–1827	Earl of Liverpool	*Tory*
1827	George Canning	*Tory*
1827–1828	Viscount Goderich	*Tory*
1828–1830	Duke of Wellington	*Tory*
1830–1834	Earl Grey	*Whig*
1834	Viscount Melbourne	*Whig*
1834	Duke of Wellington	*Tory*
1834–1835	Sir Robert Peel	*Conservative*
1835–1841	Viscount Melbourne	*Whig*
1841–1846	Sir Robert Peel	*Conservative*
1846–1852	Lord John Russell	*Whig*
1852	Earl of Derby	*Conservative*
1852–1855	Earl of Aberdeen	*coalition*
1855–1858	Viscount Palmerston	*Liberal*
1858–1859	Earl of Derby	*Conservative*
1859–1865	Viscount Palmerston	*Liberal*
1865–1866	Earl Russell	*Liberal*
1866–1868	Earl of Derby	*Conservative*
1868	Benjamin Disraeli	*Conservative*
1868–1874	William Gladstone	*Liberal*
1874–1880	Benjamin Disraeli	*Conservative*
1880–1885	William Gladstone	*Liberal*
1885–1886	Marquis of Salisbury	*Conservative*
1886	William Gladstone	*Liberal*
1886–1892	Marquis of Salisbury	*Conservative*
1892–1894	William Gladstone	*Liberal*
1894–1895	Earl of Rosebery	*Liberal*
1895–1902	Marquis of Salisbury	*Conservative*
1902–1905	Arthur Balfour	*Conservative*
1905–1908	Sir Henry Campbell-Bannerman	*Liberal*
1908–1916	Herbert Asquith	*Liberal*
1916–1922	David Lloyd George	*coalition*
1922–1923	Andrew Bonar Law	*Conservative*
1923–1924	Stanley Baldwin	*Conservative*
1924	Ramsay MacDonald	*Labour*
1924–1929	Stanley Baldwin	*Conservative*
1929–1931	Ramsay MacDonald	*Labour*
1931–1935	Ramsay MacDonald	*coalition*
1935–1937	Stanley Baldwin	*coalition*
1937–1940	Neville Chamberlain	*coalition*
1940–1945	Winston Churchill	*coalition*
1945–1951	Clement Attlee	*Labour*
1951–1955	Sir Winston Churchill	*Conservative*
1955–1957	Sir Anthony Eden	*Conservative*
1957–1963	Harold Macmillan	*Conservative*
1963–1964	Sir Alexander Douglas-Home	*Conservative*
1964–1970	Harold Wilson	*Labour*
1970–1974	Edward Heath	*Conservative*
1974–1976	Harold Wilson	*Labour*
1976–1979	James Callaghan	*Labour*
1979–1990	Margaret Thatcher	*Conservative*
1990–1997	John Major	*Conservative*
1997–	Tony Blair	*Labour*

Presidents of the United States of America

1789–1797	George Washington	*Federalist*
1797–1801	John Adams	*Federalist*
1801–1809	Thomas Jefferson	*Democratic-Republican*
1809–1817	James Madison	*Democratic-Republican*
1817–1825	James Monroe	*Democratic-Republican*
1825–1829	John Quincy Adams	*Independent*
1829–1837	Andrew Jackson	*Democrat*
1837–1841	Martin Van Buren	*Democrat*
1841	William H. Harrison	*Whig*
1841–1845	John Tyler	*Whig, then Democrat*
1845–1849	James K. Polk	*Democrat*
1849–1850	Zachary Taylor	*Whig*
1850–1853	Millard Fillmore	*Whig*
1853–1857	Franklin Pierce	*Democrat*
1857–1861	James Buchanan	*Democrat*
1861–1865	Abraham Lincoln	*Republican*
1865–1869	Andrew Johnson	*Democrat*
1869–1877	Ulysses S. Grant	*Republican*
1877–1881	Rutherford B. Hayes	*Republican*
1881	James A. Garfield	*Republican*
1881–1885	Chester A. Arthur	*Republican*
1885–1889	Grover Cleveland	*Democrat*
1889–1893	Benjamin Harrison	*Republican*
1893–1897	Grover Cleveland	*Democrat*
1897–1901	William McKinley	*Republican*
1901–1909	Theodore Roosevelt	*Republican*
1909–1913	William H. Taft	*Republican*
1913–1921	Woodrow Wilson	*Democrat*
1921–1923	Warren G. Harding	*Republican*
1923–1929	Calvin Coolidge	*Republican*
1929–1933	Herbert C. Hoover	*Republican*
1933–1945	Franklin Delano Roosevelt	*Democrat*
1945–1953	Harry S. Truman	*Democrat*
1953–1961	Dwight D. Eisenhower	*Republican*
1961–1963	John F. Kennedy	*Democrat*
1963–1969	Lyndon B. Johnson	*Democrat*
1969–1974	Richard M. Nixon	*Republican*
1974–1977	Gerald Ford	*Republican*
1977–1981	James E. Carter	*Democrat*
1981–1989	Ronald W. Reagan	*Republican*
1989–1993	George H. W. Bush	*Republican*
1993–	William J. Clinton	*Democrat*

Index

If an index entry is printed in **bold**, it means that there is an article under that name in the A–Z section of the encyclopedia. When an entry has more than one page number, the most important one may be printed in **bold**. Page numbers in *italic* mean that there is an illustration relating to the entry on that page.